The God Process

Kirk S. Boote

FriesenPress
Victoria, BC

Book of Life.

Chapter 1

1. The spectrum of life brings depth to the soul. Out of creation, out of the heavens and set upon the earth was God's plan. We taste and breathe in the depth of the soul. Beyond the spirit is the experience we take in. All that which was, all that which is and all that which will be is captured by the record that is embedded upon the life of the soul. It is the record that retains the reality of our will, desires and illusions. It is the record that retains our memory of deeds, feelings and thoughts. It is the record that life has written.

2. Out of creation was the record of life. As the word was spoken, life was given. The spectrum expanded into the void of the self to allow God to separate life from life. The record was formed and each soul took upon the self the reality that was created. Here in was the will that was willed. The will to be. In all of God's creation would we bear upon each other that reality which was recorded.

3. The heavens were separated to allow the spectrum to unfold. God looked upon the vastness that stood upon the face of the realities that was willed. As the realities unfolded, as each one choose one with the other that which they desired within the depth of their soul the fabric of life was formed. In the array of life that belonged to God came

the reality that we willed. Families were formed out of the desire for belonging. ~~We~~ We bonded one to another in the reality that we would will so that we might come to taste the depth of our own soul.

4. It was the experience of the self that we sought. To impart on one and another to taste the spectrum that stood before us. Wondorous was the life that we willed. It stood before us in colours and sensation that could be touched, and absorbed enveloped! Wondorous were the dreams that we dreamed. In each reality was a new experience. The vision daunted on our being and we were captured by its wondorous adventure. One with another we were drawn into the reality.

5. The spectrum of creation that God willed upon the heavens filled the void of space. It covered the form of thought by the limit of presence. Light converged in the density of thought to form the mass of reality that God willed. Structure and form stod before us and became the playground for the dance of life. We entered the form of light to take upon ourselves the thought of our will. Within this convergence would life emerge in the image of our dreams and desires. Upon our vision stood the mountain and the valleys, the skies and the seas, the flowers and the trees, the array of colours, sound and taste, the sensation of form, self and identity.

FriesenPress

Suite 300 – 852 Fort Street
Victoria, BC, Canada V8W 1H8
www.friesenpress.com

ISBN
978-1-4602-4029-8 (Hardcover)
978-1-4602-4030-4 (Paperback)
978-1-4602-4031-1 (eBook)

1. Religion, Spirituality
2. Religion, Theology
3. Self-Help, Personal Growth, General

Distributed to the trade by The Ingram Book Company

THE GOD PROCESS
TABLE OF CONTENTS

Dedication

To my parant's Larry and Clara Boote

May the whishper of death that separates us fade into eternity and may the lives you lived touch those that read your story.

Invitation to the God Process

The God Process is a phrase to spark the mind to the possibilities of how God uses life to mold us and shape us into who we are and what we become. How you live life and *whom* you live life with, will change you. There is a passage in Part II of this book that captures the beauty of our soul.

> *Our soul shimmers in the light that is infused onto our being from the life we live. Particles of energy like threads of light woven to form the fabric of life. Cast like a string of diamonds to solidify the garment of our soul. We shine and shimmer as God's light illuminates and vibrates from within. The very essence of who we are is both seen and felt.* 1E

Who we are—our personality, attitudes and behaviors—can be etched onto our soul like the colors of a rainbow or tainted in darkness by the choices we make. Our happiness and sadness, triumphs and tragedies, can either lift us up or cause us to fall. The process of life will change who we are. The color of our soul will either sparkle with life or will become dulled and tainted by how we live.

Most of what we do in life seemingly has nothing to do with God and yet, I think, everything that we do in life has something to do with God. Inside each of us is this mystical connection with God. The love that we feel, the relationships that we have with each other, this mystical connection to life, is the essence of God. God is both the source and the creative force, which binds the fabric of life together.

There is purpose to life, yet life is an unfolding mystery. Our life purpose and our *God Process* may not be the same thing. To see what God is trying to do may mean we will have to connect the dots. To find our *God Process,* we may have to look for the pattern of God that God has weaved in and around our life. We are instilled with goodness, a desire to help others and to become more than what we already are. Realizing our potential is what we are meant to do.

The God Process is the journey that we are all on. It is a journey we all take on our walk back to God. It is a journey of life, love, song, dance and laughter, mixed with uncertainty, tragedy and at times suffering. It is a journey of how God changes us through the process of life.

Infusing God's light into our soul sparks the creative process. We are meant to create, to dream dreams and to explore our potential. As we seek to make a better life, a better world, something in turn happens to us. We become what we were meant to be; filled with the very essence of life itself. The essence of life, the essence of God, converges on the soul.

I hope to take you on a journey through *my God Process.* My life is both normal and in some instances quite extraordinary. It is in the extraordinary things in life that tells us God is there. It is in the mystical connections between the dots of our lives that we see the pattern of God.

There are paths we take in our life that seem to be embedded into ones soul. There is this internal light that tells us what we should be and what we should do. It points the way and becomes the beacon that we follow. At times the direction we take in life is obscured; filled with crossroads that seem to lead to nowhere. Yet there is purpose and meaning; if we stop and reflect, we can discover our own *God Process* and we can discover what God is trying to do.

Our lives are filled with color. Religion, faith, people, choices and even our shortcomings and mistakes are all a part of the color; they all have a different beauty, texture, taste and aroma. Some memories sparkle and glow, while others are tainted with dullness and luster. Yet, even in that which is dull and unappealing, dark and distasteful, we know that even there are lessons that only this life can teach us. All of life's experiences help us to not only find our potential—it can also help us find a desire for God.

Life can feel like a clock. It moves like a pendulum swinging from one moment to the next. There is urgency and yet we know that the swing of the clock is only a single moment in the vastness of eternity. Certain events become embedded in your soul. Moments can be locked in time and the memory of that moment can change us forever. Time merges with eternity when moments are solidified in the space between time.

Finding a desire for God is pivotal. Looking to God can be the key to the lock that opens the door to a reality that exists in all of us. Finding God opens us to a reality that shines a light and helps us to make sense out of the why. Opening the door to God is like opening ourselves up to the light that is in our soul.

I believe in God. I believe that God actively works with each of us at our own pace. When we are ready, God is there. Discovering your own *God Process* assures you that God is actively engaged with you in your life. Seeing your own *God Process* assures you that you are loved and that you are a part of His plan. Opening yourself up to your own *God Process* allows you to see the path that God has set you on.

The pattern in which I wrote this book is a little different than most reads. When you look back on your life and you try to connect the dots, which I would call your "God lessons", you do not always see your life in chronological order. Certain events stand out. Certain people stand out. These themes, these *God lessons*, shape us—sometimes for the good and sometimes for the *not* so good, all depending on the choices that are made. When we stop and look, when we look back and look inward, our soul will speak to us. It is like a whisper that gives us insight and, if we listen carefully, we will find messages that speak to the affirmation of God.

As I wrote the book, I looked back on my life and reflected on *my God lessons,* and then tried to relate that to what, I think, God was trying to teach me. Relating life to a message of what God might speak points us to universal truths that I think are in all of us. These are the messages that speak to our higher purpose in life and perhaps to our collective purpose.

Although I am Christian, *the God Process* is not just about Christianity. God did not have us all born into *my* Christianity. I connect the dots in my life through my Christianity and for me, I see God moving in and through my faith. However, I think God moves in all faiths. Having a faith in God can lift us up. Our faith traditions are important—faith inspires us. In this mystical, mysterious and magical word we call faith, we explore God. And for those that do not aspire to the notion of "God" then perhaps the better terminology is to say we explore "life". The exploration of faith is to discover the roots of our soul. We discover that part of us that brings meaning to the self and meaning to life. In that discovery lies our potential.

I was compelled to write and to share with others my own *God Process*. More importantly, I wanted to try to give others a reason to have God in their lives. I wanted to give others a reason to look back, to look inward and to look up—to become aware that God is there and that He is engaged with us.

God whispers to us. He is there if we stop and listen. His message is always one of invitation. It is in that whisper that we find our hope and our peace. It is in the message that we find meaning.

This book has a message. It is a message to consider what God has to offer and to consider the cosmic story as God weaves the fabric of life in and around us. There are three parts to the book. The first part is my own journey of life, tragedy, family and miracles. The second part is an ethereal message, a message to consider this mystical universal truth that is seemingly obscure and yet rooted in all our lives. The third part relates my journey and *The Message* to *the God Process* that happens to all of us.

In the extraordinary moments of life we find God. When we are ready for God, God is there.

Kirk S. Boote
February 24th, 2014.

To the reader:

The reader will find numerous indentations throughout *Part I: The Journey*. These indentations which are in italics signify my "God message", a message that came from my soul and a message which spoke to me to consider this higher purpose to life, to God's Truth that speaks to healing and wholeness. These indentations are quotes from *Part II: The Message*. The actual placement of the quote can be found in the endnotes.

With respect to gender related context where the reference to God as "He, Him, Father", it is not intended to suggest the gender of God. God, I believe, transcends gender. Although we see overtones of masculine imagery both in scripture and in my own journaling, I think that using gender neutral verbiage would have worked both for and against the poetic nature of God. In reality, both male and female genders have the ability to personify both male and female personas. Masculinity can be found in both male and female genders. Masculinity points towards fatherhood, strength and perhaps authority or kingliness, but it is not intended to take away from femininity which embodies motherhood, compassion, nurturing and protection. Again, these personas are found in both male and female gender roles. Also, the use of "man", "mankind" or "sons of" points towards humankind or souls. Statements such as these in scripture can be problematic for those who are sensitive to gender imagery, however, it is not intended to create contention. The imagery of God can be complex and our expressions of God are at best inadequate to convey meaning that connects with everyone.

My hope is that as you read you will stop and consider your own *God Process*. I hope you will be compelled to consider what is "real" in God and that you will discover God for who God really is. For if God is real then what does that mean? If we are mystically connected to God, what does God have to offer? How does my life become better if I turn *to*, as opposed to turn *from*, God?

I invite you to discover *your own God Process*.

Part I

THE JOURNEY

——————— 1 Cancer ———————

For God so loved the world that He gave His only begotten Son, that whosoever believeth in him should not perish, but have everlasting life.

For God sent not His Son into the world to condemn the world; but that the world through him might be saved.

John 3:16-17

There are pivotal moments in all our lives. They can be moments which strike us like lightning or they can be moments that simply seem connected with other moments in our lives—a series of events which point to common themes.

When I started to write this book, my wife's brother Ron had just passed away; 6:30 pm on an October Thursday night. His fight with cancer ended and he was finally free of the pain.

Ron was not overly religious. He had faith in God but he was not a church going man. He had a kind gentle soul, however his life was not easy. Several years ago he stopped to help a stranger on a cold winter night whose car had slid off the road. Moments later he was struck by another passing vehicle and thrown about twenty feet. It took a year for him to fully recover.

Ron at the time was divorced and he had a fairly lonely life. He had his adult children and grandchildren that he spent time with. Still most days were filled with driving trucks. At the time he was seeing a warm and loving person. It was Shirley that helped him through the long road of recovery from the accident. She was patient and ever so attentive to Ron. God, I think, sends people into our lives at the right time to help us cope with life. Shirley became that special someone for Ron.

It was about six months before his death when the pain in his lower hip returned. He thought it was from the accident—maybe arthritis or a lower back nerve that was not behaving. There were the usual diagnostics; blood work, x-rays, CAT scans. Then the answer. Cancer.

As family and friends you watch and pray. You offer support and your love, however cancer is a lonely journey. We look to God, to our health care system and to doctors for hope and healing. However, for some, the road with cancer has no turns—just one final end.

Time does not stand still. The pendulum swings and April became May, the summer came and went. We lived on with our lives and Ron's journey was coming to an end.

September 28, 2013.

Ron was in Saint Paul's Hospital in Saskatoon. My wife Lorraine and I drove the seven hour journey to see him two weeks prior to his passing. At that time he was alert and we were able to visit and talk.

He was already extremely weak and his body was shutting down. He had stopped eating; even drinking water took more effort than he had the strength for. The pain was severe—tough to control. They were using an epidural for the pain, but the fluid was leaking out and not getting into the body.

He would close his eyes to focus and use whatever energy he had to cope with the misery that his body was putting him through. Then he would open his eyes and chat for a few minutes. We would tell him about what was happening in the world. Maybe in those few brief moments of conversation he could connect with a world which was still normal.

We prayed together and then he put his arm around his sister. It was a goodbye moment. He knew it and we knew it.

In that moment my eyes locked with his. I had seen that look before.

My father had that same look in his eyes the last time I saw him. He too was taken after a long hard road with cancer. The last thing my father said to me was, "Son, please don't go." I was nineteen.

I live with that memory and think about it often. We take moments like this in life and we look for meaning. Moments of goodbye; moments which seem locked in time. It is hard for me to shake the feeling that my father must have had when I turned the other way and walked out that hospital door on April 15, 1978. It is a feeling of longing, a wishing that time could keep sacred our connectedness, and our mutual desire to be together across the space that now seems lost.

There are lessons I think that are in each of our lives—events with common themes. They are lessons that God grants us so that we might learn and grow from. Locking eyes with Ron and being reconnected with my father was electric, like a flash of light that sparked the memory.

I truly believe that there is more to this life than this life; that we are not accidental. Events in our lives are not always accidental. "We are spiritual beings having a human experience"—one of the few quotes of Steven Covey that I remember. God is in our lives and is actively engaged with us for a purpose.

There are life lessons that we must face if we are to grow.

I often think about my Christianity and I try to connect the dots in my life through my faith. Having faith traditions help ground us in life, and these traditions guide us and point us towards a hope that help us through life's uncertainty and moments of crises. In Christianity we look to the message that life does not end in death. The walk Jesus took to the cross culminated in that single event of living and dying, but the story ends in the resurrection, the rising to new life. It is a story of God coming into creation to show creation a path back—a path of hope.

This whole process of life—the living and the dying and especially cancer, which eats you alive—seemed cruel. Yet, even there, I believe God works His miracles.

Connecting my faith to the dots, to the message of God's Truth is like medicine. You have to want the medicine if it is going to do you any good. With God's Truth, you have to want to hear the message, but more importantly you have to want the message.

I loved my father. He inspired me—he *still* inspires me. He lived his whole life doing something for someone else. I don't always do that. I loved his compassion for people and it is because of his compassion that I look to live my life differently.

His compassion reminds me of an experience when I was twelve years old. It was Christmas time and my grandfather on my mother's side was Santa Claus for the downtown Eaton's center. My father had organized the families of our church to donate toys and gifts for a care ward. This was a home where children had been abandoned to the province because they were too much to care for—children with special needs. Autism, Down Syndrome and other developmental disabilities where the children had limited response capabilities to the outer world. Parents could not cope and the kids became wards of the state. That Christmas morning instead of opening presents I went with my father and my grandfather, dressed as Santa Claus, to the care home.

One by one Santa would go to each child and I watched. There is wonder when a little child looks up and locks eyes. A simple gift, a toy—but it wasn't the toy that had the meaning, it was the love—it was the eyes. It was one soul touching another soul. Then the eyes would unlock as the child explored the mystery of the gift to discover the surprise beneath the wrapping paper.

I often think about the gift. The gift that came when my eyes locked with Ron. The gift that came when my eyes locked with my father for the last time. For God so loved the world. God's gift.

Somehow I know God is trying to break through this hard shell I put around myself. I find loving and giving both easy and hard. Part of me wants to connect with others and part of me wants to turn and walk away. There is this solitude that I would rather crawl into, rather than risk opening myself up to people who might end up hurting me.

There was a reason why I decided to write this book. Somewhere in the exploration of life, somewhere in the journey that each of us takes there are moments which cause us to look back, to look inward and to look up. I think we all do it. We want to understand meaning, to find our purpose in life and the answers to the "why". In our exploration of faith we look to God, because the hope is that in our faith we will find these answers. This is the exploration of our *God Process*—the "how" and "what" God is trying to do in this process of life—my life.

This single moment with Ron and connecting it with my father, was the wake-up call to what I now see as one of my *God lessons*. This single reminder that there is this finality to life, and to these moments that are locked in time, caused me to stop, to look back and consider what God was trying to do with my life. It was a pivotal moment along with a series of other events that compelled me to write this book. It was like all of sudden I was able to connect the dots. For me it was obvious, my *God lesson* was to find a desire to share my soul—to bring about a wantingness to open myself up and to allow others to see a message that I started some twenty years ago. It was an ethereal message written from my soul to give others a compelling reason to consider God. My *God Process* would cause me to find a deeper meaning to life.

Seeing the cancer take Ron was a reminder that there is urgency to do whatever we are called to do in life. I needed to share a message. It is a message to give us all a reason to consider God. To consider what God is trying to do in our lives.

My life took a wrong turn. It was like falling into a pit. My whole being shook inside because of certain events that were happening in my life. Events which strike us the hardest are always events that hit your own home. My life was getting caught up in corporate business and it was testing my value system. There is an expression I hear sometimes: "Business is business." It is a hard lesson. It is a dark lesson and I was getting wrapped up in it, trapped by it. I decided to walk away so that I could reflect on my own *God Process*.

It was not just corporate business that was causing this feeling of darkness in my life. There were a number of things which were not right. The world itself just seemed darker.

We know of a mother who is supporting her children through a hair salon business. She lives in Cameroon and is raising not only her own child, but also two younger brothers and a younger sister, after her father passed away in 2010. Having enough money is a struggle and so her brother, who lives in America, helps them out as much as he can. Her business was robbed and she had to pick up the pieces because there was no insurance and the law enforcement there is not always available. In fact, it is the third time that she has been robbed. Even having your money in a Cameroonian bank is sometimes not safe. If the bank goes bankrupt you are at risk of losing your savings. That happened to her as well. What do you do? Events like these can paralyze us.

One of the conversations that my wife and I had with our extended family (on the weekend that we visited Ron in the hospital) was that there is a bill that is being pushed through the provincial parliament to give the government the legal right to issue a fine to any worker caught lifting a box incorrectly. The provincial government wants to police how people lift boxes! It sounds silly, but someone in government started this process of regulating box lifting as a solution to a problem that stemmed from payouts for Workmen's Compensation Benefits. The government must be paying out a substantial amount of lost wage benefits for claims as a result of injuries from box lifting. Once passed, people will have to live in a world with less freedom and more fear of fines... well, at least when it comes to lifting boxes.

Later that same week my sister was telling me a story about a friend who was visiting her from the UK. Her friend brought her brother with her to Canada. Her brother is out of prison now after spending five years of his life behind bars for falling asleep at the wheel of his truck. He had a tragic accident that claimed the lives of a young family. The accident devastated not only his life but the lives of the victims and their families. He was two hours over the regulated hours for the commercial driving laws in the UK. He was just trying to get home. He was just trying to do his job so that he could pay the bills and that one bad decision cost the lives of this family and put him in prison for five years. His wife left him. He was full of shame and guilt. He felt like he had no one. He is imprisoned by a past that haunts him every day. He now desperately wants his life back, but he cannot free himself from the guilt, the shame and the memories.

We want our governments to enforce laws and to send a message to others. Sometimes when we see the aftermath on their lives, the price that we want other people to pay becomes just as tragic as the accident itself. There is no restitution, no resolve and no absolution when tragic choices have far-reaching consequences. We are all connected at some level. I can only imagine his pain but I know it is real. Tragic accidents leave a residue of pain with both the victims and the guilty.

There is pain when our lives become torn. There is pain when people rob and steal. I know of the struggle when you work and do not get paid, or when there is no work at all.

I could feel this darkness. I could feel it in the story of this truck driver and in the story of our friend from Cameroon who was robbed. I can see it in how our governments respond with regulations. I can see it in the workplace and it appears to be growing more prevalent in the world around me.

Something was amiss. I knew it. I could feel it. This darkness is like a cancer which consumes lives. However, it is events like these that cause us to stop, look back, look inward and look up.

To share a message about God was not an easy decision. To share a message about how God can help us, when our world grows dark and we get lost, is not always wanted.

So how does God free us? Because really, for some of us, God is our only hope from which freedom can be found. How can we find peace, hope and innocence if our world becomes dark? What if we make mistakes and become lost to shame and guilt or if we become lost to blame, low self-esteem, depression or whatever the thoughts are that haunt us? How do we get our life back? How do we get our world back? In the darkness we can become lost.

Being lost to God, or being lost to our collective goodness, is far-reaching. What happens to one can happen to all of us. Without God in our life, God can become absent in the home. The erosion of God is the erosion of our goodness and our hope. As more and more people become lost to God's goodness, our society becomes different, darker, uninviting. When our humanity gets lost, when our goodness is lost, we all pay a price. When people choose to take advantage of people, our governments enforce laws and regulations to maintain order in society. If we become over-regulated, our freedom is eroded.

When I was sixteen, my father went to his family practitioner because a mole on the side of his neck was getting larger, tender and hard. The doctor decided to apply local anesthetic and cut it out. It was sent to a lab for diagnosis. Within a week this growth was back with vengeance. The mass was the size of a small baseball. The diagnosis from the lab was melanoma—cancer. My father was rushed to the Edmonton University Hospital for surgery.

I was in high school at the time and did not comprehend the magnitude of what just happened. In surgery they cut deep into his neck and removed all that they could and then sewed him back up. He was a healthy and strong man, but by the third day he was close to death. His body was in shock from the surgery. The surgery was invasive. He was fighting for his life and losing the battle. His prayers to God seemed unresponsive.

Then came the miracle.

His spirit rose from his body and he looked down at the shell on the bed. A nurse came in and saw what was happening. My father could see her from the corner of the room as she checked his vitals. Then, all of a sudden this warmth, a surge of energy started passing through his disembodied feet. He could feel this energy beneath him as he looked down onto the room. First it was his feet; then it was his legs. It was warm and it was soothing. This energy just moved up slowly through his body.

Moments later he opened his eyes and the nurse said to him, "Mr. Boote, I thought you were gone."

He told me about what he had experienced in that hospital room about three months after the operation. He would drive me to school in the morning and he would talk to me. There was this urgency for him and he wanted me to hear it. He wanted me to know that God had spared his life for a purpose. He asked God to grant him two more years so that he might be able to do things for us, for his family, so that we would be taken care of. He passed away three years later.

Cancer is relentless and once it starts it can be very tough to stop.

There is a cancer in the darkness. There is cancer of the spirit when there is a void to God's goodness in our lives. Darkness can eat at you. It can eat you alive.

My wake-up call was more than just locking eyes with Ron. It was this overwhelming sense of being trapped in a very dark place and a feeling that life was on the wrong course. A feeling where God was becoming absent in my life and in our world. Looking to God might sound rather superficial, like a band-aid answer, but for me that was it. I knew it.

The reality is that when God is absent in us, our world can become dark. We can become lost.

God's message is one of light. God's message is a call to our humanity, a message of hope, peace and wholeness. Darkness cannot exist where there is light. Even the tiniest spark—a match or a flame on the candle—can dissipate the darkness. The darkness fades away the closer we get to the light. And there is heat in the light. A radiance of warmth as you put your hands around its glow. Even if you close your eyes it can penetrate your soul.

My wake-up call, my inner "earth-shake", was a stop and look event. It was becoming apparent to me that it wasn't just me. The darkness that I was feeling was a recognition that a lot of people are starting to feel trapped by this dark void. Our collective value system is becoming twisted. There is a silence that you start to hear after a while and it becomes deafening. It is a silence that you hear when people are fearful of speaking.

Whether it is the corporate world, our governments making global decisions or in our personal lives you can sometimes hear the silence. It is a silence that tells us that at some level something is wrong—we are becoming lost to God's goodness. The world is on a collision course on so many levels and the only way for us to stop whatever it is we are facing individually or globally, is for all of us to consider our collective *God lesson*. Maybe that sounds idealistic, but perhaps our *God lesson* is to help us make a conscious choice for the essence of goodness, peace and sustainability—a conscious choice for our connectedness. This conscious choice instills the essence of God's creative purpose; it instills the very essence of God in us.

If our world is going to survive the collision course that we have put ourselves on, it will have to come from a mutual wantingness.[1] We will have to want it. There has to be a compelling case for God in each of our lives. To recognize the goodness and the light, which calls us to do what is right, we will have to look deep into our soul to find our connectedness with the God who created us.

There are messages that compel us to consider God. When we realize that our life is at risk, when we realize that even the sustainability of our world is at risk, then maybe we will stop to consider God. When I consider God, I see the potential for life itself. The message that we should consider is in the wonder that is in God and in what God offers.

God is a just God.

Within God is all that there is. God brings to our awareness that which is just and true. God breathes life and life extends God. The fire of God is the energy that illuminates life.

Love is just as real as the source from which it came. Love to the spirit is like air to the body. The energy that love gives is vital and thrives when we abide in God. To cut ourselves off from God is to cut ourselves off from all that is around us; the earth, our home,

---

1   Wantingness is not a word in the English dictionary; however, you will find that I have used it numerous times throughout the book. On the surface one can read into it a definition of desire, wanting or willingness; however, I needed a word that captures a deep longing, a passion for, or a deep desire to have, and I wanted that word to be associated with positive energy, goodness and godliness. There is another word, wantonness, which has a definition of wanting without regard to what is right or wanting for self-gratification. There is a bit of word play in the book between wantingness and wantonness. The hope is that in time we turn our wantonness for self-gratification into wantingness for goodness, or to do what is right.

*our families, our friends. We cannot cut ourselves off from life nor can we cut our self off from the desire to belong. The desire to belong is the residue of love; we cannot cut ourselves off completely from love. Just as light, which has left its source, can never become darkness so it is that we can never totally separate ourselves from God. God is and so are we.*_{2E}

"God is a just God" is an affirmation of the essence of God. A "just God" points to a God of creative purpose who actively engages with us to help us choose peace, love, goodness and those constructs that create justice, fairness, healing, wholeness and new life.

All of humanity, no matter the race, religion or creed, is on this path back to God. Our collective humanity is being tested by the choices that we all make. Everyone is playing a role that ultimately tests our humanity. We will either enslave one another by our choices or we will free one another by our choices. Whether we are school teachers, caretakers, salesmen, caregivers, law enforcers, regulators, corporate leaders, presidents or parents, we all will have an impact individually, collectively and globally.

God's gift is in the life we live. It is in the gift we give to one another. It is in the legacy we leave for our children. It is in the world that remains both peaceful yet unpredictable. It is in the getting up, the rising up. It is in the rising up to the new life, to the life that rose from the cross.

Ron passed away on October 10, 2013. His funeral was on October 16, 2013.

For myself, if there is a message in the cancer, if there is a message in the cross, if there is a message in the dying, it is this; our connection with one another can become locked in the space between time. Our love for one another calls us to embrace life, to embrace the gift of each other and *this* connection is eternal. These moments can change us and cause us to live life with a sense of urgency—*to live life more fully, more intently.* God's word breathes life. God's word invokes light. Miracles happen when we look to the light. New life comes from embracing the light.

Darkness cannot extinguish light, but light can dissipate the darkness. I think we can cut ourselves off to the light and give into the darkness and perhaps that is the scary part. But the message that God offers is that the spark of light is still there. To free ourselves from the darkness, to heal our world, we have to want the light.

There is purpose in all things and there was a purpose in the cross. In my Christianity, Jesus took on life to give us a message. Jesus walked the path to the cross because he wanted us to accept a message. It was a message of light. It was a message about God. The road to the cross that Jesus walked was a journey of free will. A journey that he bore so that we might know God's love.

Each step we take can be a journey of love. Even in the living and the dying, we will find our desire to love and to be loved. Connecting with Ron—connecting with my dad—when I looked into their eyes for the last time, was a gift. Our eyes remind us of the eternal bond that we have with each other. It was the same gift that I saw in the eyes of the children that one Christmas morning as they looked up into Santa's eyes. That is the love that is in our God and that our God has for each of us. Such is the love that Christ had when he looked down on his mother from the cross. It is the same love that he has for us.

Love binds us together.

2 Jerusalem

This then is the message which we have heard of him, and declared unto you, that God is light, and in him is no darkness at all.

1st John 1:5

Entering the walls of Old Jerusalem is like stepping back 2000 years.

When I was growing up my mother, Clara Boote, worked at the Hebrew School in administration. Both my sister and I went there for elementary school. In June of 1976, I was at the school just passing through when I saw on the bulletin board an invitation to live in Israel on a Kibbutz (a Jewish community settlement, usually agricultural with collective principles) as a volunteer.

When you are seventeen, you want to see the world, *experience* the world.

My father's bout with cancer began in December of 1974. Within a year and a half later my father, Larry Boote, undertook to build two condominium units with nine family homes. This condominium community was my father's way of surrounding us with family and friends, should his cancer come back. Eight other families, who were close to us, were a part of this community. By August of 1976 we moved into these new homes. My aunt and uncle lived next door to the left of us and three other families from our church lived to the right of our condominium unit. Across the street were four other families; all of them knew my father well.

That summer his health was good and the cancer was in remission.

I was drawn to that poster to go to Israel. I wanted to go—I felt compelled to go, like it was something that I was supposed to do. Fortunately, I was in a position to finish high school early. Plans were made. I completed my high school requirements for graduation by December and I was on a plane to Tel Aviv with a friend named Ken by February of 1977.

Israel however, was not what I expected. Living in Canada your whole life and then stepping into a country still struggling from a long history of siege, is a culture shock. Israel was always under the threat of war. The Six Day war happened in June 1967, which was ten years before my visit. That war was a preventative military effort to counter what the Israelis saw as an impending Arab attack. The Yom Kippur War was in October 1973, a war where Egypt and Syria rose up against Israel from October 6th to the 25th. It was a joint surprise attack on Israel. By 1977 it was peaceful, for the most part, but the threat of war was constant. This constant threat of war, for me, was the realization to a different kind of world.

Within 24 hours of leaving Canada, I was on the other side of the world, away from family and in a foreign land. After landing at the airport, Ken and I were placed into a taxi and ended up in northern Golan Heights near the Lebanon border.

The Kibbutz community had a different way of life. This was a community of people that grew up together and lived for each other. The wealth of the farm was shared equally, and the people worked, played and dined together. There was no stealing inside the communal farm, no taxes, most of the people seemed really happy and they all shared in the responsibilities of daily life. It was green, lush with flowers, well maintained and life here felt like a little piece of paradise.

Volunteers like Ken and I, came from all over the world. Some volunteers came and just decided to live there indefinitely. The volunteers lived in old long wooden houses that were built back in the 1950s, which were built by the community for the community. Each house had five one room cabin style accommodations with a bed and a desk, but no running water. It was comfortable and it became home for four months.

Israel, however, became a pivotal point in my life. It was the start of a rollercoaster ride of both wanting God in my life and not wanting God in my life. Up to this point I felt like I had this connection, this desire, this faith that assured me that no matter what I did in my life, God was there and my life would be okay. Perhaps youth buys us that certain sense of innocence that shelters us from reality. However, it is only now that I can look back and connect the dots that I can see the pattern unfold. It is a pattern of coming to grips with both the light and the dark—a pattern to discover the roots of my soul.

Routine life of a volunteer in a Kibbutz is that you work for eight hours and then you are free to do whatever you want. I was placed on a work crew and my first duty was to stuff live turkeys into bird cages on trucks that were heading to slaughter. You don't just stuff one turkey into this 2x2x1 foot cage; you stuff as many as you can—three, sometimes four—and these birds would look at you... intently. I wondered what, if anything, these birds were thinking.

My sister at one time had a parakeet. It would follow you around and squawk at you until you did what it wanted. This bird knew how to manipulate you to do whatever. This bird I think had a soul; it was like a two year old, constantly wanting attention.

Stuffing turkeys into these cages for me was such an inhumane thing. However, business is business. I didn't think about whether or not if these turkeys had a soul. In fact I don't think I cared. All I cared about was doing my job.

That was really the only distasteful job I did at the Kibbutz. I worked in the orchards, in the plastics factory, the popsicle stick factory, the fisheries, and this turkey farm. They also had cotton fields, a poplar tree farm, and cattle. You would start your day at 5 am and be done by 2 pm.

It was not long after I was there, maybe three weeks, that the Kibbutz had organized a six day guided tour of Israel for all of the volunteers. There were approximately forty of us on an air conditioned coach bus with a professional tour guide who knew the history of the land and of religion. The climax of the trip for me was the Old City of Jerusalem.

Jerusalem is now a large metropolis. It is Israel's capital, home to approximately 853,000 people.[2] Back in the 1970s the Old City had about 25,000 people in total, predominately Muslims and Christians with very few Jews in the Jewish Quarter, as it had been bombed out.

The Old City of Jerusalem has over 3000 years of history.[3]

---

2   http://www.civiccoalition-jerusalem.org/system/files/jerusalem_-_general_facts_and_statistics_final.pdf

3   The area in and around Jerusalem became occupied by the Canaan-ites in approximately 2000 BC [Sacred City of Mankind A History of Forty Centuries, by Teddy Kollek and Moshe Pearlman]. Jerusalem emerges in 1200 - 1000 BC as the capital of a unified monarchy under Saul, David and Solomon in the Bible—Joshua, Judges, the Books of Samuel, Kings and Chronicles. According to Kollek and Pearlman [pg. 17], Jerusalem stems from the root word Salem, the name of the local god, so the word means "Founded by the god Salem". Of interest here is that Abraham meets Melchizedek, king of Salem, as recorded in Genesis 14:18; Melchizedek was the priest of the most high God. Zedek is the Hebrew word for righteousness. Another meaning for Jerusa-

Inside her walls the aura has not changed a lot over the years. The walls that guard her are some 13,000 feet in length, forty feet high and on average eight feet thick. The wall also has thirty-four watch towers and eight gates. The Old City is for many Christians, Muslims and Jews, the center of faith.

Our group of volunteers from the Kibbutz walked through the stone gates, down the old roads of the Old City and we took up residence inside a hostel for three days and two nights. We were told that the hostel was located directly above a prison house, historically believed to be the prison where Christ was held before his trial and his last home prior to the crucifixion.[4] The area where Pilate sentenced Jesus was around the corner and a block down the street.[5] In this area was a rather small courtyard with walls on all four sides and a single door that entered into an open air atrium.

We take life for granted most of the time. I take life for granted. We get up, have breakfast, go to work or school, come home have supper, do whatever, we go to bed and then do it all again the next day. Not every day is like that. Sometimes we wake-up go to a doctor and a week later we end up in surgery and then come face-to-face with death. For Christ, he was arrested, tried, convicted and then crucified.

As I stood in this atrium, I pictured Pilate's courtyard and I

---

lem is "City of Peace". This meaning is derived from the Hebrew name Yerushalayim, which stems from two Hebrew words Ir which means city and Shalom, which means peace.

4   I believe the hostel that I stayed use to be a hospice called Covenant to the Sisters of Sion. The prison house of Jesus prior to his trial was below the Convent.

5   Jesus was taken to the Palace of Caiaphas, the High Priest, after his arrest (Matthew 25:57). My recollections of the guided tour are reflected in my story. I believe the courtyard that I was in was the Franciscan Courtyard outside the Chapel of Flagellation. On page 117 of a Sacred City of Mankind A History of Forty Centuries, authors Kollek and Pearlman placed Jesus's trial in possibly two locations. The private part of the trial took place either at the Praetorium in the Antonia fortress or at Herod's palace, and the public part of the trial in the Antonia castle, in a courtyard open to the populace. The location that tour guides point to for Jesus's trial is station 1 on the Via Dolorosa walk, which is the final walk on the path to the Cross.

pondered. The only thing that stood between me, Pilate and Christ was time. I witnessed only stillness. The walls were silent. God was silent. Still, I imagined a podium, a basin, a stage where Pilate would have stood above Christ amongst a crowd of participants. I thought of God's justice. For many Christian's, Jesus's life culminated in this series of events—trial, the passion, crucifixion and death—then rising up again to take on new life.

There is a message that most Christians take to heart. It is the message that follows after the passion and death. It is in the sacrifice, the offering of the body and the resurrection that brings Christians a hope for salvation and a new life in Christ. It is *us* coming to terms with the cosmic *God Process*—God reaching down from heaven to reclaim us, redeem us and restore us to innocence.

To know that God is still a God of goodness and does *not* will that His creation suffers, is another message, I believe, God offers us. Suffering can torment the mind, body or heart, and it reaches the soul, but passion endured for others elevates the soul to selflessness. Even in the midst of the passion, when life is tragic, unjust and dark, we can still look to God as a refuge—as our hope in mind and spirit for healing and wholeness. The passion that Jesus endured lessens our burden, because in Christ we accept our path of passion for a new life. When we endure the inhumanity of life, God is there with us. The passion of the Christ is a witness that God is there with us; even when we might think that God has forsaken us to the cross that we might bear. Sometimes God's voice stills the moment and grants us peace.

God is a just God, setting in motion the opportunity for us to find heaven. Heaven is home. God rests in heaven and heaven goes with Him into the world. God offers heaven to those who will peace. God extends heaven to those who only know conflict.

Offering is the collection of resources that feeds the body. The offering that is collected is given back to the body. It is extended back to that part of the body that is in need. We become the collection of heaven to bring back heaven to those that are still in conflict. For heaven is not at rest so long as a part of God's creation is lost from heaven. For who would will to go to heaven forever and leave behind his brother or sister or friend who lost their ability to find their way home? We yearn for each other. I am incomplete without you and you need me if heaven is to be found for both of us. 3E

God's messages assure us that He will not abandon us and that the goodness that life has to offer can still emerge.

On first day of our tour in the Old City our guide took us through different historical points of interest. We learned of the history of the city and how through time its control shifted from one group of people to another. Jerusalem had been destroyed twice, besieged 23 times, attacked 52 times and recaptured 44 times.[6]

At about 4 pm we went back to the hostel and I was sitting on my cot. All of a sudden I felt compelled to go for a walk around the Old City. So I did. I got up, turned right outside the hostel doors and began to walk. The city streets are quite narrow, with old cobblestone walkways which are rugged yet smooth. It was a rather aimless walk, but I ended up taking a circular loop. As I was walking, I was thinking about what life would have been like back 2000 years ago and I was relating that to life today. I know this because I wrote this experience down and I had kept it all these years.

I walked for about 45 minutes and on my way back to the hostel I was confronted. I had just passed the area where Pilate tried Christ and was thinking that there really was no purpose for my walk when I was approached by a man who came right up to me and said, "*Give blood, give blood.*" He repeatedly said those two words, and he took my arm wanting me to follow him. He could not speak any English, other than those two words. So I, being young, naive and trusting, followed him.

---

6   Eric H. Cline's tally in Jerusalem Besieged., https://web.archive.
     org/web/20080603214950/http://www.momentmag.com/
     Exclusive/2008/2008-03/200803-Jerusalem.html

We walked not even a block down a side street and there before us was a clinic—it had the Red Cross signage out front. I followed him in and inside was another man; a doctor. He explained to me that they were desperately looking for a certain blood type because this man's wife was about to give birth and needed a cesarean. I am A$^+$ and I did not fit the bill, but Ken was back at the hostel and I said that I would go ask him.

The hostel was only two blocks away. I rushed there and brought Ken back with me to this clinic. Ken so happened to have type O blood, so he was a universal donor.

All went well with the procedure—a baby girl was born. So grateful was this man that he wanted to feed us. By this time his wife's brother was at the clinic and he could speak perfect English. He actually graduated from an American University. We agreed and the next evening they met us at the hostel. We walked with them down the Old City streets and we stopped to buy bread and a few other things for the evening meal. We exited the city walls and walked up a winding hill on the Mount of Olives. There outside a small two storey home was a yard with children, goats and chickens.

The man who confronted me on the street was a Muslim and he had two wives. The second wife was preparing the evening meal. We ate at a rather small table, which could only sit four people. In the center of the table was a plate filled with a mound of rice, peas, carrots, corn, onions, mushrooms, peppers and chicken. He offered a prayer in what I believe was Arabic; we broke bread and the brother-in-law translated how grateful this man was to Ken for saving both the baby and his wife's life.

Their traditions were different from mine. The men eat first and alone at the table. The wives and the children eat after the men have been fed. I learned that after the meal and wondered if I had left enough for the rest of the family. He now had eight children.

What always stayed with me from that experience is how God is at work in all faiths and in each life lived, regardless of faith. I felt compelled to go out for this walk. This simple prompting, which for me was from God, was an answer to another man's prayers. A man who was not of my faith tradition. A man who could not speak English and who was compelled to come to me, a foreign white teenager and in a street which had a constant stream of people. He chose me and I followed. It was a chain of events that speaks of a God who is actively engaged with all of His creation.

God works His miracles.

This experience changed my Christianity. We share in the cause for humanity, where one life can be a blessing to another life. Lives coming together across space and time for a single moment, a single connection. I never saw him again.

If there is a truth in this for me it was that God is actively engaged in all of our lives. He is not exclusive. *The God Process* is at work no matter who we are or what our faith traditions are. The sun rises and sets on all of the earth; on all people. Love has the potential to reach into all our lives and can touch us all equally. We can either be open to it and be moved by it or we can close ourselves off and live in a world of self.

In us is God's light. Either we can be open and receptive to a God who radiates peace from our homes or we can enclose our love to the four walls we live between and make our home a refuge from a world torn by chaos.

We cannot escape God. God is the source of life. He is there with us, in us. He is there with us and we are all connected. In Him is our true will. God wills good things and is this not our true will?

The lessons in life ultimately draw us back to find the refuge that brings peace to our soul. These lessons pull at us, tug at us, gnaw at us, until we look deep inside and take that next step towards God. To let God in, we have to let our goodness out. We have to share our soul. We have to be willing to touch another person's life.

To find God's Truth, we first have to want to hear the message. We then have to want the message. We have to want to step out of the darkness of life if we are going to find the light that comes from God. Condemnation sets us apart. Love binds us together. That light that we look for is found in *the God Process*. It is realizing that God is not exclusive. God is a participant, engaging with His creation.

We are participants engaging life with Him, in His creation. We are all in it together. What we do for others is what we do to ourselves. What we do for ourselves is what we do to others. Together, we create the world we live in.

In acts of selflessness, we find something different—we find a moment of peace.

3 War

The Lord our God is One.

The Law of God was born out of Truth. When Truth was broken the word became the law. The word was, "The Lord our God is One." In God there is no division, no duality. In God's Kingdom there is but one law, the Law of One. The Law of One maintains God's Kingdom in wholeness and in Truth. When Truth was broken the law became broken, fragmented. Man became separated from God; man became separated from God's law.[4E]

Our nations struggle with peace because we have become divided or fragmented from the root of our soul, which is grounded in the essence of love.

John Perkins, my father-in-law, served for the Calgary Highlander's Infantry Regiment. He enlisted on February 12, 1942 and came home on May 8, 1945. John would seldom talk about World War II. It brought back too many disturbing memories for him.

Yet, when he did share the stories, they echoed both the reality of war and the grace of God. He was a chaplain with the Worthington Branch Legion for the November 11 memorial services in Wainwright. For one minute after the bugle's last post, we would listen to the silence of the wind and then the bagpipes that broke the silence.

John lived with the scars from the shrapnel in his abdomen

his entire life. He never complained. There were many of his comrades, friends that never came home.

He was 23 when he volunteered. He was trained in Ottawa Lansdowne Park, a football field which was converted into barracks. They slept under the stands. He was transferred overseas in June 1942 to England.

His job was to operate a bren gun. He would carry this 34 lb machine gun along with five magazines of bullets into battle. His troop often faced heavy artillery from German resistance. On July 6, 1944 his troop landed in Port a Caen, France. Hill 67, as it was called, was one of their missions. They were ordered to take the hill back from the enemy and hold it.

Each Calgary Highlander company had a bagpiper. Prior to battle he would play. It was a prayer really. Solders would listen, say their prayers, and then go to war. Hill 67 claimed half their troop.

There is no sense of peace in picking up a gun and gunning another man down. There is no release of horror to watch a friend drop on a battlefield. It happened all too often. One would live and the other would die.

Yet there were miracles. God in His mercy somehow looked down from heaven and watched over John's life with His gentle spirit. John would sometimes tell the stories—walking against a moonlit night across open fields, finding shelter in a barn and then waking up ahead of the German's who were sleeping at the other end. Another was when he peeked his head out of the foxhole, only to be shot unconscious. The bullet hit his helmet and the helmet saved his life.

Once they were taking shelter behind mounds of dirt and then hedge hopping against artillery fire to cross the open field. They would cross in pairs. One partner would run and the other would give fire at the enemy. On this one occasion he was told to take cover, so he dove to the ground. When he had reached the other side, both the bren gun that he was carrying and four of the magazines had taken fire. There were bullets lodged in his army combat uniform jacket that he was wearing, yet he was not hurt.

John was at Falaise and at Big Bulge where allied tanks lined up and moved across France. In late 1944 he was deployed to Holland. Christmas was spent in a forest of pine trees against a snowy back drop. On New Year's Eve they drank rum to celebrate living another year and at the stroke of midnight the Germans began shooting at their camp. Suddenly, visible angelic lights of green, red and blue streaked across the heavens as the bullets sprayed through the camp and then there was silence. The night gave way to dawn and the Germans moved on. No one was hurt.

In February of 1945 they were ordered to capture Wyler, Holland. John never made it. They were attacked and John took fire. Shell shrapnel pierced him just below his chest. His partner dressed him as best he could and then he walked across a field for first aid. It was a half mile that he walked alone with shells whistling past him. He placed pressure on his wound and said the Lord's Prayer. He made it. He learned afterwards that he had walked through a mine field.

It was an Australian doctor that eventually patched him back together. The surgeon who operated on him was in a military army surgical hospital, a MASH unit. For seven days he laid on the front lines with intravenous in both his arms and ankles against the back drop of anti-tank gun fire.

He was moved to a hospital back in France. In March he was taken to Taplow Hospital in England, where his sister Edna was stationed as a nurse. John was sent back to Canada and his service ended in June 1945. He was finally released from an Edmonton hospital in August 1945 and returned home to Edgerton, Alberta to farm. He married Lillian and they had six children.

Israel. April, 1977.

I do not know of war. I never had to face war. However, to live in Israel after I finished grade 12 was to live in a nation that had this constant reality of a pending war. In Israel, peace is a day to day thing. You get up, you live your life and you put the idea of war out of your mind.

Up until mid-April, life on the Kibbutz was peaceful. That all changed one morning at 4 am. It woke me up and at first I didn't know what it was that I was hearing, but I realized quickly that it was the sound of bombs. It was a dull and distant sound, yet loud enough that my eyes sprung open in disbelief. Within about a minute, this wooden structure of a house shook. Another bomb and another. The building echoed and then shook. Then it stopped. A total of five bombs and it was over.

I got up and looked outside. The sun was just starting to rise up over the distant hills and then the birds started singing. I usually woke up to the sound of the birds. Their songs were always peaceful. 4 am was usually the time most people woke up. There were other people up and moving around, but no real evidence of panic.

By now I was living alone. Ken had moved out to live with his girlfriend, a young Jewish woman who at the time was in the Israeli army. They eventually got married had kids and moved to Canada; then five years later they moved back to Israel. He died of a sudden illness a short time after that.

Breakfast was served in the "commons" (this is what they called their kitchen and dining area) up on the hill and after breakfast people would disperse to their various work crews. There was a scattering of people, each grabbing a morning meal, cafeteria style. What seemed odd to me was that what I had heard and felt with the bombs that woke me up from my dead sleep, was not odd or alarming to others in the Kibbutz.

I sat down with one of the soldiers. Each Kibbutz had about two dozen soldiers who worked the farms, both men and women. Men served for four years in the army and the women two years.

I asked the soldier, who was sitting across from me, if he had heard the bombs. He said, "Oh yes, it is probably the Christians bombing the Sunnis." The Sunnis is a branch of Islam. The Lebanon border was only ten kilometers from our Kibbutz. You could almost see past the border from the top of the hill.

Later that day, as I was working in the orchards scraping fungus from the trees and applying a protective paint to the bark, I heard the sound of fighter jets above. Reconnaissance planes taking surveillance missions that would fly across the borders to take pictures and then fly back. I looked around—no one seemed bothered.

You can easily dismiss the war activity. There was always something going on in the afternoons and in the evenings at the Kibbutz. It was like a camp; soccer was popular, they had movies up in the commons, folk dancing and various classes such as judo and pottery. People stayed active and maybe that is why, to put their minds at ease to the constant threat of war.

That night the bombs started up again. There was more this time and they started earlier—maybe 3 am? There was a dull boom and moments later the rumble of my bed; then another boom and another rumble. I laid there and wondered who might be getting hurt? I hoped that they were bombing empty buildings. They did most of the bombing at night and I think that is why. They didn't want to hurt people. They just wanted to send a message. After about 20 minutes it stopped. Honestly, I just laid there in dis-belief. It was so surreal; almost cold to the gut and foreboding as to what might be next. I wanted to ignore and pretend that this bombing was not happening.

The next morning was different. There was a buzz in the air. You could feel it—tension. People were talking back and forth at the breakfast table. Something had happened.

Later in the orchard I had the opportunity to ask one of the soldiers that I knew, "Why all the commotion this morning?" He said, "Our fridge was raided last night." His voice seemed agitated, but I must of had a confused look as he continued, "It means we had guerrilla's in the camp." Of course being seventeen, I am thinking *gorillas...*, "guerrillas ... soldiers, most likely Lebanese, Hezbollah people. They are constantly coming over the borders, usually on a mission."

Anyone of the Israeli soldiers or even a Canadian volunteer for that matter could have been killed if they had inadvertently crossed the militant's path. The guerrilla soldiers were looking for food and that is why they were roaming through our compound the night before.

I went back doing what I was supposed to do and as I was scraping away the fungus from the apple tree, an earth shattering noise came over top of me. The noise was from a huge aircraft that looked like a C-5A. Big enough to carry tanks and it was right above the orchard, maybe 300 feet off the ground. I was thinking war is imminent and I was right in the middle of it. I looked around. No commotion, no scurry of activity. Work went on. This was definitely a different kind of normal than what I was used to.

That night as I sat at my wooden desk in my room, I held my pen and looked at the paper—a letter that I was about to write to my dad. I had to get this letter out. It was a feeling of panic and just that sinking emotion that you get in the pit of your stomach when something is not right. What was I thinking coming here? *If God had wanted me to come here for a reason, I wanted out.* It was the first time in my life that I wanted to turn my back on God. It was this foreboding emotion of darkness. I felt that if I decided to go home it would be like I was turning my back on God, but that didn't matter to me. This was such a different world and I wanted no part of it.

I put pen to paper and told my dad what was happening and that I needed to come home. I labeled the address on the envelope and then sealed it up for delivery. No sooner had I done this when a voice in my head rang clear as day.

"Your father will die in one year."

What a thought. It was almost like God's response to my decision to going home... no that's not it—it was more like God's response for me turning my back on Him. It was this deep feeling that not only was I letting my God down, but in time I would let my dad down. I discounted it. It was not something I wanted to hear.

Two days later we got news that three guerrillas were caught and shot.

Our world can be like that. Shoot first, ask questions later.

Five weeks later I was home, back in Canada. My mother didn't even know I was coming. Dad had arranged everything. I think my mom was truly nervous. She didn't like the idea of me going to Israel although she helped arrange the trip. She didn't like me flying because she was afraid that something bad would happen. It was probably better that I was flying home without her knowing.

Coming home was like it never happened. Sometimes in life you want to forget certain feelings so you just bury them; however to do that, you also try to forget that those events had even occurred. Being at home and back with family and friends was like finding heaven after a long road in hell. Israel wasn't hell, but the feelings that I had were deep and real. I think what happens is that you build up this shell of a crust over your soul to protect yourself from those decisions that could tear you apart. You choose not to feel or remember. For me God went from scary good, to just plain scary.

War is not something that you can run away from, if it is your home that is being attacked, there is no escape. Still for war to end, for the conflict to end, there has to be a healing, a wantingness for peace. A willingness to face and forgive the enemy. Although war may be regarded as mortal conflict between people or nations, its residue is left on lives long after the conflict has stopped. For people who inflict conflict—whether it is war, hatred or just selfish choices—the message of Truth is simple:

> *So as we will, so will we become. God granted us the freedom to choose but we cannot escape our choices. God is the source of life and He is always there within us. God remains with us even in the choices that would tear us apart. Yet, we can choose to place God in the shadows. He is hidden from our awareness and in our euphoria of self we are seemingly contained.*
>
> *When the Law of God becomes fragmented, love becomes fragmented. Love, which is the essence of our life force, is placed at risk love became conditional on the desire to rule chaos within the realm of order, as defined by our will. We choose who would be deserving of our love. God does not set us apart but in the midst of creation. In an instant the light can be seen when we choose to love but the darkness remains so long as we cling to our choices that would place love at risk.* 5E

Choice. Our future is always linked to the past. Our love, or even the lack of love, shapes the world that we live in. Even our choice for God, I think, can shape the construct of time. I know now that I was not bound by God to stay in Israel. But the message of my father's imminent passing was clear. It would become one of my *God lessons*. I kept it to myself.

I went back home. My father had started up his own real estate business. He loved to help people. Always doing. Always working. Dan was his partner in real estate and he helped him start the business. I ended up working with my father. I would prep houses, cut grass, paint, whatever was needed.

His illness started in October of 1977. I came back to the office mid-afternoon and there he was, lying on the floor behind his desk. He was in terrible pain, there was sweat on the brow of his forehead. His hands were clenched around his stomach. He said, "It's okay son. It will pass, just give me a few minutes."

I didn't comprehend. It just never took root in me what he was going through. By December he had checked himself into the Holy Cross hospital. He was released three days later and sent home with pain medication. They couldn't find anything wrong. He was told it was all in his head.

He laid and suffered on the couch all through Christmas trying to contain the pain, the chills and the stomach cramps.

Working was not an option now. His health was progressively deteriorating. He had no family doctor. I think he stopped seeing doctors because of the doctor who cut the malignant cyst, back in December of 1974. Maybe he lost faith in doctors?? He was pretty much all alone in his fight against cancer. I guess maybe he felt that the health care system, the doctors and the medicine couldn't save him. Maybe he had the quiet resolve that this was God's will. By February 1978, my mother had no choice but to take him back to the Holy Cross. They scheduled him for exploratory surgery.

The surgery was maybe two hours long. They basically opened up his abdomen, took one look and sewed him back together. He was too far gone. The cancer, we were told, was pervasive throughout his abdominal cavity—inoperable.

I know what cancer looks like. I spent three weeks working the turkey farm at the Kibbutz. When a turkey is sick they retrieve it from the pen, end its life and then they open it up to see what was causing the illness. That was important so that proper medication could be given to the rest of the birds. Birds that are sick are dissected and then hauled to the incinerator and burned.

Turkeys are the worst. When a bird goes down in the pen, the other birds will come over and peck at the sick bird. Usually by the time we find them, the sick bird is too far gone. You can't save them even if you wanted to.

My father was too far gone. His body had taken the toll from both the sickness and the surgery; he was too weak for saving. They sewed him up and then, after about ten days, they sent him home. I watched all this happen. After about another week at home he begged to go back to the hospital, but not to the Holy Cross.

This time he ended up in emergency up at the Foothills Hospital. He was rushed in and they found that he had over a cup and half of fluid on his lungs. He was literally drowning in his own lungs.

It was now March of 1978. Day by day he would get thinner and thinner. I would visit and watch the cancer eat him. He suffered for another six weeks. He was a 230 pound man at Christmas and now he was only 160 pounds. He had stopped eating, and even sipping fluids was a struggle.

He grasped at the metal triangle that dangled above his head—an anchor that he could use to prop himself up with. It was April 15th on a Friday night. He was alert and talking some, but still very frail, a shell of a man. My mother was there. It was just me and my mother. I don't remember much of the conversation, but there wasn't much. It was the look—the longing of his eyes as he gazed across the room to us. We would hold his hand and then came the tear. Not mine, but his. He had fought the battle, but he was done. *He was done!* There was nothing left to do but to give in to death—to let death take him.

His tear was there, but he did not want to leave us. My mother was a rock. She held his hand and whispered her love.

I let go and stood up. He turned and his eyes locked with mine, it was his look of longing to be with me that I would not forget ... "Son, please don't go."

My response, "I love you Dad and I will be back tomorrow." I left. I did not come back. Watching death take my father was too much.

There was no tomorrow. He had no tomorrow. I think he knew that it was his time. On April 17th 1978, in the pre-waking hours of the morning he passed. I miss him. I still miss him.

The sands of time are relentless. They pass us by, and once past, they are gone. You cannot go back and recapture moments to live again. You live with moments that cannot be recaptured.

Still, in all of this, God has a message. In Christianity, Jesus gasped for air and in his last breath said *it is finished*. As his head dropped to the cross, so do we also come face to face with the reality that life will pass by.

My moment that was locked in time with my father was a final plea, "Son, please don't go." Yet, in that single moment, where I am connected to my father, I am also reminded to remember my God and to not turn away from Him.

Sometimes it is the memory of the life lived that moves us to be better. It is the giving of life—the giving of one life to another. And in that giving do we find ourselves taking one step closer to heaven, one step closer to God.

And they stood and they watched on a hill, now desolate. The crosses hung amidst a pale grey sky. The air was thick and the sounds of some suffering still tormented the ears of those who stood and watched. Others who were charged with the duty to crucify became as stone to block out the death and the stench of blood. Judgment day came and went. Day after day it came and left. Another day, another life. From judgment to judgment to judgment were they crucified. Some on the cross, others in the heart and for the few who kept charge were crucified in the mind and will. Then there was silence.

As the heavens gave way to a new dawn, life emerged. Not even the cross could contain judgment against the Son of man, the Son of God. In the final judgment of Him who would judge for righteousness was the resurrection. The recreation in both body and soul to the image of what God made real in Jesus. The Christ stood at the door of an empty tomb. His life and image did not pass into death but into life eternal. 6E

Heaven's door awaits and in the last breath, in that last gasp of air, we are assured that life is eternal. With the cross, it is only in the final judgment when we stop condemning ourselves to the mistakes and choices of our past that we will find the hope for a new life. It is in that hope where we connect the dots to our *God lessons* that we will find our *God Process*—our reason to change, the reason from which we will have that inner resolve to be that better person.

I so much look forward to the day when I will again be with my father and see his smiling face—to be able to lock eyes with his and to see into the window of his soul one more time.

I look back now and I think *my God lesson* was to help me find that resolve to keep God in my life—to help remind me of what happens to my life when I turn my back on God. My *God lesson* was not a punishment, but rather a wake-up call to look and to come back to God. It was a lesson that showed me how my choices can bury God so deep into my soul to the point where I might want to walk away from God—to be afraid of God, to see God as scary.

Down deep, I think, our soul yearns for God. I also think that God wants us to have a relationship with Him. God wants us to come home. Not to heaven, but to the home which connects our soul to His essence. It is that connectedness that brings peace to our soul. It is in that reality where we will live a life that frees us from suffering, heart ache and broken relationships. God hears our heart aches. He knows when we feel lost and alone. There is laughter in home. There is dance, song and sharing of love. There are family and friends who always offer forgiveness and acceptance. God's word penetrates and calls us *all* back to Him.

—————— 4 My God Process ——————

The cross for most Christians is the pivotal turn in humanity's journey back to God. For myself, I think it is more the life and ministry of Jesus Christ that is central to the cosmic story, the cosmic *God Process*. It is a message that Jesus Christ, as the Son of God, came into creation to show us all a path back to God—that is the pivotal point in humanity's history. It is a message to bring about a hope for peace, wholeness and salvation.

Other faith traditions have a message of salvation as well which does not require the message of the cross. God I think uses many vehicles to help His creation find the path back. It is a path back to our humanity and to our goodness.

Faith traditions are important. Our beliefs, our religion, our understanding of God and how God acts on us or on His creation provides the framework through which we view life and, for many, our life beyond this life.

We are protective of our faith. Still, there are common themes that pass through our life regardless of our faith which point us towards our humanity and goodwill towards each other.

I was raised in a family and in a faith which believes in miracles. We believe that God is actively engaged in our lives. We believe that if we ask God in our prayers, God responds.

My father taught me something about prayer and it really wasn't what he said, but rather it was what prayer did to him. Prayer meant something to him. He prayed because he knew that in his prayers were the possibilities that he would invoke a response from God—a cause and effect belief. I think many people struggle with that kind of belief. I have learned that believing in prayer is a conscious decision—you choose to believe that God responds.

I often wonder why certain people are in your life. Some come and go, with others you only cross paths for a short period of time but in that brief encounter they can have a dramatic impact on you, and then there are those that you are blessed to share a lifetime with or maybe best to say their lifetime. When my father passed away his lifetime became locked in the past. Yet every so often, almost like in the movie the Time Traveler's Wife, his life resurfaces in my life.

I was inspired by how my father lived life. His example was always one of love. He had well over 300 people that showed up to pay their respects at his memorial service. My father left a wake in life. People would come up to me years later and tell me about the things that my father had done to help them out.

I am reminded of an experience about a twelve year old girl named Renny that my dad had helped. This is going back to the early 1970's. Renny was with her uncle at a gas station in Lake Louise when a gasoline hose failed and sprayed her body. She decided to go into the service bay to get the key for the washroom when the gas fumes from her body reached a pilot flame from a heater and then *puff!!* She went running outside lit up like a torch towards a young man who had just taken off his jean jacket. He grabbed her and put out the flames with that jacket. She doesn't know why he took off his jacket on that cold chilly day, but it became one of those miracles for her—he was her first angel in this horrific period in her life.

She was taken to a Calgary hospital in the back of her uncle's camper and then dropped off alone. Her legs were badly burnt; she had third degree burns with the front and back of her legs covered in blisters. It was a long two hour road through the mountains and the hills, and the blisters were sucking the fluids from her body; the thirst was unquenchable. Still she remembers the prayer of her aunt and the care that she gave her. It was that prayer that assured her that it would be okay, because she knew that God would listen to her aunt.

Her road to recovery was even longer. It was more than just the healing of the body. At the time she had no protector in life. It wasn't until she became a mother that she would find a true healing for her soul. Raising her daughters healed her of her wounds. Love does that. Sometimes it takes a lot of soul searching to make peace with life.

She wrote me a letter in June of 1994, some sixteen years after my dad passed away. Here is part of what she said:

Dear Kirk,

It may come as a surprise getting a letter from me, but after you read this you will realize that it is long overdue. I tried to express my feelings on paper many times but found it too difficult. But today is Father's day and I thought it was fitting.

My connection with your dad started when I was in the hospital. Sixty percent of my body was burned. I was not only lonely and sad, I was also very angry. I was determined to think that the rest of my life was ruined.

Then one day your dad came to visit me. He heard of my accident through someone in the church. How he came to know of my emotional pain must have been through God. He must have heard that I complained about the hospital food because he brought me a steak sandwich. Many times he would bring me a milkshake. The most memorable visit was when he filled my room with flowers (courtesy of Leyden's Funeral Home). The room had so many flowers that it depleted the air of its oxygen.

He learned that I loved football and so he went out of his way to get two autographed football programs, one from the Calgary Stampeders and one from the Winnipeg Blue Bombers. I treasured these like gold.

What he left me with was more than just presents. He taught me a whole new way of thinking. Sad thing is, I never really appreciated it until I became an adult. Sadder still is that I never had the chance to thank him.

He told me about his life when he was a boy, bed-stricken because of his asthma. Then one day a Jewish Rabbi came to visit him. In a single moment, this Rabbi's prayer healed him of his asthma. He said the gift of breath was a miracle. To be able to breathe again and not gasp for air was a miracle.

He told me of a man that was down the hallway from my hospital room who was dying of cancer and that his wife was expecting a baby. They said he wouldn't live long enough to see the baby... but he did. He lived long enough to hold his newborn son and then he died a few days later.

He would tell me stories about other people who had problems that made my situation look not so bad. I remember a motto that he gave me: "I pitied myself because I had no shoes until I saw the man who had no feet."

I thought by sharing this I could redeem myself for the lack of gratitude that I had as a child. I am so thankful for all the love and caring that your father gave to me. My own father rarely came to see me in the hospital but your dad was my most favorite visitor and a friend that I needed at a crucial time in my life. For that I am so grateful.

Your dad made a difference in my life. To you he might have been the greatest dad but for me he was an angel from God.

Renny.

I too became connected to Renny. Renny was supposed to go on a holiday that tragic day of her accident, but it never happened. A year later, my family took a trip to Disneyland and Renny joined us. We drove down the Oregon coast and I remember camping outside, eating at picnic tables and enjoying ice cream. Over the years our paths cross from time to time. There are some people in life that always stay with you. My love for Renny has always stayed with me and she is one of my adopted sisters.

People that choose to love are surrounded by people. People that push the human spirit remind us of our potential. People that stand beside us when life is tragic are angels from heaven. God's essence, I think, is about the connections. Healing each other by how we touch each other creates a better world. God's essence in my life, I think, creates a better person out of me.

Darkness, however, can trap us. Experiences like this can trap us. We can set ourselves apart from each other by how we respond to life. If my father had not chosen to take time to visit Renny, her life may have been very different. Renny's choice to see and dream the hope for life was also pivotal. Bit by bit, the choices that we all make have an influence on the very fabric of life itself.

I think back to my God Process and the choices that I have made. With most choices, I have no regrets. There are choices, however, which have caused darkness in my life. It is sometimes in those choices we find our God lessons.

In Christianity there is symbolism in the apple—it is symbolic of a choice that led to the loss of innocence in the Garden of Eden. It is symbolic of the knowledge of good and evil. The apple elevates our awareness that there was a separation between our "self" (our ego) and that part of our soul which is connected to God.

Darkness can set into our soul if we allow it. Darkness is the loss of love, the inability to love, the unwantingness to feel love. It is that cold hard feeling that makes you want to hide from yourself, others and God. Darkness is what happens when you encase yourself from both your soul and your God. It is like a cocoon that wraps around both your mind and your heart. Darkness clouds your judgment, which makes the choice to love or to be loved so hard.

In each moment, each decision and each act, there is a choice. That choice can either bind us to one another or it can set us apart. From a cosmic perspective that is the human condition. It is a condition of choice. Our conscious choice can either solidify or sever our relationships. Our conscious choice can either move us towards God or our choice can trap us in darkness. Our choice can either add to our goodness or it can hide our goodness.

For many Christians, the cross was necessary for salvation. There is a belief that it is through the cross that we are saved. Many Christians believe that God required the sacrifice of Jesus on the cross so that God could bring about redemption. For myself, *my God lessons* needed something else.

I needed to believe the cross did something different. I needed to believe that God was not a God of retribution, condemnation or punishment. I needed to believe that the path of the cross was *not* a payment for sin, but a passion endured to show me the path to innocence.[7] For me, the cross is what we all suffer when we choose to judge and condemn. Self-condemnation is the worst. We crucify ourselves, others and even our God when we inflict acts of judgment and condemnation. For me, the passion of the Christ also symbolizes the cross that we would willingly bear when we endure on behalf of others. From a cosmic perspective I think the cross was the passion endured to show us the path of selflessness—to lay down one's life so that others might find new life.

> *Greater love hath no man than this, that a man lay down his life for his friends.*
>
> *John 15:13*

It is the gift of a life. It is the gift of one life to another. For God so loved the world. The gift of passion endured.

With bad choices there are consequences and the consequences from those choices can add up. We become trapped by the error against others, against ourselves and even against God Himself. The road back to forgiveness and healing becomes complicated. There is a passage in *Part II: The Message*, which I like, as it captures the cry of our soul and the whisper of God.

---

7   Contrary to Isaiah 53:10, which proclaims that "it pleased the LORD to bruise him; he hath put him to grief", and made "his soul an offering for sin". The message that speaks for God is a message which claims that God in Christ willingly endured the passion and bore the bruises and grief as an offering to release us from sin.

It is judgment; condemnation, that has imprisoned us from Truth and separated us from God. We have crucified ourselves, our brother, our sister, our friend and even our Creator out of our desire for retribution. It was our shared guilt that imprisoned us from one another and from God. We knew not what we did. Did Jesus condemn those that crucified him? What more could God do to show that He is not a God of condemnation? Yet, the crucifixion could not claim life. Jesus was raised from the dead to show us that God is a God of life and not a God of condemnation.[7E]

Messages that speak for God remind us of the important things in life. God's message is that condemnation sets us apart, and it is love that binds us together.

Forgiving and feeling acceptable to my God was the hardest thing for me to do. My choice to turn my back on my God that night as I sat and wrote my letter to my father had consequences. To consciously shut God out of my life for me had consequences. My feeling of acceptance to my God went beyond what Christ did on the cross. It is one thing to know and believe on God's gift of passion, it is another to feel acceptable. For myself, I felt like I had locked myself to my past. This was not about God forgiving me, rather it was about me forgiving myself. Condemnation can do that.

We can condemn ourselves, we can condemn other people and in condemnation our lives can become locked to the past.

To free myself from my past I needed to believe that God was *not* trying to bring me to my knees, but instead that God was trying to lift me up off my knees. I needed to feel an end to this rollercoaster ride of my darkness, my prison. I needed a simple acceptance in my soul that would restore me to this light of healing and to wholeness. I needed this inner assurance that *my God Process* was not one of punishment or retribution, but rather these *God lessons* were there to teach me to listen to my soul—to show me *a Message* that could end the suffering that I lived with because of my past decisions. I needed to find a new meaning to life—a meaning which spoke of God's acceptance and love. I needed *a Message* that was in my soul, so that I could believe that the path to salvation was not through sin and darkness, but rather it was through embracing God's light of love, forgiveness and acceptance.

I now see the *cross* as the tool, to show us what we do to ourselves when we *choose* to live with our own self-condemnation. It is the condemnation that comes from our own self-judgment to the regrets and to the choices that cause us not to love or to not want to be loved. Without self-forgiveness, without wanting that resolve to be a different person, we become trapped in the darkness where the lack of love continues to set us apart. God can forgive us, but our self-forgiveness has to come from a choice to allow love in. We ourselves become trapped to our own *cross* as a payment for the error of our ways when we choose not to love.

God, I believe, wants to end the chaos of our lives. He wants to end the darkness and the suffering, but He cannot because we won't let go of our wantingness to *not* love. He has given us free will. We are free to choose, but we have to want to look to the light if we are going to see the message. God's message is always one of invitation. *God's light is but a spark away.* That light is the gift of love that can pierce the cocoon that surrounds our soul.

It is important that we try to connect the dots in our lives. For some of us, we need to see why we are afraid to love, why we are afraid to forgive, or why we choose *not* to come back to God.

Our lives are placed on a path to help us connect the dots. There are certain themes, lessons that reoccur over the course of a lifetime. There are moments of decision where we must choose. It is in these moments that we are tested. Our value system and our beliefs are being tested. At the very root of our soul, these moments will either define us or redefine us. When these moments occur, that is when *the God Process* is at work. These are the moments which are pivotal and it is there that we will find the resolve to change, to rethink who we are and what we are about.

Our *God Process* is our soul trying to tell us something. God is calling to us. God is trying to break the shell of our cocoon that hides His light. God is trying to have us look through these moments so that we might see the choices that bind us to the darkness, to our self-judgment of condemnation, and to those memories that would set us apart from not wanting to love. God offers us a healing. In our choice we either move towards the light or we cling to the darkness that hides us from both God and each other.

Choices which challenge us are never easy. Doing what is right might mean doing the greater good for the faceless strangers. These choices can draw us towards our humanity and liberates our soul. The right choice adds to our self-worth, to our community and it may be the right thing to do for the Earth. However, it becomes complicated if doing what is right also puts our job at risk or our job only benefits the chosen few for their own profit or power. These are moments that hit the core of our value system and we have to choose between morality, principles and relationships. People, whether it is a friend, a colleague, a boss or our family, can pull us away from the good nature of our soul and draw us into decisions which are not right.

Of course there are numerous scenarios where our choices will challenge us. The choice may be between helping people or helping ourselves. Sometimes, however, we have to realize that helping ourselves ahead of others is the right choice and we need to accept that. Conflict that creates this darkness in our soul has many different shades of grey.

The bottom line is that we know. We all know when there is something that is not quite right. We can recognize *the God Process* of life if we step out of the moment to look and see. It is what *life does to us* regardless of our belief or faith in God.

Having said all this, I now also realize that *the God Process* isn't always about the darkness and reclaiming us from the darkness. I think *the God Process* is more about growing into the light. *The God Process,* I think, is about becoming more then what we already are. It is about infusing God's light, God's essence, into our soul so that the soul might shine a little brighter. It is only about the darkness when we get lost to God and God has to help us find a way back.

If I were to count the hours of my life, I think I could honestly say I lived my life for my wife and for my children. I think most of us do that, we live our life for other people. We find the greatest joy in life from watching our children live their dreams or from helping someone else—friendship, to be a brother or sister. To follow them around to the football games, the soccer games, the basketball games, the piano recitals, to the drama performances and to their award ceremonies. It is in these events that I have my best memories. It is in the taking of time to enjoy life, the trips to the beach or to the mountains or to Walt Disney World. We live life for Christmas, family dinners, playing cards or backgammon. Good memories fill the soul.

My son, would get so excited at Christmas time. He would come bouncing down the stairs in enthusiasm saying, "Oh boy, oh boy, oh boy!!" as his eyes lit up at the sight of the presents under the tree. His love for life was carried into his passion for football. As an offensive lineman his job was to protect—to use force, grit and power to shield the quarterback. Yet in life he always manages to use words to reason out conflict. Sometimes you learn more about life from your children then you do from years of living your own life.

My oldest daughter, loved art. She expressed her soul by painting and sending us love messages through her art. She was the feisty one on the basketball court, but kept her cool even in the scraps of the game. Her way was one of laughter. The atmosphere in our home was always one of laughter when my children were around.

My middle daughter, was the serious one. She was maybe too much like her dad. She loved the piano and constantly immersed herself in learning. Her love was a quiet love. When she was eight months old I would hold her in my arms and she would reach up and grasp my earlobe with her finger and thumb to rub it. Yesterday, I was sitting on the easy-back couch next to her as we were watching TV and she reached over with her finger and thumb to rub my ear lobe. She is now 25.

Love can have a far more reaching impact on our lives than any regrets that we might have. Celebrating our dreams with one another, triumphs in our soul. Our dreams inspire us to our potential. It is in the joy of our life that our soul is illuminated.

My grandparents always took time to make memories. I wrote a poem for my grandparents. I used calligraphy on parchment paper and framed it for their living room. They too were angels of love for so many people.

> *Your kindness I can never repay,*
> *but I will take what you have given me,*
> *and I will give it to another,*
> *for what is love,*
> *but a gift from the heart.*

It's so simple to love and it means so much to others. You have to wonder why some of us find it such a hard thing to do. It is probably because of the "me"—the "me" is so hard to love.

Still *my God Process* was to come to terms with who I am. In my youth and in my innocence, God was real. As I grew into adulthood, I turned my back on God and for me that was what started this rollercoaster ride of my life. I felt responsible for my dad's suffering and passing. It was a rollercoaster of wanting God in my life and not wanting God in my life. It was about listening to my soul and then coming to terms with what was in my soul. It was a rollercoaster of wanting people in my life and not wanting people in my life. It was a rollercoaster of wanting to love and to be loved, and then building a shell around my life that would keep God and people out. *My God Process* was coming to terms with what I am willing to let other people see. I had to make a conscious decision for God. I had to make a conscious choice to share my soul.

It was only by looking back and connecting the dots that I would learn how to break the shell and find a healing. Before you can live your dreams you sometimes have to find healing in your life. *The Message* that is in Part II helped me to heal.

The cross that Jesus bore was the tool to remind me of what I needed to do. I needed to end the self-condemnation; I needed to end the self-judgments that I had of myself and against those that I found difficult to love. It reminded me of my need to allow God in and to let my soul out. The cross reminded me of the potential for new life when I look to God.

Still, to claim my healing, I realized that I would have to put the cross down and rise up to live life—to live my life for love as I quietly shared my soul through the pages of a book.

My God Process, is *my God Process*. Your God Process may have nothing to do with my God Process. The common denominator is that *the God Process* breaks through the shell that hides us from love, from being loved, from self-condemnation and from self-forgiveness. As life is lived we will change. Life's lessons will teach us, shape us and mold us. Once healed, we are motivated to engage in the creative process—to create, to dream dreams and to reach for our potential. We are engaged to infuse more life into life.

───────── 5 The Accident ─────────

Sometimes people make bad choices and those choices can make life tragic. Our ideas about why these tragic events happen to us in life can get twisted. Finding God and understanding the why is not always easy.

It was around 5 pm when I heard about the accident on the radio. Strange how it is but I thought of my mother. I had no idea. Lorraine and I were planning on going out for supper. I turned to Lorraine and I said I think we need to go home.

Back then we did not have a cell phone—there were no cell phones. It was October 1, 1982.

Shortly after we got home we got the call. My mother was rushed to the Foothills Hospital. At the time Lorraine and I had only been married for about a year and we had no children.

When we arrived she was still in emergency. She was sitting up with her arm to the side, covered in blood; shards of glass, which had sprayed from the vehicle had cut her face and body. She just got back from having x-rays. I still remembered the facial lines beneath the fragmented cuts, the deep, deep pain from what had just occurred. She kept looking at her hand, trying to move her fingers but nothing—no response.

Within minutes the doctor pulled me aside. "You are her son?

I need to show you this." The x-ray was horrific. My mother's left arm was completely shattered. The elbow was gone. Absolutely nothing left. My eyes filled with tears. I turned to my mother and the first thing she said was, "It's going to be okay."

The doctor was compassionate. He said to her, "I need you to be strong because the x-ray I have to show you is not good." He then turned the display so she could see. "We have to operate. We will see what it looks like once we get in, but I do not want you to get your hopes up; more than likely we will have to amputate."

"It's okay. You do what you have to do." Her response was one of acceptance and bravery. With my dad's passing, I had already witnessed her strength even when her life was tragic.

My mother was on the way to the mall after finishing her day at the Hebrew School. It was a little after 4 pm on a Friday afternoon. Her vehicle was in for service at Jack Carters, which was about a thirty minute walk from the school. She was offered a ride but declined as she enjoyed the walk.

A rather typical afternoon with rush-hour traffic. She was making her way south to the mall after picking up her car. She saw it all but she was trapped in between the cars as they were inching south. A black truck, chasing a gold truck heading north on Macleod Trail, bumping each other as they sped towards her on the north bound side of the road.

The man who hit her was from a town in Alberta called Hobbema; he was of no fixed address who had already lost his driver's license for drinking and driving—but that didn't stop him from getting into his friend's truck and taking off. He was already drunk by four in the afternoon. Some argument ensued and two of his buddies were chasing him down Macleod Trail at high speeds in a game of chase and catch, cat and mouse. The impact was sudden after the gold truck hit the six inch high cement meridian; his truck was airborne striking the driver's side of my mother's Malibu Buick car riding down the side and crushing her arm as it rested on the ledge of the car door window. In the process of the twisted metal and shattered windows, her car spun backwards into the vehicles behind and then came to a stop.

She was awake. She remembered people coming and consoling her. One person was able to get into the passenger's seat and he held her in his arms to calm her. She could see the man that hit her get out of his truck. He was uninjured but could hardly stand he was so drunk.

In a single moment, a single blink of an eye, her life was altered. Changed. Severed.

It was one thing to lose your husband, your companion; it is quite another to lose a part of yourself, to become an amputee. To, all of a sudden, not be a whole person.

If ever there was ever a reason to stop believing in God, to blame God for the cards that you were being dealt I think she would be justified to do so. She did not. Not once did she blame God.

I remember conversations. Conversations of why? People's beliefs can add misery to the pain. People who really do not know God. People who suggest that things happen in life as a result of sin do not know God. I remember one conversation of a friend of hers who said the accident was God's choosing, that somewhere in her past she committed sin and that sin required retribution—punishment.

In moments of despair, loneliness and even anger we ask "the why?" Sometimes she questioned God's usefulness for her. I know she spent many nights alone and in the emptiness and in the void where she would relive that moment.

"God why me? If I had only lived my life differently that day. If only I had taken that ride to Jack Carter's that was offered to me, but I chose to walk."

Yet she had faith in God. Not once did I ever hear her say that God had abandoned her. Her message to me was that God makes us stronger by the challenges we face. Still, the answers as to the *why* are never easy.

She was taken to the operating room but the surgery was only an hour or two. By 10 pm she had no left arm, only a stump. *Stump... that is what she called it. I think it was a blunt name to remind others as to how she felt.* Lorraine and I stayed with her that night in the hospital room.

She spent the next two days in the hospital, more so I think to cope with the pain and emotional adjustment to what had just happened. She asked if we would bring up her yarn and crochet needles. It was one of the strongest memories that I have of that day after the accident—watching her as she sat up in the bed, smiling and trying to crochet a block, a dish cloth. She had the hospital table up as high as possible with a pillow under her arm. She held the crochet block with the stump against the pillow. She accomplished the task, but the block was twice the size that it should be. She never crocheted again.

I know she wanted to appear strong. She wanted to be strong. Her independence and appearance was so important to her. It was the little things that worried her. She was worried about how she was going to curl her hair in the morning, yet she was back to work within two weeks of the accident.

My mother loved to play the piano and the organ. She was quite talented. When I was young I learned to play the organ. I still play. It is a gift that allows you to express what you are feeling inside. It allows a part of you to express love to the listening ear. Playing for others can bring both pleasure and fulfillment. It can also empty your soul of emotions. Hurt and pain can be released into the keys of the piano. The day she lost her arm was the day the music became locked inside her. No longer could she express her soul to hear the music. It was the day the music died.

She loved to cook. She was like her mother in that way. Always entertaining, always cooking. It was another way to express her soul to others. To have people in her life, to have people visit her home was everything to her. Her eyes would sparkle and her life would be full. Now she could not cook for family events unless she had help. She always had help. But asking for help was not her way. As the days lingered and the months became years the home became empty. Sadness has a way of not being noticed, but it can be felt in the hollowness of walls.

When you lose a limb so much has to change in your life. How you do things. How long it takes to do things. How you see yourself. How others see you.

Working at a school you are always around children. Children in their innocence and natural curiosity look and ask questions. This never bothered her. She was very cognizant of her appearance. Adults should know better. Some did not and that bothered her—so much so that she never ever went into public without wearing her cosmetic arm.

The cosmetic arm took some time to put on. You have to insert the stump of the arm into the pocket of the artificial limb. There are straps that go up over the shoulders and come down around the back and the chest. The straps would then have to be tightened to secure the arm in place. To accomplish this task she would first cover her stump with a nylon sock. She then would lay on the bed with the straps laid out flat underneath her. She would use her right hand to place the stump through the plastic pocket. This took some doing, because it was not just a matter of putting this cosmetic arm on. She had to get the fingers in place. Now that might sound a little odd but she said even though she had no hand she always felt like she still had a hand and fingers. Doctors called it a phantom sensation—nerves that send signals to the brain. She however knew differently, for her it was her spirit. Her spirit arm. Her spirit hand and fingers.

When she slept at night she had dreams—dreams where she was whole. Only in these dreams would she ever feel rested. Halfway through many nights she would wake-up because she would turn over and feel her stump. It was a horrific experience to be reminded of her reality when she was in a dream where she felt whole.

Once her cosmetic arm felt right she would have to strap herself in with the right arm. Sometimes she struggled with the straps. The cosmetic arm itself weighed about four to five pounds, but it needed to be properly secured so that it would not slip off. With her bicep severed, this piece of plastic was heavy. There was a small hole in the cosmetic arm just below her stump. She would use a metal hook to reach in and pull out the nylon sock. This created a bit of a vacuum seal and allowed the stump to better grip the plastic.

The prosthetic arm always left sores. Sores from the strap on her shoulder and back; sores on the stump, red spots and bruises. No one other than her family knew. She kept it to herself.

On the physical side she had to relearn to live her life. Tying up an apron with one hand. Tying up shoe laces. Doing up buttons on sleeves and skirts. Taking lids off jars, typing, cutting her own food and washing dishes in a sink with one hand. Try putting a plastic garbage bag into a garbage bin or grating cheese or stirring ingredients in a bowl with just one hand. All these tasks had to be relearned.

The tough tasks were tasks that caused her humiliation. Putting butter on bread in public could be quite humiliating. Her attempts sometimes ended with putting butter on her cosmetic hand. It was a loss of femininity and dignity.

In some of her memoirs, I found a few reflections that captured her anguish.

> *There are not words that can adequately express how traumatic the loss of my arm was. There has not been one area of my life that has not been affected. There is not one hour of the day that I am not aware of the loss. It is not something that will ever go away. So many pleasures of my life have been removed completely.*

My mother was in a relationship at the time of the accident and she had been with him for almost two years. He ended their relationship three months later. It was another painful loss. To feel both alone again and not whole was a struggle. Yet she was always one who accepted what was and looked for meaning. In her memoirs was a poem that I think she kept as a response to looking back on what was happening in her life.

> *After a while, you learn the subtle difference between holding a hand and chaining a soul. You learn that love doesn't mean leaning and company doesn't mean security. You begin to understand that kisses aren't contracts and presents are not promises. You begin to accept your defeats with your head held up and your*

eyes open with the grace of an adult, not the grief of a child.

You learn to build all your roads on today because tomorrows ground is too uncertain for plans and the future has a way of falling down in mid-flight. After a while you learn that even sunshine burns if you get too much. Instead of waiting for someone to bring you flowers you plant your own garden and decorate your own soul.

You learn that you really can endure, that you really are strong. You learn that you really do have worth. And you learn and you learn. With every good-bye you learn.

By Veronica Shoffstall, 1971

With every sunset there is a sunrise. In every encounter, every event, every moment comes unforeseen blessings.

Charlotta was the daughter of the man my mother was dating at the time of her accident. She was eleven when the accident happened. My mother became her second mother and Charlotta gave her purpose in life, a relationship my mother cherished. She is now my adopted sister. Charlotta has a family of four beautiful children and is a rich part of our lives. Her laughter brightens my soul.

In June of 1986 my mother met another man. His name was Charles. She called him Chuck. Our first child, was born in August of 1986. For my mother, this was two miracles in two months.

The joy, the laughter and the happiness reminds us as to the *why* we endure. It reminds us as to why we live.

I have a close cousin who I think is far more grounded than I am. He is someone who lives his life true to himself. He lives for family. He loves his wife, he loves his dog and his relationship with God is quite private. His name is Gordon.

Gordon and I ride bikes together. We would ride four to five hours at a time. Sometimes in rain and snow, with wind pushing against us like a wall as we fight to climb a hill some eight kilometers long. All along as you make the climb you think, *Why did I ever sign up for this?* Usually we bike with a group of people and Gordon could easily ride ahead of me and get to the end faster. But he didn't. He stayed with me and helped me through the hills, the wind, the rain and the snow. Then, at the end of the ride, you laugh about the torture you just put yourself through, seemingly all in the name of fun, which was not fun at all. Anyone that has ever done this or something like it can relate.

Life is like that. We climb the mountain. We run the distance. We work countless hours. We self-sacrifice and give our whole life for the jobs that we do and to the people that are around us. Sometimes there are accidents and in the process we allow ourselves to be hurt, damaged or robbed and we suffer. But we also forgive, we laugh, we sing, we dance and we move on. If it were not for that special someone in our life to help us along the way, some days would almost be too daunting.

Chuck became that certain someone for my mother. Charlotta was that certain someone. My baby daughter at that time was that certain someone. These people gave her joy and made life worth living.

Life becomes like a playground of play, fall and get up. We take risks when we climb. We take risks when we open ourselves up and give of ourselves to others. We have accidents. We become vulnerable. Our lives become vulnerable. We all do it.

The tough part is trying to figure out the lesson when things go badly. What have we learned from it? What "God lesson" have we learned? How does God heal us, how does God give us back our wholeness, how can we find our innocence after it is lost?

At the end of the day and when you look back on life, what will stand out? What kind of impact will you have had on your life? What legacy will you leave for your children? How will your life impact the world that you will leave behind?

It is out of our own free will that we jump onto the playground of life. We do so willingly. We are living this life and we have all these people in our life so that we might experience life. If we are to grow and become more than what we are now we know that we might have to risk falling off the swing. And we do fall. Constantly.

When we fall we ask the *why?* Why did we fall? Did someone push us? How did it make us look? Are we hurt physically, mentally, emotionally? The problem, however, isn't in the fall; the problem, the difficult part, is in the getting up. How do we get up, shake it off and learn from the experience?

The *God Process* is also allowing free will to take us on the journey and then knowing that God is still there waiting and wanting to catch us—to help us up. To remain open to healing and wholeness we have to want that healing and wholeness. We will never fully find healing, wholeness or happiness unless we stop the bus and open the door for God.

The man that drove his truck across the meridian and crushed my mother's arm never ever showed remorse. Not once did he apologize. She sat through the trial where he was convicted of impaired driving and criminal negligence and then sentenced to one year in prison. What really bothered my mother was that not once did he say he was sorry. Yet she never hated the man who did what he did to her—she just hated what he did to her. Sometimes bitterness overwhelms forgiveness. It is not about forgiveness, it's about living with feeling bitter—*feeling robbed.*

The *God Process* may not be biblical at all. It is not always an event where I've been redeemed or I have been saved, praise the Lord, Alleluia! Finding meaning in life and finding healing in life sometimes means you have to take one step at a time to finding the *why* to life. Meaning comes when we look back, connect the dots and find the lessons in life that change us.

To see the sunrise one has to be willing to live through the night. To appreciate what it means to stand tall may mean that we first have to fall. To become stronger, more loving, more compassionate we may have to know what it means to be weak, unloved or unwanted.

Sometimes finding a need for God—finding a desire for God— means you need to know what life is like to walk in darkness. Perhaps in order to help someone else through the darkness, you may have to be willing to walk with them, beside them in the darkness.

The *why* to life is often found in that gem that is inside ourselves. To see what is beautiful inside of us and then allowing our soul to express that beauty to others. Our courage, our compassion, our commitment, our ability to endure and overcome, are the gems of the soul. To see what we truly are capable of and that we have the potential to be more. Sometimes the gem is discovering our love for other people—discovering the deep love that we have for our wife, a mother, a father, brother, sister, friend or neighbor. To share ourselves with someone else is life's greatest gift. That bond comes from the choices we make in the playground of life.

> *What makes life beautiful comes from what is inside us. You and I are bonded together by God. But God cannot change you or I so that we recognize the bond that God has created. God cannot change you or I into something that we do not desire to be. In His gift of free will He gives us the choice. The choices are many, yet only one will prevail. In every instant that is lived only one will prevail.*
>
> *Somewhere then between what I say and do and the person that I would hope to be, is the who I am.*[8E]

We are on this amazing road of self-discovery. It is a road which can take us to the peak of the mountains or to the depths of the sea. It is a road which twists and turns and the view is spectacular. It is a journey with friends, family, neighbors and people filled with potential. We can dream dreams and experience the world in all its wonder. What an amazing opportunity we have to find the treasurers of life.

It is the simple choices that free us. It is taking time to say we are sorry. It is the reaching of a hand to hold someone in your arms to console them as you wait for an ambulance. It is the sincerity of thought with the intention to bind our lives with someone else that free us. Walk a mile in their shoes.

6 Moments of 9-1-1

I had the opportunity of spending time in New York City and have often been reminded of the day that terrorism shocked the world. One of the cab drivers I was with witnessed the planes as they struck the Twin Towers. He was taking a client to the North Tower.

The horrific events of 9/11 are a grim reminder of what people can do to people. It is a reminder of what our human nature is capable of, both our humanity and our inhumanity.[8] It testifies as to how humanity rises above inhumanity. It shows the willingness and wantingness of people who would sacrifice—people who had the courage, the first responders who raced and risked life to help others in the moment of need and crises. 9/11 also reminds us that we are all connected, one global nation who were all affected by the inhumanity of a few, unified to overcoming terrorism.

The day of 9/11, September 11, 2001, and the days that followed 9/11, ashes fell like snow on a quiet and still cemetery of a church that has stood since 1766. Saint Paul's church was at the edge of Ground Zero. It was a church where first responders would go—some to be fed, others to rest and many to be consoled. It was a place of refuge in a sea of carnage.

Darkness and light are often intertwined. When darkness invades our world God sends His light. When bad things happen there are people—angels really—who are willing to respond and help. First responders who enter the terror and the carnage to bring hope even if that hope is only for a few minutes. Our lives become immediately connected and blessed in ways that go beyond this life. It is eternal.

Snow.

---

8 Humanity and inhumanity are referenced throughout the book. Part of our humanity is the embracement of choice and with choice, we make mistakes. There are, however, choices that will knowingly inflict suffering or knowingly will put others at risk for suffering. When we engage in choices that erode freedoms, hopes, dreams or place at risk health, wholeness and peace, we are at risk of creating a condition of inhumanity.

As a child I use to look out my grandmother's window. The snow would fall and blanket the trees and the eves of the houses. At Christmas the lights would sparkle up and down the streets. Everyone had lights. There was atmosphere, a spirit that was in the air. Carols would ring in my listening ear from the television as my grandfather sat and listened to Tommy Hunter. Christmas cards hung across the walls of the room. There must have been two hundred of them.

My grandparent's names were Ted and Doris. During World War II many people found a place to stay in their home—strangers really. People who came to Calgary for training and needed a place to stay for a couple of weeks somehow found their way to them. As the years passed, the cards continued to come. Images of a baby in a manager, children skating, people caroling, Santa Claus, mountain scenes, a train. Every year people would write, some from Australia, many from Europe, most from Alberta, all to wish Merry Christmas and to share what was happening in their lives. The Christmas cards were as magical as the Christmas tree—almost brighter than the lights that lined the houses.

My grandmother in her own way was a first-responder to people who were in need. A meal, a listening ear, a bed—a roof from the elements.

My grandmother lost a child. This little baby was 9 days old. Marian was born with a heart disorder but back then they could not save her. Marian was buried sixteen days after she was born next to her grandmother and grandfather on the homestead.

My grandmother said, "You know I didn't understand why God sent me Marian to have and to hold for only 9 days, but I do know that I loved her as much if not more than all my other kids. I bonded with her in a way I could not have bonded with my other children. There were many times I could still feel her heartbeat next to my own. With each child that you have, you bond in different ways. Sometimes the bond is a memory, sometimes it's by touch, with Marian it was her cry for help. It was the sensation of her heartbeat in my hands as her tears rolled off her cheeks. You don't ever let go of those things that connect you."

They had a quiet funeral. For years it tore at her heart. Why would God reclaim this child after only 9 days of life?

We often find that God answers the *why* in our dreams. In a dream she found herself in an open meadow next to a child who was holding her hand. It was her. It was Marian. My grandmother knelt beside her and they hugged. Doris knew in that moment those 9 days were enough for a lifetime of love. She was always grateful for each day of Marian's heartbeat and the echoes of her tears which stayed with my grandmother.

Several years later my grandmother took a train to Vancouver. As my grandmother sat and watched the snow fall softly on the mountains against the click of the train on the tracks she noticed a young lady. This young woman was visibly shaken and upset. Many times we allow each other our space because that is what we think they need. In this instance my grandmother decided to go sit and put her arm around her. "Would you like to talk?"

As the conversation opened up this young woman's story unfolded. She was traveling home because her life was shattered. She had just lost her only child. My grandmother had a unique way of reaching into a heart and warming it with her love. After the tears and after holding this young woman in her arms, my grandmother said, "You know God has a way to take each life and plant its seed in us forever." The young women asked, "What do you mean?"

"When I lost my Marian, I had to live on; however, with Marian I never let go of her. With my other children as they grew I watched them move on and have lives of their own, however with Marian I never let go of her." My grandmother told her you have to hold on, to hang on tight and that things will get better. "With Marian," she said, "I never let go of her heartbeat. I never let go of those eyes that pierced my soul. Part of Marian lived on through me and I lived my life through the innocence of her eyes. I shared my life with Marian as if we lived life together."

My grandmother shared with this young lady how God grants us gifts. She talked about the gift of Marian, the gift of her dream. She shared with her the vision of the meadow and talked about how Marian touched her life and that love stays with you.

My grandmother knew that if there was ever a blessing that came out of Marian's life, it came from those few hours on that train. It was the prompting of the spirit to bring about a connection with another soul. Some of us live for 90 years, others live only 9 days. But a life lived always leaves an imprint and it touches others in profound ways.

We touch one another, even if it is only a few moments, a few hours or a few days.

Marian's brief 9 days had meaning. Her life had purpose. My grandmother sharing that memory of her has stayed with me. I think about the why and I know that often the *why* is in the brief moments in life that we become connected with others and to make a difference either in our own life or in other people's lives.

A heartbeat cannot be drowned by death. A soul does not go silent when we are separated by time and space. God does not take, but forever keeps our eternity. We live not just today, but in the space that exists between today—the space where time and eternity converge.

Snow.

My mother, Clara, married Chuck on August 5th, 1988. They met each other through a local singles group and spent a lot of time in the mountains. In the summer they would hike and in the winter they would cross country ski. Clara and Chuck often would take my daughter, cross country skiing with them. They had a sled and she would ride behind Chuck. Being in the mountains brought them a sense of freedom. To see and breathe the majestic nature of God's creation was her way of finding peace.

My mother stopped going to church. Over the years much of my extended family stopped going to church. Religion had lost its flavor. Their songs and their prayers that once filled our church are now absent. What was the corner stone of their lives became replaced by other things. Not that their faith in God had changed because it was still there. I know by conversations with my mother that she always had faith in God. Yet people were not finding God in church. Maybe it would be more accurate to say they stopped looking for God in church. The sad part for me is that I miss them. I miss seeing them. I miss hearing their voices and their prayers when I am at church.

On Friday January 26, 1990 we had our very last family dinner together with my mother and Chuck. It was a spontaneous event because my sister, who lives in Vancouver, just happened to be passing through Calgary. Everyone was there—my mother, Chuck, my grandmother, my sister, Lorraine and I, and our two daughters who were three and one. We didn't know it at the time, but that would be our last meal together with my mother. The memory of that evening was a rich experience for me because there are some memories which never fade. Her laughter and smile will never fade. I am a grateful for that moment.

Snow.

Two weeks later on a beautiful Sunday morning the mountains were calling to my mother.

Lorraine and I were up north in Irma, Alberta visiting Lorraine's sister and their family. My last memory of my mother was her giving me a ride to meet up with Lorraine. As I stepped out of the car I had another premonition—a message, a voice in my mind—*this will be the last time you will see your mother alive.* I dismissed it.

I often think about premonitions. I do not have them very often, but when they do occur I now recognize them as gifts. To know that God has a plan is a gift. Knowing that God has angels and that they walk beside us is confirmation to me that we do not walk through life alone. If there ever is a compelling reason to know that God is there it is by looking back on your life and seeing the *God Process.* No one can take that away from you.

February 11, 1990

Clara, Chuck and three of their friends decided to go cross country skiing through Healy Creek, a trail that starts at the base of Sunshine Ski Hill in Banff National Park and works its way west. They started their trek at about 10:30 am on a rather warm winter day. The snow was falling that day. Large flakes would land like feathers on the white sugary landscape. Others had broken the trail before them and they followed the tracks in. Approximately four kilometers in, one of their friends was feeling fatigued and decided to turn back early. That saved her life.

When the avalanche was triggered it was shortly before 1pm. They had crossed the clearing of trees a half an hour earlier and had stopped for lunch in the tree line on the opposite side of the chute. Avalanches were common here. But this was not your typical avalanche; this was a 500 year occurrence. It was triggered on the far west side of the bowl at the top of the mountain, way above the tree line. The snow gave way and swept eastward across the bowl of the mountain and then turned back on itself on its one kilometer path down the chute. Except the snow wasn't contained in the chute. It entered the tree line breaking the 200 year old spruce trees like tooth picks as it ravished everything in its path. 9 seconds. 9 seconds from the time it started to when the wall of snow struck them. People who have witnessed avalanches describe it as the sound of thunder.

All four of them were trapped, nowhere to go. No time but to turn and look. Struck and buried under three feet of snow in a snow pack that was now eight feet thick. Carried some twenty yards down the mountain from where they had stopped for lunch. Instant darkness. Instant burial.

We got the call at about 6 pm. If it were not for my mother's friend, who had turned back, we may not have known for weeks as to what had happened. This friend was waiting and waiting and then finally she asked those who were coming off the trails if they had seen or passed a group of skiers. That was when she learned about the avalanche.

First responders did what they could the first day, but they quickly learned that this was a recovery endeavor. They were found two days later—Clara (Bates) Boote-Coombes, Charles Coombes, Charlie Lorenzo and Verne Powell were claimed. Lilly Collins, their friend, was spared.

Snow.

I am reminded of the *snow*. The ashes that fell like snow on New York City. The snow that fell on the mountains as two people came together on a train to grieve in the loss of a child. The snow that fell like feathers on a wintery landscape that called my mother to the mountains. The snow that swept her away. The snow that landed outside the window, on the trees, on the eves of houses as the lights of Christmas colored my listening ear with carols when I was a child.

With every goodbye we learn. We learn that the darkness is intertwined with the light. That life does not end in death. That humanity is found even in the midst of inhumanity. That goodness overcomes and soars above carnage. We see that beauty can only be fully appreciated after we have travelled the landscape. We plant the garden of our soul by the choices that we make. We enter the playground so that we might know the joy of playing, falling and getting up.

The scars of our inhumanity can be difficult to heal. Scars that sit in the depths of our soul are difficult to bear. When the fabric of life has been torn, God enters in to work His miracles. God works His miracles by giving us back the fabric. When we tear the fabric, when the tapestry of creation has been torn by our choices, God goes to work.

He does not set us apart, but in the midst of creation, to recreate the opportunity that restores life. The opportunity to heal our hearts and minds. To blend our life with the ones we love and provide the opportunity to reclaim love in the loveless.

We choose to come. We choose to walk in the darkness so that we might show others the light. We choose to walk with others through the darkness so that they do not walk alone. We are not afraid of the darkness because we know of God's light.

The waters move and reflect the rays of the sun. The sun in all its splendor is illuminated as it becomes one with the water that it touches. The dance of light begins and lasts all the day long. But when the night came, were the oceans consumed in the darkness? No, for the darkness cannot contain the water. And where is the sun? Has it moved from its place? Do not despair in the darkness for it cannot consume you. Nor has God moved. Turn then to God, for in Him will you see what is just. For natural is His light and His splendor will illuminate even you.

Begin again and allow a just God to find a home in you. 9E

With every sunset there is a sunrise.

Behold, day has come! The sun rises on the landscape and touches all the earth that stands in her wake. The trees, the rocks, the birds and the lakes reflect her rays. Who would hide in the earth to escape her warmth? Arise and feel the radiance of what burns but is not consumed. Look with your eyes to see the life that draws strength from the sunshine. God is like sunshine. His light brings warmth by the radiance in which it burns within His creation. We are His creation. He burns in us and we are not consumed. Behold, day has come, and today we can emerge in Him. 10E

─────── 7 The Dream ───────

I had a rather normal life growing up. I had good parents. I was grounded in church. I had good friends and good schools. I was the well behaved son every parent dreams of having. On the other hand, my sister whom I love dearly, use to torment me.

My sister was good at her antics. When I was nine, I was in her space so she kicked me. I went to my mother for revenge as my mother was pretty good with the spoon, but my sister had a quick tongue. Her excuse, I should watch out when her foot is up. We have a long history of tormenting our siblings in our family. My mother would tie her brother to the leg of the stove when she was young, so my sister came by her loving ways naturally.

My sister and I when we were young were two very different kinds of people. I was very much into the "Kum Ba Yah" churchy kind of behavior. She was the free spirited 60's child. My mom use to worry and fret over the kind of friends my sister had and if she was getting into trouble. My dad on the other hand took everything in stride as he was the trouble maker child in his youth.

Funny how life comes full circle. My parents were called by the school for something my sister had done. My father showed up at the school with my sister, the principal took one look at him and said, "Oh, it's *you*—that explains a lot!" The principal was my father's shop teacher when he was growing up. My dad was a bit of a back talker and knew more about engines than this shop teacher did. Correcting and telling your teacher that he's doing it wrong in front of other students apparently didn't sit well with this guy. One of the engines that this shop teacher was working on back fired, creating somewhat of an aftershock. My dad turned to him and said, "Told you so." Anyways, my dad decided to move my sister to a different school.

My father use to be a police officer before he went into sales and then into real-estate. He had a really strong sense of right and wrong. My sister had a leather coat stolen from her once. She knew who took it, so my father went to the house of the parents to confront them. The man who came to the door did not take the accusation well. Basically he told my dad to go to hell. My father pushed him back, opened the front hall closet and there was the coat. He handed it to my sister and bid the man a good day.

I think that is where my sister gets her great charm from. She is very good at putting the truth in front of people when she knows they are lying. She can be cutting with her wit, but is usually right with her actions. She also has a great way about her. She can easily win people over and is a far easier person to talk to and be with than what I am.

I spent a lot of time with my grandparents on my mother's side when I was young. My grandmother had a strong faith and it is because of her that I believed in a God of miracles.

Family was important to my grandmother. We had many family gatherings for a meal after church on Sundays. With her children and grandchildren there were thirty-two of us. Family gatherings could get rather large. We were a close knit family, bonded together by her faith in God.

It always amazed me as to how many stories she had. Stories of how God intervened—miracles, visiting angels, healings, near death experiences and past life recollections.

The most memorable stories were back on the homestead. Her family moved to Canada in the early 1900s to Loon Lake, Saskatchewan. Her father was able to acquire the homestead from the Canadian Government. There her family built a small two storey farm house, which was quite a distance from the closest town.

Her father joined our church soon after coming to Loon Lake and took God and prayer quite seriously. One winter my grandmother's brother, Albert, came down with a severe ear ache. After several days of this, my great-grandmother Martha knew it was time to get something to help out. With it being winter, taking Albert to the nearest town to see a doctor was not an option. Traveling for them would have been on horse and buggy with seat warmers with very little protection from the elements. Roads would be covered in snow and temperatures could be below minus thirty degrees. The best home remedy would be to warm flaxseed oil which you place into the ear. However, there was no flaxseed oil in the house, so Albert's father went to the neighboring farm yard on foot to ask if they had flaxseed oil. On his walk across the prairie farm he stopped and knelt to pray to ask God for a blessing.

I think in the old days people were more reliant on God for help. Back then you didn't have access to physicians or clinics or health care. You looked to God. You prayed for blessings.

Having a deep need for God, being reliant on God is a call to God for miracles. God's response is usually one of blessings.

The story goes that at about the same time as Albert's father knelt and prayed a man, who looked like Santa Claus, came into Albert's bedroom. Albert was so excited to see Santa Claus that this man did not scare him at all. Santa Claus sat beside him on the bed and had a brief conversation with Albert, and then reached over and touched him on the ear. Santa Claus told Albert to be good and go to sleep, then left the room. Moments later, Albert could not contain himself and went running to his mother. "Mommy, Mommy I saw Santa Claus, I saw Santa Claus." He then stopped mid-stream and said to his mom, "My ear ache is gone".

This blessing, this Angel, came to Albert as Santa Claus so as to not frighten him. God works His miracles in a way that sometimes we are not even aware of it until after we have had them. Sometimes we do not recognize them as miracles or as gifts until much later in life.

As such was my dream. At the time I did not know why I had the dream or what the full meaning of the dream was. I was fifteen, sleeping, yet it seemed as if I was awake. I was very much aware of everything that was happening to me; vivid, lucid and surreal. In this dream, this vision, I found myself trapped. Trapped in a void, a darkness that just encased my entire being. I was fully aware as to what was happening and I was drawn to look at my life. I had these feelings, these thoughts, these memories. In the dream...

> *I looked deep within myself and saw the mirror of my soul. It was a vision that I had seen before, but I was unable to fixate myself on its image for it was clouded, distant and elusive. As I was drawn into the vision, I became trapped by the shadows and the darkness that mystified my whole existence. I was lost within a sea of nothingness. Drowned by the lack of light.*

> *Time stood still. In this reality time had no meaning and I was faced with only my memories. Yet even the memories were but shadows. I choose not to look, not to remember, for it seemed as if so much of it was painful. My memories seemed wrenched with a guilt that I could not fathom. I was lost to God. I knew that I was lost to God. Not by God's choosing, but by mine. Silence. My thoughts became numb. What was I to do? I called out into the mist to a God that I knew was*

there, somewhere—But time stood still.

Then, the vision shifted. It seemed as though the vision itself was being dictated by a consciousness that was not my own. I felt a presence and I sensed a voice. No words, just thoughts passed between me and the personage that I could not see. The personage knew me, his beingness seemed capable of captivating all that I was. What I could not look at myself was now in plain view to him. Through him was I allowed to see what I had forsaken. A valley appeared below me. The hills were lush with color, colors unimaginable, colors that one could touch, feel and taste. There was water that rolled through the land and its sound trickled and soothed my listening soul. I could hear laughter, children. I saw people that I knew and that I longed to be with. Their souls danced and their spirits were pure. I knew that their lives were full of love and that they had shared themselves by the choices they had made.

The vision shifted again and I saw a mountain. The mountain was illuminated by the light which emanated from a city. It was a city of light. It was my home, a home that I walked away from long ago. It was being offered to me again by the life that I now would live.

Then the vision slammed shut and I was once again in the mist and the darkness with the personage beside me. A final message, the personage said that with this life I must choose and with that I awoke.

This tiny instance of a mystical experience has stayed with me my entire life. So real was this experience that even from the eyes of my youth, I knew that this life would have an impact on my soul.

At the time, I didn't quite understand why I had the dream. I was living a good life. I had a faith and belief in God. So why the dream, why this vision? And what choice was the dream referring to?

Now I think I know. Now I think I see why I was given the gift of this dream. This gift of a dream caused me to think about everything I did in my life. It heightened and maybe over-sensitized my soul to pay attention to my "God lessons". This dream was the catalyst to connect the dots of my life so that I would not lose sight of my soul. It is only after travelling the landscape and looking back that I would be able to see the *God Process*, the reason why, the answer to my purpose in life.

I know now that I was not responsible for the suffering and death of my father. When I sealed that letter the night saying that I wanted to come home from Israel, my premonition of my father's death was not God reining punishment on me or my father. God was not punishing me for turning my back on Him. Rather, that premonition was a gift to tell me that God was in my life. He had a plan for my life—a plan to help me reclaim the essence of His presence that was buried deep inside of me. What a gift!

I know now that both the tragedies and the joys that I shared with my father and my mother were to show me that *God lessons* are not about what happens to us in life, but rather what **we do** with what happens to us in life. It is in the courage to get up, to rise up to the challenge and to become more then what we already are.

I had to make a choice. We all have to make a choice. There has to be a conscious choice for God.

This dream would point to the choice that I would have to make. My choice was whether or not to tell my story, to share my life and to share how my belief in God has impacted my life. My choice would be whether or not to share my *God lesson*, my *God Process*. It would be a choice as to whether or not I was going to share a message that was and is in my soul. It would be a choice as to whether or not I would write this book.

Looking back, looking in and looking up can be a lifelong *God Process*. In my youth I looked to God and I would pray. As I grew, the God of my youth faded. Watching my father in the death process introduced my soul to the silence of God. I became almost indifferent—his death left me with a lot of questions. Watching what happened to my mother with her pain and suffering caused even more indifference. Yet down deep it did not make sense. My soul would not stop searching for God. To see and be a part of lives that you love and knowing that you cannot change history, knowing that you are powerless to heal their pain, means you have to either accept that God is either indifferent to His creation or that He has a higher purpose, and in time we will see His purpose.

For me, it came down to a choice of whether or not I was going to allow the God of my youth to be a part of my adult life. I had to make a conscious choice to accept God into my adult life. It was not until I was in my thirties that I would come back to God and find God in my soul. However, even then it was a cyclical on and off process. Moments of where I would look to God and moments where God seemed so distant that I would not make the effort to go look for Him.

My struggle with life was always one of swinging back and forth between this pending darkness that I felt and allowing myself to be open to this mystical vision of God's wondrous message of Truth. It was such a mixture of hope and despair, light and darkness. My everyday life was the same way; giving to others and yet feeling that I was being taken advantage of. It was this constant swing of wanting people in my life and yet feeling so vulnerable to getting hurt by them. There are stories there, however they are dark and I would rather bury them in the past. But I can identify with people who have been betrayed and robbed by other people.

Finding God and seeing God in your life becomes complicated especially when you get hurt. Especially when cancer claims the people you love or accidents irreparably alter your life or when life is compounded by avalanches. Yet, I knew that I had a choice as to how I was going to allow these events to either *shape or shake* my belief in God. Even with all the extraordinary events and messages that came into my life to tell me God was there, I could still easily dismiss God. To find and have God in my life required a conscious choice and a wantingness to have the light that God offers.

Darkness in our lives can often seem overwhelming.

Often I think that there is a pending darkness that we all could be facing. Our world, our global consciousness could gravitate towards a darkness, if we collectively become lost to God. If collectively we become lost to God, we all could be at risk. Our families are at risk if we allow darkness to overtake our lives. Without God's goodness in our soul we turn on each other; we turn our backs on each other. Each to his own. No more helping hands. The light in the world grows dim. Sometime you see it on the news. At times you can feel it in the air as the world becomes polluted, the ice caps melt and the waters rise. The world seemingly teeters at the edge of its sustainability.

As darkness creeps into our society, we live with governments that want to over regulate and over tax our lives. People want entitlement; they take advantage of and look to crawl above others in the race to get ahead. Our freedoms get eroded and our hands are tied. At risk are our children who cannot find meaningful work, and yet the cost of education strips away opportunity for some and only a lifelong debt for others. Our world is becoming complicated and dark.

Having said this, I know that collectively we still have great potential. That gloom and doom is not necessarily our global fate or destiny. Almost in the same breath of darkness, one can also see the light. We see people living for people and doing good for others. We see so many organizations actively engaged in great causes. Whether it is the Red Cross, World Vision, the Shoe Box Campaign, Toy Mountain, the Mustard Seed or Samaritan's Purse; there are people and organizations doing good things to promote life and healing. Most of us are doing what we can to make a better world.

The bottom line is one of choice. We all have a choice. People in the position of power have a choice. To dispel the darkness whether it is in our lives or in our world, requires a choice. We have to want the light or the message that will dispel the darkness. We create the world that we live in.

For me, the dream was the catalyst. Connecting the dots between Ron and my father was the trigger. I needed to share a message that I had written, but was put on the shelf some ten years ago. It was an ethereal message that came from my soul. It was a message for the cosmic *God Process*.

The soul has a language. Our soul will speak to us if we are open to it. Not necessarily in audible terms, but in thoughts and in dreams. Our soul gives us direction and encourages us to make certain decisions when we are not sure what to do. Our lives are like a test sometimes and we have to choose whether or not to listen to that good voice that is inside us.

There is a light in the messages that come to us through our soul. There are messages that brighten our mind and help us to see ourselves and our world differently. Our soul calls us to God and tells us of the reality that exists in God.

We need God. We need the humanity that exists in the goodness that we identify with God. Down deep we know that if we lived with goodness at heart, our lives would get better. Our relationships would get better, our lives would get better and our world would be better.

The ethereal message that you will read in Part II is a cosmic revelation that speaks for God. It compels us to consider the cosmic story of this universal reality we call life.

God is present. In His wonders, in the possibilities, we find the potential of God to work His magic and to set in motion His miracles for our life. Believe, for the Truth will set you free. Of such is the promise that was echoed by Christ 2000 years ago.

There is a reality that exists in God and His truth calls us to that reality. When we focus on the light of God, the light becomes the beacon. Just as the star of Bethlehem leads us to the manger scene, so does God's light lead us to God. We are drawn to it for in that light we find the Source of life. Truth draws us to that reality that exists in God.

There are messages that lead us back to God, that lead us back to the reality that exists in God. Messages that compel us to have God in our lives can help with healing and wholeness. The *God Process* comes from a child holding our hand, a song that inspires our heart, a passage that enlightens our mind and laughter that cases our stress. These simple expressions can alter our awareness to draw us away from ourselves and back to each other. Our eternal journey is the journey with God. It is the journey of our soul. It is the cosmic story as it converges on life itself.

There are messages in life that leads us to peace, hope, wholeness and purpose. We only need to be open to them.

The spectrum of life brings depth to the soul. Out of creation, out of the heavens and set upon the earth was God's plan. We taste and breathe in the depth of the soul. Beyond the spirit is the experience we take in. All that was, all that is and all that will be is captured by the record that is embedded upon the life of our soul. It is the record that retains the reality of our will, desires and actions. It is the record that retains our memory of deeds, feelings and thoughts. It is the record that life has written. [11E]

There is a cosmic purpose for life. This earth and all of creation were created for a reason. There was purpose in the life of Jesus Christ and his purpose was and is to help all of humanity. The centrality of Christ can bring meaning and hope to all of us. As we explore the life of Jesus Christ we find new meaning in our own lives.

God's messages are given to us in a way that allows us to have room to breathe, because that is what God does. He gives us room to breathe. He gives us room to either accept or reject Him. Such is the *God Process*.

The decision to share my *God Process* and this ethereal Message was another one of those "God lessons" in my life. Do I share my soul?

I choose to share. The lesson was that life takes on a deeper meaning and that darkness fades away when we share our soul. The lesson was that I would find healing and wholeness in myself when I chose to open myself up to God. The lesson was that the conduits of love open up as we choose to love both ourselves and others. The very conduit for life is in the living and sharing that part of us that is a part of God.

Messages that point us to God shines a little more light into our world. As God grants us more light we will see a shift in our collective consciousness. We will see a shift in how we perceive God. We will see a shift in how we believe God interacts with His creation. We will see our cosmic purpose and hopefully that shift will create a better world.

Part II of this book is called *The Message.* It is an ethereal book. It is a message that compels us to consider God. Discovering messages that compel us to consider our *God Process* will resonate in our soul. When we open our soul to God, God finds away into our life.

Part II
THE MESSAGE

The Hope of the Message

For unto us a child is born, unto us a child is given.
And the government shall be upon his shoulder and his
name shall be called Wonderful, Counselor, Almighty
God, the everlasting Father, the Prince of Peace.

Isaiah 9:6

If ever there was a reason for hope, if there ever was a potential for *Peace on Earth*, it will come from the Word, the message that speaks for God. We look to the gift of a child who came in the meridian of time to set in motion His Father's work for *Peace on Earth*. We all hope for that day when that reality will be seen. A day where life is lived in peace, a day where the world is free of war and a day where hearts are not torn apart.

That hope starts with a message. It begins with a whisper of peace. It is the ringing of the bells on Christmas morning with the echo of "can it be"?

——————— 1 Source of The Message ———————

Rather than just jump into *"The Message"* which, starts on page 97, I wanted to ground the reader as to what this ethereal message is and why I believe I was being compelled to share it.

What is an ethereal message? Sometimes, an example is far better than words:

For unto you is born this day in the City of David is a
Savior, who is Christ the Lord.

Luke 2:11

Luke 2:11 is a fulfillment in prophecy to an ethereal message found in Isaiah 9:6 (above), which was written around 730 BC. It is an ethereal message because it is mystical and it illuminates our minds to the surreal—to a reality of possibilities, one which is of cosmic purpose. Ethereal messages do not always come to us through the normal conscious human mind. Ethereal messages come to us through dreams, through our higher consciousness or through some mystical connection with the Divine. To the critical reader, this process is inherently flawed for a number of reasons and to be viewed with skepticism. Yet, all ethereal messages written that have merit to the soul would have been received in this manner (compare Psalms 46:10, Genesis 1: 1-31 and John 1:1-14).[9]

Authenticity of an ethereal message is usually a subject of source—can the source be trusted? Again, to the critical reader there needs to be some proof of source. We are curious and yet we are quick to dismiss, unless there is proof. Ethereal messages are not readily accepted, as they need to stand the test of time and they need to be scrutinized by the "faithful", *or* God Himself must sometimes bear witness to the message if it is going to gain acceptance.

There are a lot of competing voices in the world that would want to speak on God's behalf. People that say that God has spoken to "me" and say this is what God said, are at risk of crossing the line. Praying to God is normal. Asking God to help us is normal.

---

9   Psalms 46:10 says, "Be still and know that I Am God." It is both the recognition and affirmation to the creative force—a poetic message to a reality we acknowledge, yet can only be grounded in faith. The physical reality of such is accepted by the faithful.

Genesis 1:1-31 tells the cosmic story of Creation... "In the beginning." Of course no one in human form could have witnessed these events, so it is a mystical vision of the possibilities to the creation story.

John 1:1-14 also tells the cosmic story from the perspective of who created. That God created the stage; history was preordained—scripted or constructed with purpose. It points to the ethereal, to the surreal and to our cosmic origins.

Saying that God has spoken to "me" is *not* normal. It is not normal because that is not how God works. People that say they speak for God can be problematic. Messages speak for God. Messages that compel us to consider what God has to offer will resonate. Messages that resonate and stand the test of time are messages that the soul recognizes.

The Message was written through a process called *spiritual journaling*. Spiritual journaling is allowing thoughts or messages to be written on the page without consciously directing the flow of thought of that message. Spiritual journaling is very personal and quite common. A lot of people do it. For the most part, these kinds of messages are really only intended for one person—the person that penned it. Spiritual journaling messages are not necessarily messages from God. We are compelled to share our soul, but that does not necessarily mean that the voice or the inner thoughts from within is from God. It is up to both the conduit (the writer) and the recipient (whoever hears or reads the message) to use reason and discernment.

We all have access to our soul. In fact our best creativity can come from our soul. Good music, rich literature and higher knowledge of science may in fact be sourced from the ethereal (through the soul) which is the creative process. Great music such as Handel's Halleluiah Chorus (from his *Messiah* composition) would have been heard in his mind long before he put the music on paper. God however does bring light, knowledge and beauty whether it is art, music or literature that is brought into this world, according to His design or through the inner appreciation of our soul, but it requires a willingness on our part to be both conduits and recipients of that creative process.

Messages that are ethereal in design should resonate in our soul. We quickly become in tune with great music because it resonates, it strikes a chord. Words on the other hand require a far different process because we each have a filter that accepts or rejects what we read or hear. Great literature takes us on a journey. If it is written in the form of drama, comedy, adventure or fantasy it will take us to amazing places like Asgard (*Thor*), Hogwarts (*Harry Potter*) or the Capital and District 12 (*The Hunger Games*). When we read, we are both disconnected with the story and yet fully connected, feeling and seeing ourselves as observers to these mystical fictional places. On the surface we are entertained by the action, the drama, the comedy, adventure and fantasy however at a deeper level we are moved because we recognize the cosmic struggle of light and dark, good and evil. We identify because on some level it elevates our awareness to the "what if". What if we have the power? What if we allow evil to fester in our society? What if we give in to hatred? What if we were immortal? What happens to the good guy and the bad guy? What would it be like to be rich or poor? What would it be like to live through the apocalypse?

Ethereal messages have a different element of the surreal because the alternate reality itself is the unseen reality of this eternal journey of life. By design we are supposed to pay attention because in that message is something of critical importance to the soul. We are not supposed to be the observers but rather participants. The life of Christ is perhaps one of the most supercharged ethereal messages of humanity—a man claiming to be God. What made it real was that God bore witness of the man. "This is my beloved Son, hear him."[10] In the man we call Jesus, we find the Christ—Emmanuel, God with us. In Christ was the revelation of the cosmic story, it was the cosmic *God Process* coming to rest on humanity itself. It was the Creator of creation coming into the human condition to give us a message of how to come home.

I began to write *The Message* in 1992. I was compelled to. I would wake-up in the middle of the night with these images, these words and I had to write on paper what was coming into my mind. I would sit down with a pencil and write. There was nothing in front of me—no Bible, no books, just a pad of paper and a pencil. After 194 pages of continuous text and twelve years later I put this manuscript up on the shelf.[11] Maybe to those that write books

---

10   Matthew 9:7.

11   The reader is also referred to Part III The God Process: 1 Passion is the Path to the Soul for more discussion on the source of The Message.

all the time that is normal, however I cannot consciously write without cutting and pasting, scratching and rewriting. From time to time I would take *The Message* off the shelf and read it. It resonated each time that I read it—*The Message* compelled me to look at my life and to reassess my own relationship with the Divine. It caused me to study scripture and read books to explore the mystery of this mystical universal truth.

When I first started this work, spiritual journaling was foreign territory. Although I do have a very deep faith, belief and wantingness to be connected with my God, I would be the first to say that I am not schooled in scripture. I do not have a degree in religion nor have I studied the Bible to the nth degree. Yet, *The Message* for me was compelling.

After ten years with *The Message* sitting on the shelf I was drawn back to it; I was being prompted to take it down and to share what I had written with others. I have little to offer to the reader as to the source of this ethereal message other than to say that I believe this message was written into my soul long before I was born and it is one of my life purposes, as God willed.

There is a reason why ethereal messages like this are coming to us. Something is happening. Something is different. In a single generation we have all watched this explosion of our collective consciousness. We are all plugged in, connected and exposed to the world. News reaches every corner of the world in seconds. But it is more than that. The cosmic veil is lifting with the surge of books and testimonials of life after death, life before life and case studies under hypnosis that talk about the journey of our souls. There are these ethereal messages from the other side of life that are coming to us. We are being given new insight, new light, a new reason to believe in the creative force we call God and I believe that we are being shown this for a reason.

Strange for me how it is that some people can live life without an active faith or belief in God. For them, the God of the universe, whom we say created all this, *seems* to be void in the very creation that He created. This mystery of God is so elusive that perhaps we can live our lives and completely choose not to believe or realize that He is there. Yet, I think, in the very depths of our being we also know something else. We know that everything we do in life is pivotal on this mysterious connection with this something, this God that we cannot see.

There are common threads throughout these messages that point not only to the reality of the light and the dark, but also to a life beyond this life. We are learning of this mystical cosmic message, this universal truth, that tells us something about our God, His plan and "the why" to life.

The veil of our eternal journey is being lifted to perhaps help us with choices that we have to make now in this day and in this time. To help us understand how choices impact not only us individually, but our families, our communities and our collective destiny on a global scale. Our choices have an impact. Our choices impact our goodness, our hope, our peace and even the suffering that we endure. We have an impact on ourselves, each other and on God.

If God is real and if He is actively engaged in His creation, then maybe He is trying to send us a message. Maybe God is trying to infuse more light, more understanding into our world to give us a more compelling reason to live our lives differently. Maybe God is lifting the eternal veil to help save us from ourselves. Our governments and world leaders almost have too much power in their hands and it is at a push of a button. Even social media can give people too much power.

Maybe we need to live our lives differently so that we can *save our planet*. We see that our world is changing. Every year we see a little bit more how our world is changing. The balance of our eco system is shifting as the oceans become fished, as the ice caps melt and cataclysmic storms rage destructive forces across the planet. Our global society is impacting the earth. How we live our lives is having a global impact. Our sustainability is at risk.

Maybe God is lifting this eternal veil to help us with these difficult decisions on what we need to do differently. Our corporate leaders are at the forefront of decision making and maybe they need these ethereal messages to help give them the will power to make changes. But it is not just them—it is all of us. It is our collective consciousness that needs to shift so that we all will have enough resolve to recognize what needs to be done when it comes to clean energy, clean disposal and making peaceable sustainable decisions. By looking to God, by looking to His light, we might just see things differently.

Peace on earth should be everyone's prayer. Everyone should want a clean and renewable earth. If we have the mind and willingness to want it, we can have it. The answers are in the light because in the light is a knowledge that resonates with God. Christ taught us the peaceable Kingdom. If we are to instill into our minds the belief that God can bring a little heaven into our world, then together we need to look for that peace that is in our soul. We need to live with our soul if we are going to realize that dream, that reality of *Peace on Earth*.

There is a cosmic purpose to life. There is a reason to why all this and why things happen to us in life. There is a reason why God is seemingly hidden from us and why our humanity has the potential for inhumanity. There is a reason for the suffering, but there is also the hope that we can bring an end to that suffering.

If we are going to understand the cosmic *God Process*, if we are going to understand what God is trying to do, we need to connect the dots. We have to look back and see the cosmic story. We have to consider what caused the problem and what brought us all to this point. Somewhere in this mysterious mystical universal truth is the answer. It is an answer that can only be found by connecting the dots. It is an answer that is hidden from all of us and yet seemingly we are all fully aware of that universal truth.

——————— 2 The Cosmic Story ———————

The Message starts with *The Beginning*. It starts by showing us the creative process and that God breathed life into our soul.

> *In the beginning God created. God breathed life and life extended God. The life force of God was extended.*

Life has to have a life force, a source from which life sustains life. Just as love extends love, life draws life from life. We are nurtured by God, for God is the source of life.

In the beginning was the word and the word rested with God. The word was God. The word was Truth and Truth was wholeness; Truth being the word of what God wills. What God wills is the reality that exists in God. In Truth we see God, for that truth brings us back to that reality that God would will.

In the beginning there was wholeness across the face of God's creation. The reality that God willed was a tapestry of heaven beating in the oneness of our soul.

*Yet in the silence, as the thought of man emptied himself into the void of his own will, God's reality became forgotten. Truth became buried deep within our thoughts as our will gave way to that will which God would not desire. In creation, God placed life within our soul, creating us in His image. Out of that gift He gave us our voice. A voice which would echo the identity that we would create.*_{12E}

There is a part of us that is a part of God. Our conscience keeps us on that good path, because it is the voice of our soul and our soul is a part of God. Our conscience tells us when we are at risk. If we silence our self and listen to our soul, which is the voice of our conscience, we can hear that message that compels us to consider God.

Most faiths teach us something about our creation. *In the beginning...* We know we had a beginning and that beginning happened long before our birth. In faith we look to God because we say God created. We are because He is. Out of God were we created.

The construct of what we are, is that God created our soul in such a way that our soul could be connected to and yet be separate from God. We in turn created a voice for self. We became conscious, we became aware of the "me". In life we choose an identity. We willed in the "self". We willed for our self. That voice became our ego. It is a voice which is separate from our conscience. As we took on life, we formed our own voice, our own identity, and it was a voice which was separate from God. From a cosmic creative perspective God created a soul and in turn we created the self, God – Soul – Self. Our essence, the "who I am", is a dimension within a dimension within a dimension. A dimension of self, a dimension of soul and a dimension of God, all connected and inseparable.

Buried deep inside each of us is a soul. Our soul is like the electricity to the power source we call God. The electricity is light, the electricity of our soul is love, the life force of our soul is the goodness that gives voice to our conscience. Our soul is a part of us and it is our soul that is connected to God. The voice of our soul is our conscience which speaks to us—whispers to us. It is the internal voice that pulls us back when we are tempted to make bad decisions. To hear our soul we have to silence our self.

Our soul speaks to us about Truth because in Truth is the message for God. To recognize Truth, we have to still the self and listen to the whisper of our soul.

There is a reality which we know about and it is deep inside us. That reality is that we know that there is more to us than just us. The more is God and we are connected to God. When God created us, His life force went with us. He is there. He is always there. We are because God is. The path back to God starts with knowing that deep inside of us is a soul and that our soul is connected to God.

The Message illuminates our mind to the mystery of the soul and how darkness was woven into the fabric of God's creation and how it is that we can become trapped by darkness if we forget our God.

> *What we create gives meaning to the self. Our identity is born out of our own free will. It is the spilling of life onto life such that life takes on meaning.*

> *Out of life was the fabric of God created. The relationships that we nurture in life becomes the fabric*

of God. When we do good the fabric of God is woven in the array of God. When we lack goodness, the fabric of God is at risk and can be torn by our actions. The bond of life can be fragmented if we create fear and distaste towards each other. When the fabric of God is torn, our soul can become lost in a void. We hide ourselves from each other and from the darkness that we created. In Truth, love was our reality, yet our relationships became severed and the array of love became lost to our vision. _{13E}

The Message also shows us the path back. The path back is in the choices we make. The past is locked, but in the possibilities of tomorrow is a new day.

All that we do in life comes from choice. God gave us our free will. It is our free will which defines us. It is out of free will that created movement either from God or movement towards God. In our choice we either are a part of God's creative process or we set in motion choices that can tear apart God's creative process. We set in motion our will.

There is a message about *The Beginning* in the creation story. It is a message that tells us of the *fall*. Adam and Eve took the apple from the tree of knowledge and they ate. They became aware of their nakedness. They sinned and were cast out from the garden of Eden. It is metaphoric story for the loss of innocence.

There is, however, a cosmic reality to the story. There is a reality which exists and we know it exists because of the condition that it created. We know that we are no longer innocent. We have all lost our innocence to a certain degree. Our human condition is such that we are not always good. We make choices that are not always good. That is what makes us human. Yet in our children we are reminded of the beauty and purity of innocence. The purity of our human soul survived the garden.

When we make bad choices we are at risk of tearing the fabric of God. The degree to which we make bad choices will determine what kind of impact that we will have on ourselves, our relationships or even our world. Acts of inhumanity by a few can have a global impact on the many—*9/11*.

There was a cosmic message that rang clear with the events of *9/11*. The moment the planes struck the Twin Towers, we all woke up to the awareness of how the acts of a few can have a global impact on all of us.

In 2006 a transatlantic plot by terrorists to detonate liquid explosives on board at least ten airliners was foiled by British police. On August 9, 2006 eleven of the twenty-four suspects were arrested. The actions of governments around the world were swift with restrictions and tightened security. The acts of these twenty-four suspects impacted billions of people on a daily basis and we all paid the price. We are still all paying the price.

Our human history is tainted time and again with acts of inhumanity—*Hitler*. There are people with influence, people with the power to inflict, people who want to take control and they put us all at risk. ***But that is not the problem.*** The problem is the condition that created the problem. We are on a course that is bound to repeat itself unless we can recognize and correct the condition.

It starts with the "one". It starts with planting a seed into our collective consciousness that tells us when we are on the wrong course. It starts with each one wanting. *Do unto others as you as you would want them to do to you.*[12]

It sounds simple but it becomes complicated. Especially when we have to choose between doing what is right for the faceless many or choosing a path that buys us reward with the chosen few. To see choices for what they are we have to first recognize that we have a problem.

We have a condition of self. It is a condition based on beliefs, illusions and half-truths. It is a condition of "want", the want that can give us profit, gain and power at the expense of others. It is a condition where we can convince others of entitlement and exclusivity. And when things go wrong we can just rewrite history,

---

12   Key message of Matthew 7:12, Luke 6:31 and Mark 12:31.

we can rewrite our version of the truth and rewrite what happened to justify our actions. When things go wrong we can place the blame and responsibility on someone or something else. We can create a condition of semi-innocence.[13]

It is a condition where the soul has become so buried under this shell we call our ego that at times we don't even know our soul is there. Our soul is buried so deep that we do not always hear or listen to the whisper that it speaks. We need to wake-up. We need to be aware of our soul. If we are going to be able to hear the message that leads to peace and for the healing of our earth, we need to stop and listen to our soul.

The Message is constructed to pierce through the image of self and help us to see the Truth that exists in our soul. If we are to break free of our inhumanity we need to want the reality that God created in our soul.

3 The Use of Time and Eternity
———— in the Cosmic Story ————

Time is the construct of movement. We are defined by the movement of time. Our truth, the truth that we stand for, the *what* we do in life, will stand in the midst of time. Our time defines who we are. The images of our will, the desires of our heart and the impact of our lives leaves an imprint. We cannot escape the reality that we create.

What we have willed in the past shapes the reality of time that stands before us. We are all connected. We look to one another for

---

13   Semi-innocence is a common theme throughout The Message. Young children are innocence when they have no knowledge of right or wrong. They cannot consciously error until they have been taught error. Semi-innocence is the acceptance of our innocence by choice. It is the choice of innocence by proving (or convincing) ourselves and others that we are not guilty. There is another state of innocence called restored innocence. In restored innocence there is no desire to do wrong or to hide the "error", because we are forgiven. Our innocence, our humanity, our goodness is restored or maintained because there is no longer a desire that is in us to be inhumane or deceitful or to put others at risk for the sake of personal gain.

love and support. Others, in turn, look to us for love and support. Insomuch as we nurture each other, our common reality forms peaceful memories. It is only when we place each other at risk that our world falls apart. When our choices create memories that seem more like nightmares, life becomes precarious. We cannot escape, run or hide from the world that we have created. The memories and the feelings—whether they be full of joy, emptied by regret or intensified by our passion and our wantonness—will have an impact on our soul, on others and on the fabric of time.

The reality of this day will stand in the wake of time that has already moved.

There is a construct to time. In the very deepest part of our inner being we know that we are here for a reason, that there is purpose and meaning to life. There is this cosmic purpose that governs the why and where we are going.

Our true refuge comes from facing God in the reality that we have willed. If we are to grow and to become more than what we already are, it will have to be lived out in the construct of time. There has to be a physical reality to our dreams if we are to reach our potential. We can't just wish ourselves to be. We have to create. It is the fire of the flesh that leaves an imprint on the who we are. It leaves an imprint on our soul.

Unfortunately with "soul development" we do fall down. When we do fall down it is easy to allow our soul to become lost in the process.

There is a message in Truth that speaks for God. The message is this.

> *God did not create us to find a just cause from which to destroy us.* So God went with us. He planted Himself deep inside of us and we drew life from Him. We could separate ourselves from Him by our beliefs and illusions, but He could not separate Himself from us, for He created us and continues to love us. *14E*

There is something that is inside of us and it calls us back. There is this mystical message of Truth that calls us back to God.

That Truth bears testimony to the reality that God would will. Truth is a message that speaks for hope, for oneness, for healing and for peace. Truth calls us to wholeness in ourselves and in our relationships. Truth speaks for honesty and for innocence.

> *Truth bears testimony to the reality of God that exists in God. When all the illusions and fears that hid God from us are gone, then all that will remain will be Truth. The awareness to that Truth, which liberates and restores us to wholeness, resides in our willingness to look for God from the very depths of our soul. God is the source of life. From Him was life created. God created. He is and so are we.* _{15E}

There is a path back to God. There is this mystical path back which heals us of our selfishness, our ego. It heals us of the badness, the temptations, the unwanted hurt. There is a path back to love and to the healing of our hearts and relationships. There is a message that can release us from pain, guilt and suffering.

The problem is not with the fall. The problem is in the getting up. The problem in our collective consciousness is how do we get our lives back? How do we heal ourselves?

> *Truth in its purist form will always release us. When we look for Truth we give ourselves back to what we desire to be real in us. We desire to love and be loved. We desire peace and acceptance. Only in fear do we hide from Truth.* _{16E}

The word "Truth" points to "God's reality".[14] When you read the Truth in scripture it is pointing to the reality that exists in God. There is a spectrum in the good and evil that we find in the human condition. At one end of the spectrum is a reality of the goodness that is present in God, as the essence of God is goodness.

---

14   The reader will find that "Truth" is sometimes capitalized and sometimes that it is not capitalized. When "Truth" is capitalized in a middle
of a sentence it is pointing to a specific meaning which is "the reality
that exists in God". When truth is not capitalized the meaning to be
conveyed is honesty, truthful or our perception of reality.

Truth points us to the reality of goodness. At the other end of the spectrum is evil. Evil leads to alienation, separation, infliction, destruction and creates a condition of suffering.

So how does knowing this help our human condition? How does knowing this help us with this condition we call "self"? How does it change how we think? How does this help us with choice? Can this simple knowledge impact our destiny?

If we change the condition of "self" we can change the world. If we can change how we perceive what has true value to our self, we will see our world differently. What has true value to the self is the love that makes life full and meaningful. What has true value to the self is what resonates in our soul. If we choose to listen to our soul, we will find a shift to what brings value to the self. To live our dreams, to bring about creative purpose, to love completely and to look to God is what resonates in our soul. It is not in the money, it is not in the possessions and it is not in the power. Rather it is in the use of our money, it is in the sharing of our possessions and it is in the serving of power for the greater good.

Our choices impact the construct of time. The reality of this day will stand in the wake of time that has already moved. Tomorrow's reality will be governed by today's decisions. Our collective reality of peace and a sustainable earth will be governed by our collective choices. If we plant the seeds today that allow us to pierce through the self, so that we might see the light of our soul, then the reality that exists in God *may* just surface to show us the way.

Having said all this, we still have a problem. There is a fly in the ointment. There is a flaw in the process. The problem is, "who cares?" How do we get people to care? Why should we or anyone else care about God or about becoming aware of our cosmic purpose or reality? How do we get others to wake-up and pay attention to a message that speaks for God so that we might *all* have *Peace on Earth*. What is in it for them?

There is an answer that is obvious to all of us. The answer is in the tick-tock, the clock that both moves forward and seals the past to the past. The answer is in the fact that we know we have an expiration date. Our world could have an expiration date, if we don't change. The freedom, the gift of our hope resides in understanding as to how God uses *Eternity*.

To look for meaning, to look for why we should care, we have to look at how God uses eternity.

> *Just as time brings movement into creation so does eternity find the stillness that resides in time. In eternity, time matters not. Yet time was created because we moved from God. Since it is God's will that none of His creation be lost from Him forever, God placed in motion the time necessary to restore us back to Him.* 17E

If there is a bridge as to the "why" we need to pay attention, the why we need to wake-up, it is in the realization that time does not stand still. Yet, in the vastness of eternity, time does not matter. This single day is but one of a billion days that stand before us. Time is endless and if it takes forever for us to find the path to the light then so be it. The cosmic reality is that God uses time to give us both the space and the free will to discover for ourselves. God cannot change me, or rather, God will not violate my free will to change me. Only I can change me and I have to want the will to do that.

The condition of the self, for the exclusivity of self, is entrapment for suffering. Acts of self that tear the fabric of God creates suffering. Acts of poor choices, wantonness, hatred and all acts of inhumanity creates suffering. What we do to others is the world that we create for ourselves. God's path to healing is that He gives us the fabric back.

If God created, if God has a plan and if we are a part of this cosmic plan, then either we will make choices that move us towards the light or we will live with choices that will trap us to the darkness. The choice is ours. It is only in the light that suffering ends. God created time to allow us the space to find the light and, if we so desire, He will give us all the time we need. The movement of today is but a click away.

We resist God when we stop looking for Him. We resist love when we stop loving. That is the reality that we will when we simply don't care, when apathy sets in, when we stop loving and think only of ourselves. In that reality there will be no movement towards the light. We become trapped by the darkness that keeps us from loving. We will be trapped by the darkness that keeps us from God.

> *We resist God when we resist the call of another who looks to us for belonging. Resistance bears no fruit from which fruit can be born. To resist love, to resist healing in our relationships, is to resist God. If God is love and we resist love, how can we find God? If it is God that you seek, if it is heaven that you seek, if it is salvation that you seek, then love must find a way to work in you.* 18E

We are all on this path of discovery. To become more than what we already are. To become more we have to create. Yet in our soul development, if we get trapped in the darkness, our creative condition becomes marred, tainted and self-serving.

Time is a product of eternity. Each deed and each word is preceded by thought. Each thought is born in part from belief, in part by illusion and in part from Truth or the reality that God would will. Thoughts that are born in belief have an element of time. Thoughts that reassure us of Truth remind us of eternity. Each moment is caught between the now and what was or what will be. Time happens when either the past or the future determines our salvation. Time matters not when eternity meets each moment and we live each moment in the eternity that God has granted.

The Message is structured to help us break through the human condition that traps us to suffering. *The Message* helps us to rediscover our true creative purpose. It is structured to break through the ego and the illusions that keep us from God. It is written to break through the image of self and to help us see the light of our soul.

There is a Christian expression to the presence of God. It is called the Holy Spirit. When our soul is connected to God we recognize God's presence. We call that connection, that presence, the Holy Spirit. The Holy Spirit is an awareness to God's presence in our life. The Holy Spirit brings to remembrance that desire of good which is the essence of God. When we become aware that God is there, we find that there is this pull. We are drawn to Him. His persistence continually works on us until we come face to face with that desire which binds us to God.

Jesus came to teach us of God. His ministry was the path back. "I and my Father are One"[15] is the promise that the fullness of God can reside in the human condition. Just as the Spirit of the living God came to rest in Jesus so it is that the gift of the Holy Spirit can be present in all of us. The path of one becomes the path for all.

In Truth we will see that God is real and that hell is the illusion. Hell is real when we make God an illusion. When heaven is restored in us, our salvation is made real. When hell seems real, our salvation can only be found out there somewhere in the void where we believe heaven awaits. Hell then exists, but only in the framework of time, not eternity. For in salvation time matters not and in time will God restore His creation to salvation.

Time only masks eternity where God is. Bring heaven to the framework of time and eternity will be restored. In Part II: *Eternity* we read:

> *Rethink time. Each moment of each day is broken into routines that define our movement. Yet our movement is caught within timelessness. Our thoughts carry us forward and our memories recreate the past. If we fear the future and hate the past, there is hell to pay.*

> *Where in is there hope if hope carries no meaning? Our salvation remains out there somewhere, but where? Gentle is hell's descent within time for it places us firmly on the illusion that tomorrow is another day and yesterday is not yet gone. The illusion persists so long as tomorrow has no hope and today is only a reflection of yesterday's memories. The illusion is intensified when tomorrow is feared and yesterday is our only reality. The now becomes displaced when our*

---

15   John 10:30

*illusions entraps our identity, our memories, our hopes
and our dreams. God's reality becomes displaced when
our identity becomes lost to what was or what will be.*

*Yet in time God will bring you full circle. In time your
journey will cause you to search your soul. The inward
journey is realized in your search for meaning, to make
sense out of that which makes no sense. In that search
you will find Truth. Not the truth that makes sense out
of the senseless, but that Truth that brings you back to
God. In that Truth, found deep within the soul, is the
remembrance of the reality that rests in God.*

*From remembrance of a time when love was our home,
we begin to see what moved us from the creation that
we were created in. A sparkle, a glimpse of love that
shone deep within assured us that God would call
us back. From the nothingness that trapped the soul
within the confines of time will we remember. From
the nothingness where our value was lost to what had
no value will we remember. Here it was, all along. We
stood in the face of nothingness only to see and to
learn from its heartlessness.*[19E]

Things that have no eternal value have no eternal meaning.
In our giving of ourselves to what has no eternal meaning, we
learned that no meaning could ever come of it. Our possessions are
nothing. They are nothing because our possessions cannot love us
back. They have no eternal meaning. They have no meaning other
than the meaning that we place in them.

Time then becomes the stepping stone back to God. Each day
we are given the opportunity to create, to re-create, to bring healing
and to promote wholeness. Each day we must choose to love, to
end the conflict and to dissolve the guilt. Each day we can allow
God to look through us so that we can see how God sees. Each day
is a day for innocence, a day for Truth. Rework the fabric of time
and time will rework the fabric of God.

4 The Message of "*The Message*"

God's messages are about invitation, healing, wholeness, redemption, possibilities, creation and salvation. *The Message* is the eternal path of restored innocence. *The Message* tells the cosmic story of how God is actively engaged in this process from creation to salvation. It is the cosmic God Process of how God instills His essence back into our soul. God is actively engaged with each of us. God is actively engaged in the eternal path of our soul.

The Message illuminates the cosmic story. From our creation, to the stage that was set upon the earth where life would be played out, to the call of our salvation to be a part of the Kingdom of Heaven, we discover this mystical wonder of life. It is the story of our humanity, as co-creators with our God, in the journey of our soul from a cosmic perspective.

It is a message for possibilities, to give us reason to consider God. *The Message* compels us to consider what God has to offer. The promise that is offered is that as we look to God, God offers healing and wholeness. As love finds a way, suffering will end.

The Message opens us to the reality that exists in God. When we focus on the light of God, our life becomes illuminated. It is this idea of Truth that draws us closer to God. Truth helps us understand the "why this"—the *why* "all this", the "*why me*" and the "*who I am*". It helps us to understand our own *God Process*.

The Message affirms our salvation, for there is a part of us that is drawn to God. When we look to God it compels us to look to each other. Love becomes the magnet and the more that we see the good in each other, the more we will see the good in ourselves and that God *is* in our life. The more that we are attracted to is that part of God that is in each of us.

The Message compels us to explore, to ask questions, to seek that part of ourselves that is connected to God. Down deep we know that the goodness that resides in us, the very source that we draw life from, comes from God. God is not on the outside looking in but on the inside looking out.

We are all on this path that leads us back to God. Even when bad things happen in our life, even when our lives seem to be going in wrong directions, the message is that God is there with us. When bad things happen God is already at work to bring about His miracle. When darkness overshadows our lives, God sends His light and He sends others to help us along the way. It speaks to the journey of our soul and opens us to the possibilities of what God is trying to do.

It is in the light of the soul that we will find the answers to life. As we draw closer to the goodness that is in all of us, we will see a shift in our collective consciousness. We can bring peace into our world. We can make the choices that can end the suffering.

If ever there was a reason for hope, if there ever was a potential for *Peace on Earth* it will come from the Word, the message that speaks for God. God sent us the gift of a child who came in the meridian of time to set in motion His Father's work for *Peace on Earth*. In the centrality of the Christ, in the message that Christ brought will we find our innocence. Today can be that day when we will see that reality. A day where life is lived in peace, a day where the world is free of war and a day where hearts are not torn apart.

Our hope starts with a message. It begins with a whisper of peace. It is the ringing of the bells on Christmas morning with the echo of "can it be"?

> *For unto us a child is born, unto us a child is given.*
> *And the government shall be upon his shoulder and his*
> *name shall be called Wonderful, Counselor, Almighty*
> *God, the everlasting Father, the Prince of Peace.*
>
> *Isaiah 9:6*

To the reader:

On the following page is the start to the ethereal message. I hope you will find *The Message* inspiring and compelling, however *The Message* is not a story book read; it is a poetic read. It is written from three alternate perspectives, intertwined to tell the cosmic story as it unfolds. The first is from the perspective of us as an observer looking at the canvas, the second perspective is with us as participants in the canvas and lastly it is written as if the Christ was the messenger giving us again a different perspective to *The Message*.

The Message looks at creation, the birth of our soul, the journey of our soul, the reality of God, the dimensions of God, God's Kingdom and Salvation. Although the focus of the cosmic story is on the centrality of the Christ, the message of salvation is one of having a desire for God and allowing God's essence to penetrate our lives by how we live life and love others. Having said that, this ethereal message does point to reincarnation as part of our *God Process*. In scripture, we have Jesus telling Peter, James and John the brother of James that John the Baptist is the reincarnation of Elias or Elijah (see Matthew 17:9-13). *The Message* also points to Adam and Jesus as being the same soul entity. This may or may not be acceptable theology to some people.

In the exploration of *faith*, in our desire to understand the roots of our soul, there are many ethereal messages that are surfacing through books on *Life After Life, Life Between Life, The Messengers, The Journey of the Soul* and other writings.[16] Reincarnation is becoming mainstream—there is a reality to our soul journey; we do not live just one life. The veil of our eternal journey is lifting and people are looking to God. However, they are finding that religion is not necessarily aligned with this ethereal reality. Our beliefs and the ethereal reality need to be aligned if we are to fully embrace our faith.

What is written is written with purity of mind and heart through the process of spiritual journaling (please see *Part III* for more discussion). Ethereal messages are intended to provide inspiration and a spiritual connection with God, rather than to tell a story. Yet, I believe there is a cosmic story as it relates to the journey of the soul. My own personal story picks up again in *Part III: The God Process*.

Rather than interrupt the flow of *The Message*, I have added footnotes to provide the reader with some context where I thought it would be helpful. That context will provide some definition to words or additional meaning to the text and sometimes it is a personal note or reflection. The footnotes in *The Message* will provide insight and

---

16   See Part III: God of Reincarnation, for the authors of these books.

are recommended to be read. Please note that the actual manuscript of *The Message* was shortened quite a bit and rearranged. Some paragraphs were omitted and others were paraphrased.

The reader will find numerous indentations throughout *The Message*. Unlike in Part I and in the *Hope for the Message*, where indentations signify quotes from *The Message*, the indentations in Part II are intended to signify a break in the flow of thought to either introduce a shift from third person to first person or a shift of thought to a poetic message.

Again, with respect to gender related context God, I believe, transcends gender. The imagery of God can be complex and our expressions of God are at best inadequate to convey meaning that connects with everyone. Please refer back to page xv in the *Invitation to the God Process* for comments related to gender use.

THE MESSAGE
The Eternal Path of Restored Innocence

Creation

——————— 1 In the Beginning ———————

In the beginning God created. God breathed life and life extended God. The life force of God was extended.

Life has to have a life force, a source from which life sustains life. Just as love extends love, life draws life from life. We are nurtured by God, for God is the source of life.

In the beginning was the word and the word rested with God. The word was God. The word was Truth and Truth was wholeness—Truth being the word of what God wills. What God wills is the reality that exists in God. In Truth we see God, for that truth brings us back to that reality that God would will.

In the beginning there was wholeness across the face of God's creation. The reality that God willed was a tapestry of heaven beating in the oneness of our soul.

Yet in the silence, as the thought of man emptied himself into the void of his own will, God's reality became forgotten. Truth became buried deep within our thoughts as our will gave way to that will which God would not desire. In creation, God placed life within our soul, creating us in His image. Out of that gift He gave us our voice. A voice which would echo the identity that we would create.

> *In God was I created. Just as God breathed life into Adam, so it is that the breath of life comes from God.*

> *In my beginning, God created me. He is my source and*

I am of value to Him for He created me.

In the beginning, the life force of God was planted deep inside of me. He created me in His holiness. I was holy to Him and whole in myself. Yet as I sought an identity, I willed for myself. The self took on meaning. But the meaning was without form, without substance. To grow as God created me, I in turn had to create. To add value to God's creation, I had to add value to life. When I added value to life, my life took on meaning.

So I willed for myself. My thoughts took form and the substance that I created out of both will and desire defined my identity. Yet what I made, what I created was of little value unless it had an impact on life. It was my impact on life that brought meaning to myself. What I willed defined the who I am. It defined my identity.

I became what I willed. I created and my creation defined the who I am. Every thought, every deed and every action had an impact on life. I have an impact on life. Every decision I made became a reflection of how I valued life. How I valued others relative to myself. Somewhere then between my thoughts and my actions is the identity that I created. Somewhere between what I willed then and what I would will now is the "who I am".

Source: Book of Truth

———— 2 Born of Light ————

The source of all life emanates from light. The essence of the soul, the encasement of self and the embodiment of who we are is magnetized in light. Our light is infused into the spark of the Divine and it is through our alignment with God's goodness that the soul is illuminated in colors.

Vivid, dazzling, translucent in form, a myriad of colors is the garment of our soul. Each particle of energy draws from the essence of the Source. What we become in heart and mind, through desire and will is the embodiment of the soul as seen in the garments of the light that we wear. Each particle is formed and shaped by thought and desire of who we are and who we desire to be. Our light vibrates the ethereal plane into a form that is both visible and radiant.

We are what we have willed to be. Our soul shimmers in the light that is infused onto our being from the life we live. Particles of energy like threads of light, woven to form the fabric of life. Cast like a string of diamonds to solidify the garment of our soul. We shine and shimmer as God's light illuminates and vibrates from within. The very essence of who we are is both seen and felt.

Life from light. All that we are, all our hopes and our dreams, our love and our compassion, our determination and our strength, our pride and our ego, our humanity and our godliness is captured in the form of colors that radiates in light. As we draw close to the Source, as we draw from the essence of God, in both goodness and deed so it is that our light is intensified. We are infused with God's image by both will and desire.

The soul within is intensified and radiates light from life when we choose God's goodness. Visible in all its forms. So it is in both heaven and earth. Our personality is as colorful as the garments that we have sown. No two souls are alike. We are etched in color which echoes the image of our soul.

In the beginning our souls were born of light, we are children of the One. Created in innocence, our souls radiate in the purity of white—colorless, yet we sparkle like diamonds of dust on the new fallen snow. We are nurtured in love, a sea of warmth awaits. Possibilities. Dreams upon dreams fill the senses, to live, to choose, to become. Wondrous are the possibilities. The landscape is endless and we are drawn into the path of creation.

Life from light. Each life is a stage. A backdrop to add color. A test to infuse God's essence. We come. We seek. And by our choices will we be illuminated. No life is lived where color is not added. Even in the shadows of darkness where inhumanity is present are colors, particles of energy that will permeate our being to shape us and mold us. Even there, God is present.

From dawn to dusk. From the rising to the setting of the sun. From our birth to our death, in the incarnation will we be tested. Each day is a test. Each day can add color. As the spark of God illuminates our thoughts and our desires so does our actions radiate His presence. Our image permeates creation for all of creation to see who we are. Our being of light is both seen and felt.

So as we will, so will we become. Our dreams create the backdrop to the landscape of our potential that we all can walk. With God all things are possible. God paints creation; the fabric belongs to God, yet we enter His creation to dance on the stage. His essence with us and in us, we are free to choose, to will, to become. Out of free will, will we choose. Out of free will is the voice of self. We are illuminated by will and desire to fulfill God's purpose, so that we might construct the beauty of our soul.

In life before life we prepare. Life incarnate becomes the test. We set in motion the trials of the flesh. Through the fire of the flesh is the spark of God stoked into our being. All the attributes of goodness, purity and strength are at play. With God we plan the stage. We enter into life as participants in His creation. We take upon ourselves the cloak of humanity to prove our goodness, purity and strength. As God's essence is etched, so does our image become illuminated with God's intensity.

Look to see the dawn of creation. It begins even now. Your dreams are your possibilities. The very essence of God will dance in the light of your potential. All that is, all that was and all that will be is a constant stream of motion which is created out of the very movement of your will and desire. Step by step, breath by breath and beat by beat it begins. It starts today.

Source: Book of Light

3 Convergence of the Soul

Creation is the combined energy of thought and form. The creative process instills our dreams and desires in the form of reality as we willed. It is our beingness which creates the impact on life. We are constantly creating. Our movement is active and is engaged in the creative process. This is our beingness.[17] Our presence becomes the power, the force, the influence that moves.

For the creative process to be magnified requires the construct of thought and form to be realized as having value. We make sense out of the visions and dreams. Our visions and dreams move us and the creative process begins. It begins from within and moves outward. As a new reality is set in motion so it is that we become active participants. We become a part of the very creation that we willed. As movement is shared, creation expands. Its impact can be like an explosion detonated from its core or it can be like a wave that radiates quietly across the sea washing itself upon the sands of time.

In time, we learn to work with God in our creation. We expand our beingness into God's creation by sharing our lives with each other. Insomuch as our lives expand into God's creation, insomuch as our lives touch the lives of others, so will it converge back upon the core of our being. The light that shines forth is the light which is instilled. As the light of God's being expands through us so will His light become our own.

Beingness is the creative form of self. Separated between illusion and reality our beingness expands and contracts as it impacts upon the lives of others. God's presence illuminates our beingness by dispelling the illusions that would darken our world.

Illusions are a false reality. Illusions exist in the mind and the

---

17 Beingness is not in the English dictionary. This word is intended to mean both the self-awareness of our "being" or our soul and the invisible extension of our soul, which extends outward beyond the self. Our beingness is both centered in our soul and radiates beyond our own soul, mind and feelings to influence the creative process. Our beingness blends into the people we influence and the movement we create.

heart. Illusions are not real. Reality is a construct formed in time, space and beingness and illusions cannot fill all three dimensions. Within time is hope, within space is healing and in our beingness is God's presence. Illusions form a false reality because only God's reality is the reality that God would will. In time all illusions will dissipate, in the space that God grants will be the wholeness that we desire and in our beingness will we find the oneness of self with others.

Yet, beingness is the construct of self. It is the form of self as seen by both ourselves and others. We define our beingness. It is the "we" aspect of our beingness which converges upon the "who I am." What we impart in our lives is what converges upon our soul.

This life recreates the self in the form of our beingness. We become what we will and we will what we become. To recreate the image of God in the form of self requires the presence of God in our beingness. As our humanity is explored and tested, as the taste of our inhumanity becomes bitter and shameful our souls are cleansed. Our beingness finds rest in the peace that binds our hearts in the illumination of God's Holy Spirit, God's Holy presence.

This life expands and contracts on our beingness. It is our impact on each other which contracts, converges on the image of self. We see what we are by how others respond to our presence. We see our beingness by the impact of our presence in the wake of our movement. This touch of our humanity or inhumanity either brightens the lives of others or casts shadows that are borne in fear and mistrust.

Illusions are a false reality. Illusions are the *images* of fear, mistrust, hatred and anger. They exist in our mind and our heart and project a will for a false reality. Illusions rob us of our identity with God and consume our beingness with a false reality. Illusions entrap us because it forms a beingness on our soul which converges. All images that we create, all images that we project is the reality that we ourselves become participants in. All images converge on the soul.

Only in the desire for wholeness, forgiveness, healing and love can the images of these illusions be dispelled. The construct

The God Process

of this life recreates the conditions by which we can dispel all illusions. God grants us the time and the space to rework the fabric. We are given the opportunity to remold our image, to heal our relationships, to seek out our forgiveness, to restore our innocence and to find God in our hearts.

The Book of Life is open. By looking upon the pages of our life we can see the presence of our beingness and the convergence of God's light in our soul. Through the corridor of time we can see the movement of our soul by the reality that we willed. Heaven awaits our next step.

Source: Book of Life

———— 4 The Dance of Life ————

The spectrum of life brings depth to the soul. Out of creation, out of the heavens and set upon the earth was God's plan. We taste and breathe in the depth of the soul. Beyond the spirit is the experience we take in. All that which was, all that which is and all that which will be is captured by the record that is embedded upon the life of the soul. It is the record that retains the reality of our will, desires and actions. It is the record that retains our memory of deeds, feelings and thoughts. It is the record that life has written.

Out of creation was the record of life. As the word was spoken, life was given. The spectrum expanded into the void of the self to allow God to separate life from life. The record was formed and each soul took upon the self the reality that was created. Here in was the will that was willed. The will to be. In all of God's creation would we bear upon each other that reality which was recorded.

The heavens were separated to allow the spectrum to unfold. God looked upon the vastness that stood upon the face of the realities that were willed. As the realities unfolded, as each one choose one with the other what they desired within the depth of their soul, the fabric of life was formed. In the array of life that belonged to God came the reality that we willed. Families were formed out of the desire for belonging. We bonded one to another in the reality that we would will so that we might come to taste the depth of our own soul.

It was the experience of the self that we sought. To impart one with another, to taste the spectrum that stood before us. Wondrous was the life that we willed. It stood before us in colors and sensation that could be touched, enveloped and absorbed. Wondrous were the dreams that we dreamed. In each reality was a new experience. The vision of incarnation was daunting, yet it captivated our being.[18] One with another we were drawn into that reality.

The spectrum of creation that God willed upon the heavens filled the void of space. God covered the form of thought by the limit of presence. Light converged in the destiny of thought to form the mass of reality that God willed. Structure and form stood before us and became the playground for the dance of life. We entered the form of light to take upon ourselves the thought of our will. Within this convergence would life emerge in the image of our dreams and desires. Upon our vision stood the mountains and the valleys, the skies and the seas, the flowers and the trees, the array of color, sound and taste, the sensation of form, self and identity.

We entered the spectrum in the reality and will of God. Our joy was filled with the beauty of creation and the interaction of life where we shared the experience of the structure and the form of the reality that was created. We interacted with life, one with another maintaining the fabric of God in wholeness as God willed. Willing what God willed, our desire maintained the fabric of God.

Wholeness stood on the heavens and God's creation was bonded by the life that connected us one to another. We stood with our Creator and willed as He willed. Yet in the innocence that blends children to children our form knew not of the ego that willed

---

18   There is a spectrum of emotions that this passage is intended to convey from the vantage point of the soul that enters into the incarnation. To leave the spirit world where the soul is surrounded by love and acceptance, to enter the incarnation of structure and form, where the soul is encased from this connectedness, can generate emotions of apprehension, a sense of being overwhelmed, uncertainty in the self, fear of failure and yet for some they are fearless, excited with anticipation and unstoppable to the dreams and visions that they want to experience.

the self in an image separate from God. Our wholeness was formed in innocence, out of the purity of light from the source of life. In heaven, light emanates from within. Convergence is magnified by the glory of light, shining, luminescent and transparent. Life blends with no boundaries in form. Heaven was our home from where we all came.

Our celestial home is a Kingdom of light. Just as we are infused with the sparkle of light by the garments that illuminates our being, so it is that the City is created by energy, particles of light, manipulated to form structure and substance. Homes, gardens, rivers and trees sparkle and glow, radiate and permeate the soul. Wondrous creations that dazzle the senses transcend the landscape. It is ours. It is our home. When we vibrate in the oneness of our God we can vibrate to see the Kingdom of light.

Our vibrational energy, our living energy, cannot be manipulated without the Creative Force. It is infused in us by God through the free will of self, through choice. We are illuminated by the fire of the flesh, when we will to be. As we wear the breastplate of our humanity, God's essence takes root. It is our choice. The will to love in both desire and deed will either be intensified in light or tarnished and tainted in the shadows of choice to reflect either God's goodness or the lack of God's goodness in us.

In the beginning darkness had no taste. The realities that stood before us were structure and form, encased light separated by shadows. As we took upon ourselves the life of form our eyes became dim to the light of the soul that emanated from within. In the reality of form, as our movement defined both time and space, the eternity of heaven became distant.[19]

---

19   I would suggest the reader consider that the context here is to point towards what created movement. Normally we think of movement in terms of time, however, in this context think of time as a "reality of form" itself, like a series of frames on a movie reel. From a cosmic perspective the spirit moved from eternity into time where time became separate—set apart from eternity. There was awareness to movement or awareness to time. This is a very important frame of reference to consider; from our earthly perspective we think of eternity as "forever" as opposed to a concept where time is not measured. For example, we gauge time from the rising to the setting of the sun; we

It was in this darkness that the ego emerged. It was in this reality that elation was born.[20] It was in this reality that we came to know of fear, self and wanting. Light was encased and heaven became at risk. As our choices placed one another at risk, the Law of One was sacrificed. The darkness became embedded upon our being; our soul. The light of our soul was dulled by the choices of our will and desires.

The identity that was created in the image of self tore the fabric of God. Heaven itself became split. The reality of heaven was

think of time in terms of days, hours and minutes. What if in spirit there is no rising or setting of the sun? What if there is no frame of measurement to gauge the hours and the days? Where this becomes important is in our understanding of eschatology. Eschatology points to an eternal judgment of souls; the meaning implied is one of finality. In this passage we see the eternal as the constant stay of the moment or the inability to measure the movement through time. Eternity takes on new meaning as in "not forever" but rather the constant stay of the moment or no awareness to the movement of time. To take it one step further, eternity could imply a constant state of being, a solidification of the soul until the soul is ready for change. For the soul to infuse change (growth) there has to be a willingness and wantingness for change. To grow back into God, to infuse God's essence, there has to be a willingness and wantingness to have that light.

20   The word "elation" is used a number of times in *The Message* as being closely associated with our ego. It has a connotation of being a pathological emotion in the cosmic story. Elation in this context is the emotion used to describe the euphoria of self, to become proud or to feel exalted. It is the inward swing of pride when our exultant gladness puts the self on a pedestal. Elation is pathological when one gets caught up or consumed by the emotion (i.e. to become narcissistic, to be considered exalted and to be full of pride). In the cosmic story elation is used to suggest the emotion that starts the pendulum, the swing in the knowledge of self. In our humanity we embrace our emotions, even emotions such as anger, frustration, hate, or emotions created by defiled language, etc. Our emotions, even negative emotions, can bring strength and character to our soul; they can intensify our resolve for force when force is needed. Left unchecked these emotions can become destructive and work against the creative process and our soul development. Our ego magnifies our self-awareness and pulls us towards the exploration of these emotions and tendencies. God sends us into the playground of life to learn and explore, to find and discover our "self", even those emotions that have negative connotations.

lost to those that lost their desire for heaven out of the taste of the darkness in the reality of structure and form. As the shadows were lifted and their spirit left the form that they took, they saw for themselves the garment of their soul that was tarnished by the choices they made. Innocence was lost. They could not return home for they tasted the shame of their ego.

The vision of heaven became lost and out of fear they returned to the structure and form where they could forget once again. Heaven was severed. Part of God's creation became lost to God. Anguish vibrated the heavens, for out of time and space God's creation became lost to eternity. Out of free will did they choose that which God would not. Separation was born out of identity, out of the image of the self, out of the ego that willed elation. It touched the soul and spawned darkness that could be seen in the very garment of their being. For those that fled heaven to take refuge in the structure and form of the encased reality, knew not how to return. They knew not how to cleanse their garment that had become tarnished by their ego.

The plan of God was to give meaning to life, to intensify life by giving depth to the soul. Out of structure and form would we come to know a deeper meaning of self.

To bring meaning to the self, glorified heaven. To experience the self in both structure and form, under the confines of time and space was wondrous. We could test our choices; test the strength of our will against the desire of our being. This reality was necessary for God willed that we would grow and come to know wisdom. As we did good and sought to add value to the fabric of God, our garments that clothed our souls became brighter. We beamed in intensity with the light that emanated from God. God's presence in us became visible. For those that returned home from the structure and form of this reality, having added value to the fabric of God, beamed from their inner being the light that had formed out of life.

Such was God's plan. Yet the risk that was formed by the ego weighed heavy on God and on heaven. Those that became lost to God, those that became lost to the darkness, weighed heavy on God. As innocence was lost, the work of redemption began. The record of each life was written so that the choices that were made could be reviewed in spirit. In spirit could we learn from one another how choices had an impact. The record would allow us to experience in part what was felt, what was known, why they did what they did, and how each choice impacted both them and those around them. The record would prepare us in spirit, so that we could draw strength in life.

Together would we return. From spirit to the life of structure and form. We were known as the children of the Law of One, for we brought the image of heaven with us. We sought to restore the remembrance of what was forgotten to those who were lost to the light of God. The sons of Belial, the children of the lie, were lost to the ego of the self in the illusion of their own elation.[21] The memory and desire of God for them became dimmed.

God, who could not leave His creation, knew of the cold and anguish that daunted the souls of those that were lost. No longer could they hear His voice, yet He was there with them, in the darkness of their own souls. God withdrew deep within their souls, for He knew that His very presence would cause them to run and hide further into the darkness of their reality.

Lost were they—lost to the reality of the self that knew more of fear and wantonness than of the bond that desires for one another what God freely gives to each of us. Beyond the shadows of the

---

21 References to the sons of Belial are made sporadically throughout the Bible (see 1st Samuel 2:12, 30:22). In the cosmic story there is a division, a split by choice to the Creative Force. We find this both in scripture and in mythology. Souls (even souls that were regarded as angelic in nature) that wanted divergence from free will were inclined towards subjected will. The "lie" was in the illusion of goodness, where goodness could be maintained by subjection, an expected reverence to the divine or rather to divinity—to bow down to, to be subjected to deity, suggestive of lesser souls being subjects of the Creative Force. Innocence and beguilement led to entrapment as souls became subjected to influence. The cosmic story for the fallen spirals downward from there as free will became perverted to do whatever to whomever without reprise on self and ignorance to consequence. Most of the cosmic story found in both scripture and mythology is told in parable, yet again we know that there is an imagery of reality which reflects upon both the record of souls and the destiny of souls.

reality of God, His children hid, yet the light of God still shined. Into this reality, in the shadows of structure and form, would God work the plan of redemption to restore innocence to those that were lost to semi-innocence.

God, in His plan of redemption, would restore His own. Out of free will would He reach into the darkness to reclaim His own. We who were the children of the Law of One would go with Him to reach once again into the hearts of our brothers and sisters. Together would we bear both humanity and inhumanity to reform the spirit and the garment of those who were tarnished by the will and the desire of the ego.

Source: Book of Life

The Dimensions of God's Creation

—— 1 The Six Dimensions of God's Creation ——

There are six dimensions to God's creations. Three dimensions which divides heaven from earth and the earth from the abyss and three dimensions to allow for God, soul and self. Three dimensions form the space and structure through which reality is defined and three dimensions form the creative essence of life.

The first dimension is filled by God alone. It is a dimension defined by light, purity and Truth. It is the first reality and the source from which all realities exist. As the will of God moves the vibration of light takes form to become the realities that we experience. Only he who is one with God can move light in the pattern which can alter the fabric of creation to restore wholeness. We, who enter into the fullness of God, taste and feel the presence of God's light which vibrates from the first dimension.

As God moved, a second dimension was created. It was the dimension of thought divided, a dimension divided to form a voice unto its own. Life and spirit is the dimension of thought divided. God Himself cannot be divided, created a dimension within a dimension where He could reside yet His will could be stilled to allow the will of His creation to co-exist. This is the dimension of the soul. Like God, this second dimension is a primary dimension. We who seek God, wills the desire of God in their soul.

Out of the second dimension came the third. It was the dimension of self. As the soul formed, we in turn created a dimension within a dimension, a voice where the dimension of self was explored.[22] All of creation resides in the experience of the self. To return to God, to return to the dimension where our soul is whole and complete we must find and refine our self. We must seek and allow the first dimension which is the dimension of purity and Truth to take root in our soul which exists in the second dimension. Both the first and the second dimensions are present in the dimension of self, but the self must seek God if the soul is to be illuminated. Without the desire for God, the vibration of the second dimension becomes heavy and grey. God is always present through our soul with the self, but the self must find God in the soul to be present with God.

The soul is our life force. It is always bound to God. Our soul aspires to the Truth and the oneness that we were created in. All our dreams and visions which seek to add value to God's creation comes from our soul which is in communion with God. God inspires us to do good through our soul. It is in our soul that God retains our innocence. It is here that God resides and it is here that our innocence cannot be disturbed. It is only in the mirror of our soul that our self can find the wholeness that would make us complete.

As we moved in thought and desire to find self-meaning and an identity, the dimension of space and matter took form. This is the fourth dimension. The pattern of self was formed and it became the home of our soul. Each of the three dimensions where God, soul and self co-exist are dimensions of thought divided. We

---

22   Think of the dimensions of "God—Soul—Self" as "Source—Conduit—Giver". If God is love (where love is one of the binding forces of the universe) then the soul becomes the conduit, the channel through which that love force enters our will. The self becomes the giver, the filter from which love must pass through if love is going to be realized or experienced. From a cosmic perspective God's light or love must pass through the three dimensions from God, through the soul and into our awareness which we call self (we equate the self with ego or identity but it is also elusive as it is our personality, our talents and the image of what we are and we are not). If the self blocks the light, the soul cannot be charged or infused with the light that comes from God. Our ability to love, our wantingness to love and be loved must pass through the filter of self if the soul is to be illuminated by God.

retain a multitude of images, dreams, aspirations, hopes, desires, feelings, motivations and convictions because each of these three dimensions co-exist to form the pattern of self, soul and the essence of God in the dimension of space and matter. We are granted space and the pattern of light forms the vibration of our soul which can be seen, felt and measured.

The fourth dimension is our eternal home. It is heaven from where we all came and the home to where our spirit looks and strives to return. It was out of this dimension that creation was expanded and formed the other two dimensions. As we interacted with God and each other to explore the visions of our dreams through the reality of space and matter, we took upon ourselves the limits of form to test our self-will and to find our own self-image. We moved in and out of space and matter, out of bodies of form to set in motion the creation of our thoughts and desires. It was in the dimension of self through the dimension of form that the soul became lost to our own self-image.

The dimension of form and matter split God's creation and tore the very fabric of God. Heaven became split and an abyss was created. It was a willful act of self for self alone, which created the desire to hide one's self from God. Unlike the second dimension, where the soul was created as a separate entity from God, the abyss formed a dimension of exile which placed the self in darkness from the soul that God created. We ourselves became split. We became of two forms, one which co-existed with God for God was present within, and the other which sought to hide God from our own awareness. The abyss became a dimension of duality and conflict.[23]

---

23   Heaven is both a place of structure and form and a condition where oneness of self, soul and the essence of God can co-exist. The abyss is a created dimension of formless exile to hide light in darkness, almost like a lucid dream sleep. It is the willfulness of want to hide from God, to deny God's essence, a pause or stay of anger where emotions themselves take form in the darkness that is willed. It is a curious state where fear has dissipated and the soul has lost its desire to sense connectedness with others. Souls in exile become trapped out of blind willfulness in defile to the creative process, and they blame God or others for creating the condition of their state of being. The fire is the internalizing of the anger which in itself also takes form and con-

Since the self cannot be divided, separated from soul, they sought to hide in the abyss from both God and others.

The abyss was the dimension of illusion, a false reality of self for self, exclusive to the self alone. Because of the abyss, a rift was created to separate this dimension from heaven. It became a dimension of exile not out of God's will, but out of the will of the self to hide from God. God created the space to allow the self to exist in the illusion of separation. Because of the abyss, the fifth dimension was created as a bridge, a conduit between the abyss and heaven. The fifth dimension forms the reality on earth. It is our humanity that hides the pattern of light to infuse the souls where light was tarnished. Unlike the fourth dimension, where space and matter took form through the pattern of our spirit, the fifth dimension became the bridge to restore those who were lost to the abyss, the sixth dimension. The light of heaven and the darkness of the abyss that existed in the soul would be hidden and forgotten in the incarnation, the fifth dimension.

Humanity became the vehicle through which God could return to His creation and restore His creation to the oneness and wholeness that He created us in. Here His light would be hidden in form, but seen in spirit—hidden in the third dimension of self but seen again in the second dimension of our soul. Those who were lost in the sixth dimension could find God again in the fifth dimension and be restored, redeemed to come home to the fourth dimension.

The fifth dimension is the corridor through which we pass through. It is here that the image of self can be tested and be measured in the form of our humanity. We who can endure God's vibration can sustain that reality where God's fullness can be seen

verges. Again we find that these are souls of influence, shifting in consciousness according to the illusions of want for self. Unlike the fourth dimension where God's light is illuminated according to the essence of God endured, the sixth dimension has a different form where God's essence is hidden, forgotten in soul. The light of the soul is tarnished, blackened, festered and demonized—taking the form of the image internalized.

and felt. Here we will learn what we must learn. Here will we return to be tested and to be quickened, so that we might know God in the image of our self.

As the glory differs from the sun to the moon and from one star to the next so are the realities that now exist between the fourth and the sixth dimension. We are separated not only according to our vibration, but also by our willingness and wantingness to be restored to God. The reality that we perceive is the projection of the dimension from which our state of being exists. The reality and dimension that we find ourselves in is both by choice and by desire.

We co-exist on many levels and move between dimensions according to our awareness and the vibration to which God can move within. The who we are, the self that we will, sets in motion the vibration that is seen in us. It resonates and illuminates, or dampens and dulls the dimension of our soul, which is the only corridor we have to connect with our God. When we live with God our soul is seen, felt and vibrates through the dimension of self. Without God's presence our soul becomes silent and retracts to draw strength from God by hiding itself deep within our core. God goes with us within the life force of our soul, even if the self chooses the abyss where our illusions overshadow our awareness to God's presence.

The sixth dimension is both a stay of reality and a state of being. It is a place where the past is relived and relived. It is a place where our form is lost, but our presence can be seen. It is a state of being where conflict is imprisoned by our unwillingness to seek our God. It is here that we see ourselves for who we were, for what we willed and for the emptiness and pain that we created. There is a void in the sixth dimension. It is a darkness that hides the light of God. The one who wanders in the darkness of the abyss knows not of one's own soul. The self cannot be divided, separated from soul, and so the soul waits to be awakened. It is there in your soul that you will find God who holds you still in the grace that is yours.

God places within the human mind a state of forgetfulness. The memories of the abyss or the sweet aroma of heaven is forgotten and in the fifth dimension life begins anew. God reaches into His creation to restore His creation. The vibration of the soul is hidden within the body and the form that is expressed can be shaped by our humanity. The vibration of the soul can be quickened by the presence of others in our lives. God living through our soul is seen in the self. Those who were lost to God can find God through those who are in communion with God. From the very relationships of our humanity can divinity be seen and felt. When God is seen and felt, the soul is awakened and the abyss is lifted.

Baptism is the symbolism of our renewal of life with our God. However, it is our humanity that vibrates God's image. Our humanity is the expression of our compassion, our caring and our love for one another. Baptism without humanity is a waste. Humanity without baptism is still godly. Baptism with humanity fills the soul and illuminates the self. Heaven awaits.

Our walk back to God is with God. God reaches into our soul and sparks the revelation of His presence in our lives. God awakens our soul from the abyss of our self to place into communion His will. We only have to listen with our heart and allow His call to guide our lives. All are called, for God excludes no one.

Source: Book of Life

——— 2 The Realms of Structure and Form ———

The realms of reality were separated to allow life to unfold in the spectrum of touch and sensation. God's interaction in His creation would be borne by creation itself. We would carry God with us by allowing His image to work through us. Insomuch as that image was borne in us, determined the construct of the reality that stood before us. This life determines the construct of our reality that stands before us. What we see, what we feel, what we receive is a reflection of the construct that we impart to others.

To taste the sweet grass upon our feet and to smell the fresh fragrance in the air that surrounds us can be captured by the vision that illuminates our soul by the image of our God. His image rests in the reality and is as vivid and real in this life as He is in the next life. God's light does not leave God's creation, but the form of the reality determines the degree of illumination. The glory, the intensity, the electricity of God is dampened upon the distant spectrum of realities that God created. The further we move from the likeness of God determines the reality that does exist in the darkness of God's creation. This is not punishment from God, but rather grace to allow you the time and space to recreate the desire for God within the confines of your own free will.

Behold, God's glory is the infusion of God's light. It pulls you from the darkness that you created from the inhumanity of your will. God's light is the beacon. In all the realities that stand in God's creation, God's light emanates to bring a release from the darkness. To see God's light one must look beyond one's self. The form of darkness that encases our spirit from God's light was created out of this illusion that we are separate from God; we are not.

The light of God is repelled by the exclusivity of the self. The darkness that emerges is the images that are created in the realities that we will. As we leave this life, all images converge upon the fabric of our soul. The law of spirit dictates convergence. In this life, where structure and form encases both the light of our soul and the darkness of the self, we choose out of free will. We emanate both desire and will. We emanate either God's light or repel God's light. Darkness is formed out of desire for the self, for self alone, for the exclusivity of the self as the ego wills. But the law of the spirit dictates convergence. In death that which was imparted converges. By the images of this life which are reviewed in spirit will we see. The record of life stands before us.

The light of God is glorified in us as we will for others that which promotes life. As we uphold one another and seek to bring humanity into the lives of those whom God has called us to serve, God's light is infused into our very being. The Book of Life bears testimony, for insomuch as we impart God's goodness is God's goodness infused into our very being. In death, in spirit, God's goodness converges in our being and His glory, glorifies our image. We shine; we are illuminated by His light.

When one's life is lived in the exclusivity of the self, at the expense of others, darkness encases ones soul such that God's light cannot be seen. The images of this life which if lived in darkness must also converge on the very fabric of your soul. God's promise for release can only occur out of a desire for Him. Without your desire for Him the darkness cannot be dispelled. The reality that will stand before you will be the reality that you created. You with others, who are of like will and desire must walk together.

Let the beacon of God's light dispel the darkness that you created. The Book of Life will bear testimony of your goodness if you'll will for others. The Book of Life stands as a record. It is both embedded upon your soul and is recorded on the scroll of time. The record cannot be changed or altered but its conditions can be recreated.

The reality that takes root on the inside of our soul is the reality that is created, seen and lived in the world that is without. Beyond the self is the image of the self that we project. The reality that we create today, is the seed and the construct of the reality that we will live in tomorrow. Death is not the escape but the fruition of the reality that we created in life.

In death, the life is reviewed. We stand in the light and the images of our life now past, is reviewed in spirit. Here you will see and feel all that was done. In full view will be your thoughts, your actions and your desires. Here you will see what kind of an imprint your life has had on yourself, others and your God. All will be borne in witness to yourself the image you willed. God who stands beside you in the light sees His image in you, even through those times in your life which were marred by inhumanity. We impart upon God and others life and in death God instills His presence upon us by allowing us to see our humanity as our only true desire. We desire to relinquish in anguish our inhumanity. God's forgiveness will always stand whole but our free will and desires are ours to hold and to mold.

The realm we choose with Him in death, in spirit, is our home according to our wants and our desires. The creation or reality that stands before us in spirit is a reflection of who we are and what we desire to become. We go not alone. Family and friends in this life and lives now gone by, walk with us. Yet there is a separation. Just as we are separated from those in spirit when we are born so it is that we are separated from those in this life when we die. Similarly in death or in spirit we can become separated in time and space from each other because of the choices that we make. The garment of our soul projects the light of our God. As the image of God shines through us, our garment is glorified by the love that dwells in us. The image of God, the image of love can be seen and felt like the warmth of the sun.

The realm that we choose is God's grace that brings us full circle to the restoration of our true image. By our will we choose with God. For those who resist, their journeys are arduous and long. The path is marred by the imprisonment of their own inhumanity. The images of their elation and ego, bars and traps them to the reality of others who are of like mind and desire. Together they will bear upon each other their acts of inhumanity until their inhumanity can be released from their will and desire.

God cannot set us free from the fear, despair, hatred and rage until we let go of the self-justification and condemnation of wantonness, greed, apathy and blame. Those emotions and desires go with us in death. Where there is no desire for release, these emotions intensify. Born in us and of us, they take root like a weed in the garden that God created. The weeds cannot take root when the soil is toiled. It is the desire to keep the heart and the mind pure and innocent that maintains the garden as God created.

Life does not rest in judgment to God's law, but rather the gravitation of God's law. Our lives either move in likeness to God or resist God's likeness that is in us, by the images we create. We either move towards the light or repel the light that God placed in us. When we move towards the darkness the pull of God is intensified. Listen carefully to the pull from God for it is the conflict that is in you and you cannot escape it. Abiding the conflict and living the lie only prolongs the suffering. It is your choice but in your choice will be the creation you create. Separated from the light, the images that were created in darkness will remain in you to be faced again until the desire for them becomes bitter and distasteful.

Within the fabric of God we can recreate the conditions. The shadows of the past must be relived in their fullness to reenact upon ourselves that will that formed the darkness. By and by, our true will for God's presence pierces the darkness of our past by restoring God's wholeness back into lives. So it is that the record of life bears testimony again. In testimony, the testament of God's promise comes to rest. The restoration of innocence is granted by the passion of the fruit.

Source: Book of Life

God

─────── 1 God is a Just God ───────

Within God is all that there is. God brings to our awareness that which is just and true. God breathes life and life extends God. The fire of God is the energy that illuminates life. Love is just as real as the source from which it came. Love to the spirit is like air to the body. The energy that love gives is vital and thrives when we abide in God. To cut ourselves off from God is to cut ourselves off from all that is around us; the earth, our home, our families, our friends. We cannot cut ourselves off from life nor can we cut ourselves off completely from the desire to belong. The desire to belong is the residue of love; we cannot cut our *self* off completely from love. Just as light which has left its source can never become darkness so it is that we can never totally separate ourselves from God. God is and so are we.

God is a just God[24] and as such He does not give us an unjust life. Our life has purpose and meaning. It is fulfilled within the plan of creation that God wills. Out of free will we struggle. The struggle is magnified when we choose to hide ourselves from God. We cannot hide from God, but we live with the belief that we can. In our hiding we feel safe. Yet, unknowingly, we still draw life from God and God continues to sustain us. We only need to look

───────────────────────

24   "God is a Just God" is an affirmation of the essence of God. A "just God" points to a God of truth, reason, justice, fairness, principle, peace, love, creation, construct and all the attributes which bring light and energy into creation.

around and we can recognize the calmness that radiates from life itself. God moves, and in His movement we are sustained. His will sustains us even in that darkness where we would not have Him be.

This life is just. It is just because it can bring us back to God. The lessons that we learn and the people that we live with are all part of the plan. Amazing, isn't it? In the very instant that we stop and consider all the lessons, the people that we love and the people that we avoid, can we not see how we have changed? Can we not see how God is trying to show us what we painfully hide? When we avoid God's Truth and build up walls between us and others, does not our life become more difficult? Does not our pain increase, and do we not solidify our beliefs to find a refuge? Does that refuge not encase our identity? Have not our lessons also shown us that as we forgive and help others, we too are released?

As we reach for Truth, healing is granted. Forgiveness dissolves the anger and frustration and in helping others we find peace. When we choose to love, love becomes a part of us. There is less tension, less stress and our desire to be with one another increases. Those beliefs that would hide us from one another lose their meaning as Truth is restored. God's grace sustains us, because His grace patiently allows us the time that we need to work through those beliefs that would keep us from Him and from each other.

Can we then say that God is an unjust God? Can we then say that life is unjust? For if God moved and we moved with Him, would not love follow us all of our days? And what more would we ask of Him? It is only in our choice for conflict that we speak of injustice. It is only in our own duality that we would justify ourselves to an identity that we do not want. For either we hear the voice of God or we listen to that voice which would set us apart. It is that voice that keeps us from God that would speak of injustice. Listen carefully, for either you are strengthened towards God or you become entrenched in the injustice that you would make real.

God, who is just, sets you in an environment that you choose to provide you with the challenges necessary to help you become a reflection of His image. Yet you go not alone for He is there with you. We weave the fabric but the fabric belongs to God.[25] When we tear the fabric, God gives the fabric back to us to try again. Together we choose and God, who is just, will allow us the time to rework the fabric—rework the relationships until they are whole again. We mold the relationships, but our relationships belong to God. It is the relationships that God gives back to us. It is in our relationships that we are challenged to find God. We find God when we find God in each other.

God is a just God, setting in motion the opportunity for us to find heaven. Heaven is home. God rests in heaven and heaven goes with Him into the world. God offers heaven to those who will peace. God extends heaven to those who only know conflict.

Offering is the collection of resources that feeds the body. The offering that is collected is given back to the body. It is extended back to that part of the body that is in need. We who hear God's voice become the collection of heaven to bring back heaven to those that are still in conflict. For heaven is not at rest so long as a part of God's creation is lost from heaven. For who would will to go to heaven forever and leave behind his brother or sister or friend who lost their ability to find their way home? We yearn for each other. I am incomplete without you and you need me if heaven is to be found for both of us.

When a just God is found, then that part of God that is in you will find a home. Without Truth we have no home, for Truth is the only home where heaven is found.

Where do you will to be? Do you will to see God as a just God, who would extend heaven to all or do you will a God of justice, who saves only the elect few? Choose carefully, for in so choosing, you choose for yourself. For the God you see is the God you worship and in your beliefs, Truth will either find a home or it will continue to elude you. In so choosing you either become God's offering to a world in need or you become exclusive to God's offering clinging

---

25   In my journaling this phrase was "We *mold* the fabric but the fabric belongs to God". It is a different imagery, more like the potters clay. I liked this imagery because it gave a more three dimensional construct to the fabric.

to the duality that makes you special.[26]

Build the temple of God inside you where a just God can bear witness to the world. Just as the sun shines upon the earth and the earth comes alive in the array of life and color, let God shine through you. In you is His light. Your eyes become the doorway to your soul and your hands become the hands of Christ. In your witness will the world know of the love of God. As the world sees a just God in you, so will the peace of God find a home in the world.

Jesus said, "Abide in me and I in you. As the branch cannot bear fruit of itself, except it abides in the vine, no more can you, except you abide in me."[27]

The waters move and reflect the rays of the sun. The sun in all its splendor is illuminated as it becomes one with the water that it touches. The dance of light begins and lasts all the day long. But when the night came, were the oceans consumed in the darkness? No, for the darkness cannot contain the water. And where is the sun? Has it moved from its place? Do not despair in the darkness for it cannot consume you. Nor has God moved. Turn then to God, for in Him will you see that which is just. For natural is His light and His splendor will illuminate even you.

26 The word "duality" in theological terms has numerous overtones, including the co-existence of good and evil, or a state of being both divine and human (i.e. to be of a dual nature). Our humanity (goodness) co-exists with our divergent potential to be inhumane (evil). In the context of this sentence it is the belief or that voice which would suggest we are special, entitled or exclusive to God's favor for whatever reason (as in birthright, race or religion). God sets us apart and loves us more because of... i.e. we think we are favored **which is not** the nature of God. The affirmation of God is a God that embraces all people regardless of faith, religion or creed. Our faith traditions and religious beliefs can add both diversity and culture to our worship. However, dogmas can create elements of exclusivity to God which, if not tempered, can be divisive. When we choose our worship, both faith and humanity should point towards our connectedness as the Creative Force is present in all life. Peace on Earth only happens if we embrace each other in our diverse faith expressions for God.

27 John 15:4

Begin again and allow a just God to find a home in you. His peace will magnify your true identity. This is the process that brings release and establishes God's righteousness. Seeing a just God is the link, the thread that will allow you to pierce through your beliefs to find the Truth. A just God is the reflection seen in Jesus Christ. A just God is the vision that brings your awareness to that part of you that is still a part of God. Seek what is real and your reality will change. For what is real is pure, as pure as a just God whose love is unconditional.

Source: Book of Truth

——— 2 The Essence of God Must be Found ———

From the moment that the spirit of you was formed out of the essence of God, you were retained. God emptied Himself yet filled you with that which was divine. The spirit which was of God was emptied of His will, His desire, His image, so that you might choose for yourself. In this emptiness did He give up all that He was so that you might find your own image, your own desires and your own will. Yet God could not empty that which was divine in Him. God's light went with Him into His creation. In you, God is. His presence is forever with you, for God could not empty that which was divine in Him from you.

The fullness of God is the essence of life itself. Strip away all that which is not of God and all that will remain is God's fullness. The light of God is the divine within. Herein is the innocence that is retained in you. God's essence is pure, restoring God's Truth through that which is divine. From the source of light all that which is retained *is* life restored.

> *I am the way, the light and the Truth.*[28] *Peace goes with me. It will shine out of the darkness that hides my spirit. From the recesses of the mind, from the emptiness of the heart, from the solitude of the soul,*

---

28   Similar in message to John 14:6.

as the self is emptied into humanity will the divine be restored. God's oneness claims again God's creation[29].

The fall from heaven was the illusion of our inhumanity.[30] Humanity was set in this reality so that the Divine could once again touch in you what was lost to free will. All that was you was retained in God; everything else will be released by grace through your humanity. If you claim humanity, you claim grace. Grace is the free gift of you in the image that is reflected in the mirror of God. From the image of God, all that which is divine is reflected in you, through you and of you.

When humanity and divinity converge, the Law of One will be restored. Just as God emptied Himself in the image of Adam to create humanity, so it is that Jesus emptied himself from inhumanity to restore the divine—reflecting back the essence of

---

29 This is the first of numerous "poetic" use of first person statements that the reader will find in The Message where the message in the spiritual journaling is suggestive of a quote from Christ or from God. To be true to the journaling exercise the thought as penned (or written) was based on the thought received. There is a risk that some will see these statements as crossing the line in the journaling exercise as I did not have any physical manifestation that was Angelic in nature (that I was aware of) nor is there direct evidence of a quote in canonized scripture to confirm the statement. As such, these statements are not placed into quotations. Yet the essence of thought is pure and consistent with the Christ message. The intent of The Message is to compel us to consider God and the possibilities of how God inspires us to consider what He offers.

30 This sentenced has always caught my attention—the illusion of the "fall from heaven". My own perception of reality is based on what is real, what really happened. The twist to think about is that an illusion is a "false reality" or rather a reality that God would not will. The illustration is that what fills our consciousness or our awareness to a particular reality is grounded by what we make real. What we make real is not necessarily what we see and touch, but rather what we take in, what we feel, or how that impacts our destiny. As an example, if we think people are going to attack us our natural response is to protect ourselves. Our perceptions may or may not be real, but our response will create the reality. The act of inhumanity created this belief that God would not want us and so therefore we are cast out, fallen, lost, doomed or maybe robbed, imprisoned, exiled, hated. The choice of the self is to either run from or to turn to God.

your spirit that was formed by the hand of Him who holds you still.

I am the way, the light and the Truth.[31] He who follows me will not walk in darkness.[32] For I am present, forever beside the shadows that hide my image. To look upon me is to look upon yourself. To see me as I am is to see you as I created. To find my wholeness is to see your humanity.

To embrace your humanity is to accept the gift of grace. Grace by humanity restores the divine that binds God to you. Life from life restores life to life. Life from your humanity restores life to the light of the divine that is within.

Herein lays the hope for all mankind to be free of the self that wills for the self alone. To be restored in self to the will of the divine that restores us all to God. As the divine brings unity and wholeness from within, each one restores each other to the divine that restores community to the whole. From light to life. Light shines from within and restores life to the whole.

All are called to the divine love that binds God to each of us. God in you and me, recreating the image of the reality that exists beyond the illusions that binds self to self. As each one gives back the self, as each ones empties the self from the self, will each one be set free.[33] From one to the other will the whole be restored.

God's hope extends into the darkness to call all who could not choose in life, to choose in spirit. Out of the pure desire for God will the resurrection emerge. Silence and the darkness will be broken out of the desire for life—life from the desire for light, God's light. Claim that which is held sacred in Him. God hold's your innocence

---

31 Similar in message to John 14:6.

32 Similar in message to John 8:12.

33 This sentence structure is about the imagery of looking at ourselves in a mirror. It is coming face to face with who we were, who we are and who we hope to be. There is a part of our self that thinks only for our self and another part that embraces selflessness. In our conflict to choose between our selfish nature and our selfless nature we come to terms with the fact that we cannot escape our choice. All of who we are will face God.

sacred in Him and seeks to give it back to you.

For those who choose God will find God's light.

Source: Book of Law

───────────────────── **3 Truth** ─────────────────────

God's Truth brings us back to that source of knowledge that breathes understanding into life. In that Truth comes peace and acceptance. Truth takes us back to God. Truth bears testimony to that reality that God would will. Truth is a message that speaks for hope, for oneness, for healing and for peace. Truth calls us to wholeness in ourselves and in our relationships. Truth speaks for honesty and for innocence.

If in God there is one guiding light then that light can be recognized in that Truth that brings us back to God. When all the illusions and fears that hid God from us are gone, then all that will remain will be Truth. Truth bears testimony to the reality of God that exists in God. If God is real, Truth will bear testimony of Him. The awareness to that Truth, which liberates and restores us to wholeness, resides in our willingness to look for God from the very depths of our soul.

God is the source of life. From Him was life created. God created. He is and so are you.

Truth in its purest form will always release us. When we look for Truth we give ourselves back to what we desire to be real in us. We desire to love and be loved. We desire peace and acceptance. Only in fear do we hide from Truth. We fear each other. We are afraid of our past. We are afraid to take the first step towards love and healing. We are afraid to look into the eyes of our neighbor, our friend, our brother and our sister.

However, it is only in Truth where true healing and true wholeness can be found. This Truth is the reality that would restore our relationships. This Truth would speak of our desire to be accepted, loved and forgiven. This Truth brings us back to God and to each other.

Since God is the source of life, the source of our healing, God will not allow us to wither away in the pain and the illusions that we created to hide ourselves from Him and from each other. *God did not create us to find a just cause from which to destroy us.* So God went with us. He planted Himself deep inside of us and we drew life from Him. We could separate ourselves from Him by our beliefs and illusions, but He could not separate Himself from us, for He created us and continues to love us.

Without the desire for Truth, we cannot free ourselves from the illusions that we cling to. God will not violate our own free will.

Truth resides in God. So must it be if we wish to be free from our illusions and our guilt that God must abide in us. All that we do and say must be a reflection of that Truth that has been planted deep inside. It is in God that our true identity takes on real meaning. Our identity becomes free because Truth illuminates our thoughts, our feelings and our actions. God moves through us and we are not consumed by Him. Nor are our thoughts, feelings and actions dictated by Him. Truth sets us free to be, without guilt.

> *I see within the wind the movement of God upon the earth. The earth listens without recognition to its Creator. But I know that He is there. I hear His voice. He is in me, for I feel Him. His Truth calls to me and bids me to come near. His desire for me is pure and I long to look upon myself as He would look upon me. Father in heaven, set me in your Truth for without it I am lost. May I look to you in all that I do and say, so that I might be a quiet reflection of the peace that was present in your Son Jesus Christ. For with Him I would gladly spend all of my days.*
>
> *Source: Book of Truth*

————————— 4 The Law of One —————————

The Lord our God is One.

The Law of God was born out of Truth. When Truth was broken the word became the law.[34] The word was, "The Lord our God is One." In God there is no division, no duality.[35] In God's Kingdom there is but one law—the Law of One. The Law of One maintains God's Kingdom in wholeness and in Truth. When Truth was broken, the law became broken, fragmented. Man became separated from God; man became separated from God's law.[36]

The Law of God binds us to God. God's law binds us to the life force of life; the source that extends God. In life, this life, we become witnesses to order and chaos. Our understanding about God's law is lost when we see law within the confines of order and chaos. When order is broken chaos ensues. When law's in a society are broken, chaos sets in. To bind man to man's law, man in turn binds chaos to order. Chaos is imprisoned and order is used to measure injustice. In man's understanding of law, Truth is sacrificed and is used to lay claim to order. If in Truth we are set free, how can Truth be used to imprison? [37]

God's Truth sets us free and God's law binds us to God. The

---

34   The word "when" is used as a change in state as opposed to a reference in time. An example would be, when someone falls, they are no longer standing. A change in state requires a new set of rules or rather the rules of the former state no longer apply. For example, you can no longer run until you get back up on your feet.

35   In The Message the reader is to consider "oneness" and "duality" as not polar to one another but rather the co-existence of "oneness" within the human condition even though our human condition is of a dual nature. In the context of the language in this paragraph, "no duality" simply is referring only to the essence of unity or a natural state of harmony and oneness. With respect to heaven, there is no division or "duality in love" in God's Kingdom. In God's Kingdom people do not love only half the people—they would not love someone openly and then secretly not love that same person.

36   Separation here is one of choice. We have free will, so we are not bound to abide by God's law or God's Word or God's Messages. Yet we become what we will. Our creation defines the "who I am". In time we must face what we created. Gravity dictates what happens when we fall. Creation or miscreation will dictate time in the construct of what we will.

37   See page Part III The God Process: Section 5 Commentary Notes on The Message which discusses the author's perspective on the Law of God as it pertains to society, regulators and enforcement.

Law of One calls us to God's creation. We are called to be of one heart, one mind and one purpose, which fulfills the Truth that brings value to life. We are called to be the children of the Law of One. One with God, living in the Truth that promotes each other as we seek our true identity. The Law of One does not bring order to chaos, but instead allows us to see God within the chaos. In turn, the chaos finds stillness as God is revealed from within.

In creation we were born of God's image, but the image of God became distant to man. Man became lost to Truth when beliefs were formed to replace the reality that we willed and the Truth that we forsook.[38] The law became fragmented. Our understanding of what bind's us to God was buried deep within our soul. The image of God was fragmented for God became a reflection of what we feared in judgment. Sin was established and retribution was weaved into the image of God.

To break free from sin, to break free from those beliefs that sets us apart from God, the Law of God must be strengthened within your heart and within your will. Sin in our beliefs separates us from God. God cannot look upon sin because sin is an illusion

---

38 The construct of belief by definition is a conviction to truth. Yet also by definition there is a mystery, an uncertainty in that reality that we call truth. We give ourselves to our beliefs. Beliefs are powerful as they form the foundational basis through which we see and judge ourselves, others and our world. Our human condition is such that we do not have perfect knowledge, so we look to our beliefs. However, beliefs can be transient in design and may differ from one believer to the next. If our beliefs point us to the reality that does exist in God then our beliefs are grounded in Truth. Beliefs that are not grounded in Truth can be considered illusions and illusions which oppose Truth are constructs which will hide God's reality from us.

We believe in Truth, yet we know there is a mystery or an uncertainty in knowing God and it is in that mystery that seems to maintain God at a distance. Yet what is real is real and that reality cannot be altered. God is real. All other convictions which are not grounded in reality are, in fact, illusions. When we make God an illusion, beliefs will hide God from us. Beliefs require analysis, exploration and reflection to assess if they are constructs which bring us back to God. More importantly we need to assess if our beliefs bring us back to the reality that exists in God or God's reality—Truth.

to set us apart from our God. Wantonness split's the self, which retains the vision of chaos and order. Both chaos and order are transient in measure, relative only to the self.

The norms measured by the self moves ones identity in and out of chaos so that semi-innocence is maintained at will. Yet within the perception of chaos and order, sinlessness—innocence— cannot be restored. Separation from God by the perception of sin is maintained and we believe we are hidden from the very God that we draw life from. Man cannot give himself back to God because the Law of God cannot be found in wholeness. The Law of God has been fragmented and man's understanding, based on chaos and order, retains God's law within the realm of judgment.

Within man's understanding of sin and transgression, man is bound to chaos and order. Order and chaos demands retribution to satisfy the error against God. Yet, it is only out of our beliefs that we demand retribution to satisfy the error against God, self and others to maintain order. True forgiveness demands no retribution. It is our beliefs that binds us to the laws of chaos and order that in turn hides us from seeing the pure image of God. If we cannot see God's Truth, we become powerless to know and understand God's judgment. We become unable to release ourselves from those beliefs that separate us from Him and from each other.

Wantonness is the thought form, and sin was born in the act. Sin was the imprint of our wantonness, a mistake now visible to God, self and others. Sin was set apart in time, irreversible and unchangeable. It is our ego however that keeps sin alive and keeps us apart from God. It is our ego which replaces God's image with our own euphoric self-image to uphold our beliefs, and even in sin it freely grants us our own semi-innocence.

Our ego goes to the root of our soul and covers the soul with beliefs and half-truths. Our ego entraps us. Our will is etched, our ability to love is etched, and our personality is etched. Our very self-image is etched, and we become trapped within the walls that were built out of our beliefs to restores us to our semi-innocence. The cocoon has been formed and we are lost in our ability to find God's Truth and to restore our true innocence. It is our beliefs that protect our ego, our self-image. We become imprisoned in the fear of our illusions that we would make real.

Our ego builds a belief system; it is a paradox of thoughts and feelings to hide sin in semi-innocence. We are free to be as we choose yet in the paradox of our thoughts we are trapped by the beliefs that hide us from God, self and others. We mask ourselves with an identity and rewrite the past to justify our actions or lay blame and denial in the wake of others. Instead of looking to God for release and forgiveness to restore our self-image and to heal our relationships, we look to our belief system. In turn our ego fortifies our belief system where chaos is imprisoned and order is maintained in semi-innocence.

The ego was created by the self to protect the self. It becomes the voice which fears both God and others. We build our own form of order to protect ourselves from each other, to protect ourselves from the chaos we created. The walls of semi-innocence form the cocoon around the self and the self is protected. In sharing our beliefs we extend ourselves to those that will accept us and protect us. We hide ourselves from both God and from those whom we fear.

Wantonness takes us away from God and into the downward spiral where the self becomes wrapped deeper and deeper into the cocoon that would hide our soul from the light of Truth. Our ego would hide us from God but God won't let us go. Even though the Law of God has been fragmented, we still cannot escape it. For as the darkness appears to close us in, the Word of God daunts upon the ego.

The Lord our God is One and the self cannot be divided.[39] We cannot separate God from our soul and be whole in our self. Only in darkness can we hide His light. So God goes with us into the shadows of our mind where He is hidden.

---

39   This is a key message to our cosmic nature. When Jesus proclaimed, "I and my Father are One", it was the fulfillment or embodiment of God's law, the Law of One, where oneness and harmony had overcome the "self". It was the desire and will to embody God's essence and yet retain the "self", to retain individuality, personality, identity or self-image singular in beingness to the Creative Force.

In order for there to be a healing, God has to break the illusion that was created by our wantonness and the imprint left by sin which binds us to fear itself. Since nothing can ever separate us from the love of God, God must look upon our wantonness and our ego as chaos. Chaos breaks us, fragments us, torments us and eludes us along a journey that we do not want. Would God will that we remain in chaos? So it is that the punishment of sin is chaos itself. God would end chaos, but He cannot, because He has given us our free will.

So as we will, so will we become. God granted us the freedom to choose, but we cannot escape our choices. God is the source of life and He is always there within us. God remains with us, even in the choices that would tear us apart. Yet, we can choose to place God in the shadows. He is hidden from our awareness and in our euphoria of self we are seemingly contained.

When the Law of God becomes fragmented, love becomes fragmented. Love, which is the essence of our life force, is placed at risk, love became conditional on the desire to rule chaos within the realm of order, as defined by our will. We choose who would be deserving of our love. God does not set us apart, but rather He sets us in the midst of creation. In an instant, the light can be seen when we choose to love but the darkness remains so long as we cling to our choices that would place love at risk.

The Law of God is constant, persistent and permeates all souls.[40] The Law of God defines the value of the soul as seen by God. Our ego, however, swings like a pendulum either glorifying our self-image or crucifying us in our remorse and guilt to retain our beliefs which upholds our semi-innocence. We cannot free ourselves from the pendulum when the ego devalues God, self or others to uphold our glorified self in semi-innocence.

---

40   There is a reality to our soul nature. It is a reality of the life force that we were created in. It is the reality of the essence of God within us. We are drawn towards oneness, inclusiveness and harmony because that is the true nature of our soul. For our soul to be at peace, we have to be at peace with God, others and ourselves. We are drawn to God because God resides within. Therefore, to be at peace with our "self", we have to find a way to make the essence of God real in our lives.

The Law of God glorifies wholeness. The ego devalues God's law to glorify the self. The Law of God brings us back together by forming bonds which become unconditional. Wantonness would break our relationships to satisfy self-indulgence. Fear entraps us when wantonness creates an imprint of sin. Chaos sets in. Relationships become conditional, and order is formed with no apparent boundaries. God's law is founded on Truth, yet when Truth has been forsaken, our beliefs set us in judgment to the exclusion of self.

God's law is fragmented when life is lived in duality. God's law is obeyed in partiality. God's law is kept sacred with some relationships, but not all. Where our relationships are maintained whole, where love is not placed at risk but kept unconditional, the law is kept. When our relationships become conditional, set apart by chaos and order, God's law has been broken. Our vision becomes obscured and no longer are we able to see others as God sees them. The Law of God becomes obscure and our vision of law is reduced to retribution. No healing can be found when relationships are held in bondage to retribution. It is the self that is held in bondage, for as the self sees, so shall the self judge. Judgment comes back on the judge. Judgment entraps, for condemnation cannot restore us back to innocence.

It is only when we look back to God can the Law of One break free the bondage of judgment. Since the law of man, which was formed by order and chaos, only has meaning when judgment is made to condemn, how can we break free of condemnation without seeking God's law? God's law connects us to one another. Judgment serves no purpose if in our judgment that judgment condemns the judge. God's law allows us to see the difference between the beliefs that set us apart and the Truth which binds us together. God's law becomes the only law where judgment sets us free. God's law frees us by binding us all back together.

The Law of God is strengthened in you as you release yourself from the desire to attack and defend those who would challenge your identity and those beliefs that would place your relationships at risk. Your defense is the wall that guards your semi-innocence.

It is a wall of fear. The voice of the ego speaks to you and inflames your emotions to protect what you have claimed. It is the nothingness that you claim which must be realized if you are to break free from those desires which either attack or defend. For the Law of One binds us to each other and releases us from the nothingness that we placed our value in. In the form of the attack of what we defend do we give ourselves to that which has no value from which value can be found.

The Law of God rests in the desire to love the Lord your God with all your heart, mind, body and soul, and to love your neighbor as yourself. For he who is born of God, must desire that which God desires. In you rest's the desire of God, and to be a part of God, God has to be a part of you. The Law of One must be kept whole and sacred. You must uphold others as sacred even as God upholds you as sacred. For what is sacred is kept whole in God—holy to God, for God's holiness is extended.

The Kingdom of Heaven is at peace for the Law of One is kept whole in God's Kingdom. The city of light shines forth for there is no darkness within. When the desire for God is made real, Truth is restored and the Law of God brings healing. When the Law of God finds rest within, sanctification is complete—the atonement is complete. We become free of judgment, and God's judgment sets us free. The Final Judgment will come when our innocence in Him is proclaimed. We will become one with Him for there will be no duality within us.[41] No conflict. We will be of one heart, one mind and one purpose, serving the purpose of creation.

Source: Book of Law

---

41   We end duality when there is no desire to judge others harshly and judgment does not come back on us, in our final judgment we are free from the temptation to judge or condemn.

The Plan of Redemption
The Journey of the Christ

——————— 1 The Plan of Redemption ———————

And I, Adam, was called forth to be the father of humanity. For I was with God, the Father, in the beginning having been begotten of His spirit, I was one with Him. From the source of light would I take upon myself the form of the earth. Out of the dust would I rise to begin my Father's work. Through me would flesh encase the light of the soul. In me and through me would the spirit of all mankind learn humanity. Out of humanity would the desire of God be rekindled and the heart of heaven be reformed.

From the dust of the earth will the light of heaven be restored. Here in is the record of heaven given that the Book of Life might be opened. I and my Father are one. I came into the world to restore in flesh what was lost in spirit. To restore innocence through the image of humanity. To bring full circle the divine by washing the garment of each soul with the will and compassion of the flesh. To release each one from the judgment that bound them to the retribution of the self.

My path was the path of restoration. I stood upon the earth and begot the sons of man. The children of the Law of One would stand with the sons of Belial, the children of the lie, and the light that illuminates the garment of the soul would be hidden so that humanity might bridge the spirit to rekindle the desire for God. Out of love and compassion in the setting where fear and hatred can be seen in form will each one see for themselves the path that will lead them back to the light.

By my own flesh and blood would I stand upon the earth as a witness to God. I would take upon myself the image of the fall, so that in Christ I might complete the work that restores each one in innocence.[42] The record of heaven is open so that all might see the restoration of one is the redemptive process for all. I am the way, the Truth and the light. No man comes unto the Father but by me. It is through my humanity that the spirit which resides in the divine can once again be whole in the self.

42　This is the first statement in The Message that Jesus and Adam are the same soul entity. This message is both one of cosmic purpose and one of soul choice. For most readers this will be an introduction to a theological consideration which is not prevalent in Christian theology. This may appear as divergence; however reflection on scripture brings us closer to the cosmic story and to our own soul development. Scriptures like: "I am Alpha and Omega, the beginning and the end" (Rev 21:6), "I am the first and I am the last" (Isaiah 48:12, Rev 1:17), "And the Word was made flesh and dwelt upon us" (connect John 1:1-13 with John 1:14), the Word resonates with the Creative Force of both Adam and Jesus. In 1st Corinthians 15:22 it is written, "For as in Adam all die, even so in Christ shall all be made alive." See also Part III: God of Reincarnation for additional discussion.

Although it is not penned in any of my own spiritual journaling work, I believe that just as Jesus and Adam are the same soul entity, so are Eve and Mary the same soul entity. Eve, having offered the fruit of knowledge to Adam, became the conduit of purity for the Christ through the incarnation as Mary. The birth of both Jesus and Mary through innocence is symbolic of life from light, where ultimately we are all quickened from within by God's light. Life restores light to the soul. The miracle that we are to embrace is that God is actively engaged with His creation and is part of the cosmic story, the God Process of creation.

Light will emerge from within. Darkness will part as each soul relinquishes the bondage that was created out of structure and form. Pain, suffering, fear and the inhumanity of will and condemnation that tainted the color and light of the soul with shades of dullness will be the shadow of your flesh standing behind the light of your redemption.

From my fall as Adam, to my resurrection as Christ, will the image of the Son of God be reformed. Relinquish the Father of man from that image where sin is held in bondage from the presence of God and from there will the vision of heaven be seen. Just as you release Adam from the fall and see in him the image of Christ so too will the shadows of the flesh stand behind the light of God. As you see the spirit of Adam converge in Christ, knowing that Adam stood and willingly partook of the fruit that brought the knowledge of your nakedness, will you find the purpose of your humanity was to restore you back to God.

You were created in the form of light. I was created, and emerged from that one eternal spirit that still resides in you. As I took upon myself the image of Christ, the Spirit of God was formed in me restoring wholeness and innocence to my soul. I am in the Father and the Father in me. The Law of One binds me to Him and I draw life from Him. My innocence flows from that pure desire which tasted of the darkness of the ego but no longer clings to it. I am released from the illusions of elation for its form no longer is appealing. I am void of the self that willed for self alone and filled it with the will and desire of God which wills for others. I am fulfilled in creation, for creation was fulfilled in me. I am the light, the way and the Truth, for the restoration of innocence is the reality of God, as God willed.[43]

The plan for salvation was created so that God could once again walk with those who walked in darkness. The separation was made real when those whom He created lost sight of God. Within Adam, man's eyes were closed to the glory of God, but the innocence, which allows man to see God, remained with Adam. Because Adam chose to touch the darkness that worked elation into the heart of God's creation, God was able to show man that innocence can be restored.[44] For after the pattern of Adam could those who walked in darkness find hope. And after the pattern of Jesus was hope fully restored, for innocence is brought back when we remember our desire for God.

The image of Adam and the image of Jesus Christ is the image of humanity restored out of free will. Each stood as a witness for

---

43 Writing ethereal messages requires a certainty in one's own soul as to the truth of what is being penned. This passage set my soul on fire. I knew in my own being as to the truth of what was written. Yet there were times I would stop the journaling process to look for collaboration. It was a short time later that I started to read books on Edgar Cayce who also gave ethereal messages of Jesus and Adam being the same soul entity. Finding collaboration of sorts was reassuring. I have little to offer to the reader as to the truth of certain passages, but I do believe this work was written into my soul long before I was born (see also the *Hope for the Message* and the *Passion is the Path to the Soul* in Part III). Allowing *The Message* to be written required openness to God—a trusting to God's purpose. I could have stopped *The Message* at any time from being penned or published but if I did I would have had many sleepless nights and this constant uneasiness in my soul. Similarly, the reader has a personal choice as to what to take and apply of this message to their own life. The critical reader also has a choice to vocally denounce this work, but I hope that no one will do that. There is a choice, a resolve that each of us has to make, for we are either compelled to consider God and the messages that God offers or we can ignore, turn a blind eye and even stand against such messages. However whatever one chooses will converge on the soul.

44 Elation has been used numerous times in the Message as being a pathological emotion in the cosmic story. It is not a bad emotion. Please see footnote 20 from *Creation: 4 The Dance of Life*. Again, elation is used to illustrate the emotion that puts into motion our euphoria of self—the pride of self. Happiness, self-confidence and a state of wellbeing are positive products of elation, and these emotions are what we hope for when we instill God's essence. As we grow into God the pendulum stops swinging, as our ego has no hold on our wellbeing.

God and God stood in the midst of both. As Adam stood apart in free will, by willing to taste the very structure and form of life which limited one's presence to the awareness of God, Adam came to know of the choice of self. Adam whose essence was full of God tasted the darkness of structure and form. From Adam came the image of our humanity. From the union of Adam to Eve to the children that were born to stand with them in this creation, our humanity and inhumanity would be seen both within and without as our actions and desires were imprinted on the very lives that we lived.

As Adam began the work of our humanity, the life and testimony of Jesus as Christ was set apart to bring an end to inhumanity. Jesus who took upon himself the image of God, having fully immersed himself with the will and desire of our Father, offered Himself as a living sacrifice to show to the world that judgment and condemnation leads to inhumanity and the inhumanity is borne by the cross.

Within creation, Adam took on the will of man. For in the beginning Jesus was with God and of God, one with God—he came from Heaven to be the Father of man, being both the Father and the Son. God Himself as seen in Jesus Christ was present in the soul of Adam, having created Adam in His own image. In Adam, was the image of innocence lost. Adam tasted separation and the earth became the home for man so that we might once again find God. Yet in Adam, Jesus was never lost to God, for Adam knew God but chose to walk within darkness to make way for those who were caught in darkness.

The essence of God speaks to us. His spirit beckons us to the light of creations purpose. It is the remembrance of the Truth that we were created with. From the dawn of creation when we emerged in the thought and the form of the self, in the glow of our innocence, we seek to become. Life out of the form of our dreams, our desires, our hopes and our wantonness. Creation, out of the will of our heavenly Father, is ours to hold and mold. Life out of the form of our humanity, as we witness one with another the creation of our hands, the desires of our hearts and the will that wills for each other.

Truth bears testimony of life, and life is what God wills. It is the reality that sets structure and form in harmony with the Law of One to bind us all back to God. When Truth shines into the shadows of the illusions that we created, life is restored. Light from life. The record is written and upon it rests the image of our past. From its remembrance will we embrace God's reality as the image that God created. It is our image in God that we have desired all along, yet from the remembrance of our past came the knowledge of good and evil. The shadows are broken by the light of our God that now resides from within.

> *A piece of me is embedded on the record of life. It is there, written upon your soul. It is of me, created by my hand and imprinted upon the fabric of God. I have touched it, tasted it, molded it and shared it in the presence of God. The record of my life is mine to hold and reshape, forged by my will and my desire but I stand not alone. Nor is my life set apart in glory from you. My image has been forged and its presence stands as a testimony, a witness to the humanity of God by the compassion of His love.*

> *Source: Book of Life*

2 The Garden of Eden

Adam and Eve stood before the tree of life and in their innocence they partook of the passion of the fruit. In God's image did the body of spirit take up structure and form out of the dust of the earth. Life from light. The body of spirit became encased in the body of flesh and the light of God was hidden. The spectrum of God's realities converged into one to release God's creation from the darkness that was created out of the desire for self.

Here in this reality would the Law of One be played out against the backdrop of our humanity. Adam and Eve stood in the midst of self to taste the passion of desire and will beyond the presence of God's light. Yet within Adam and Eve was the fullness of God's light. Both the reality of God in the body of self was fully present as Adam and Eve came into this reality where man's eyes are covered.

Adam and Eve willed for God. The tree of life is the symbol of both the roots that enter the soil to draw life from darkness and the branches that reach to the light to absorb the life from the heavens above. Adam and Eve willingly partook of the tree of life, to enter into this reality to rework God's restoration of innocence back into His creation. Out of wantingness to taste the freedom of will separate from God, Adam and Eve simulated the fall in the form of the fruit that God Himself created.

In temptation did God allow the choice to co-exist with His Spirit.[45] In the form of Adam and Eve where God was present, even as with Christ, did the form of the illusion illustrate the fall of man. God enclosed upon Adam and Eve the separation of self from self, the voice of the soul from the voice of the ego. The son and daughter of God separated from God in the form of a reality where the Law of God could be seen and heard again.

The form of man would encase and enclose the glory of God, the illumination of God. In the beginning of this creation, this history, which began the work of restoration, God did set Himself

---

45   This is a paradoxical statement since our understanding as to the nature of God is that sin or temptation does not exist within the essence of God, yet we have the co-existence of choice through free will within God's creation. I thought about taking the phrase out completely or changing the phrase to something more palatable; however, there is imagery here that I also thought needed to be explored. When the soul is created, the essence of God remains in the soul. For the voice of God to be present in creation, that voice must be created in the form of a soul (in particular, Christ—yet not exclusive to Christ). The essence of God is magnified out of choice. The cosmic story is one of choice—allowing choice to exist. It is the giving of free will from the Creator to His creation. This passage, I believe, is intended to point to a condition that existed prior to the incarnations on earth. The meaning to be inferred here is that God did not intervene to stop temptation, to stop evil, to stop our inhumanity, to take away free will. It is because of temptation, which was formed from choice, that His Spirit co-exists within the illusion of self as separate from the Creator. Since the essence of God goes with His creation we have a condition of duality within God's creation.

in the very midst of the land of Eden. He with Adam and with Eve to allow the choice of wantingness and desire to rework and recreate the conditions that simulated the fall from heaven.

Temptation became the backdrop to the illusion that out of choice man was separated from God and chastised from Eden. Eden was not lost to man but rather man became lost to Eden. When we took upon us the form of reality before Eden was created, the soul was tarnished by that will and desire which grew out of the ego. The fall began. Once fallen, separation took root, innocence was tarnished, and many became lost to God. They who entered the playground and lost their innocence became trapped to the playground.

So the fall was recreated. The stage was set, and Adam and Eve became the first. God Himself, in the presence of Adam and Eve, stood upon the creation of Eden. In the garden, God placed the tree of life, the hope for life anew. In the symbol of the fruit where freedom of choice was allowed would the fall be illustrated. By the temptation to partake in the choice of one's own free will would the illusion of being separate from God begin. In the condemnation of self, to hide one's self from God by the choice to leave Eden was Eden symbolized to be lost.

In Adam and Eve did God illustrate the fall from heaven. What was real and did exist in those that had already fallen and were lost to the presence of God was symbolized by the fall of Adam and Eve. Yet, here in is the message that restores God's creation in wholeness—God still loved Adam and Eve. The presence of God stood with Adam and Eve. In their lost innocence, God remained. His light and His Spirit was forever there.

Out of free will and desire, Adam and Eve reached to God. As so were they free, so are we. The record and the illustration bore witness to Adam reaching for God with Eve by his side. With the fruit in one hand being given to the other both were tempted in will and desire, yet out of temptation with innocence lost would they reach together to be restored.

The undoing of what was once done was the work of Adam and Eve bought by fruition through the life of Mary and her child. Out of innocence borne, God *with us*, is born *in us*. Out of life would life be recreated, restored to us. By every act and every deed would God come. For the very purpose of creation was not to condemn but to restore. To undo what was lost out of free will, by restoring our true will, which is the will of God. God's act in Jesus was one of presence. God with us is restored in us. His presence, His Holy Spirit is present with us, even in the darkness where we would not have Him be.

Jesus became the light of our restoration. Our redemption was the restoration of God's light in us, as was illuminated in the presence of Jesus Christ, the Son of the living God. Innocence lost in the image of Adam was restored in fullness through the image of God, as lived by the life of Jesus Christ. God with us and for us is living in us and magnified by us as we choose to live in His light. Jesus is the way, the Truth and the light. His path is our path. His restoration is the recreation of the image of God as our own likeness by the desire of our own free will.

The Book of Life is the record of God's reality restored to God's creation. Out of time, out of the movement of self from God and through free will, restored to God is eternity recreated in us. The final judgment comes to rest as our inhumanity is expelled from both our will and our desire. We, in God, are restored through the grace and love that exists in God and dwells forever in us. Just as the image of God rested in the life and ministry of Jesus Christ, so will that image be present in you, your brother and your sister. One voice, one will speaking in unison as to the creation of God restored.

The path and the way were guided by God's presence but the walk was made by choice. Jesus in free will chose the path and became the way. With every step he took a footprint remained. His life was imprinted upon the sands of time. A record for all to see. His was the atonement of self made perfect. Not in sacrifice to sin, but to the wholeness of self in the presence of God.

To release the image of God within the breath and act of life is to write upon the Book of Life. Its record stands in witness to you that your image is restored in wholeness. By God's light, as you stand in His presence, are the shadows of your past, which were hidden in darkness, illuminated. Seen for what they are with God by your side allows you to see yourself with its compassion. Knowing that the path you walk is not unlike the path that God walked with Jesus of Nazareth is a witness to you that you are not alone.

God's presence is the reality you seek. Not in some secluded corner of a church where piousness can dispel the image of inhumanity. Not in the prison of walls and bars where inhumanity can be locked away and sin is repaid for the debt once owed. Not in remorse, grief or despair where fear can hold only the captor. Not behind the image of fame, glamour or grandeur. Not in war or hatred or insult. Not in distaste, distrust or dishonesty. And certainly not in the image of sin where the form of sinlessness paints only perfection that can never be seen.

God's presence is the reality of life. Present and visible in every act of our humanity. Present in acts of kindness and every gesture of love. Present by the softness of our hands as they gently touch the lives of those around us. Present in the eyes that pierce those that long to be looked upon. God's presence is the reality of our good desires, written in the Book of Life, the record of life.

Source: Book of Life

────── 3 The Path of Restored Innocence ──────

The stage is set and from the heavens it begins. From Adam to Christ, the promise of Aaron[46] and Melchizedek[47] and the vision of Enoch[48] would the gift of eternal life be restored to innocence.

46   Refers to the promise of eternal life through the sacrifice, the offering of the Lamb, the Messiah (Leviticus Ch 9).

47   Refers to the promise of eternal life through the sacrifice, the bread and wine, the Messiah (Genesis 14:18-20). Also Christ fulfilling of both the Levitical and the Melchizedek priesthood (Hebrews 7:11 and Hebrews 6:20).

48   Hebrews 11:5. I would refer the reader to the writing's on Edgar Cayce

Just as Adam fell so it is that Jesus was restored. Just as innocence was lost in Adam, so it is that innocence was restored in Jesus. Just as Adam having been created by God became man, so it is that Jesus being a man became the Christ, God with us.

We then who are created by God, being also the sons and daughters of Adam, are restored in God when Christ lives in us. When God lives in us we will see as God sees. We will see ourselves as God sees us and we will see in others what we would will to see for ourselves.

From the beginning to the end, from the birth of the self to the cross which we bear. Only in the journeys end do we see life restored. Transformed out of death to a new life. Just as we fell in Adam to humanity's desires for self and wantonness, so are we risen in Jesus as the desire for God sets us free.

Just as God created man in His image, having created Adam as our Father, so it is that the very Father of man became the Son of man to show man the path back to God. As we bear the cross of the self, as we bear the cross of self-judgment, will the Father meet the son. It is the cross that we bear willingly that allows us to let go of condemnation, it allows us to meet our Creator within His creation. As we find God in each other, God finds a home in us.

The life and ministry of Jesus Christ was first to the healing and restoration of our spirit to God our Father and second to the wholeness of the person in the body. In Jesus Christ we are made whole, first in spirit and second in body. This is servant ministry; the healing and restoration of the spirit by extending the image of God back into God's creation. Restoring life by extending the source of life. Restoring innocence by extending innocence.

Oh, how great is His plan that we can be purified by His image within our own free will. To be free to choose for Him and for His eternal mercy, which suffers with us until we have freed ourselves from those images that chained us to order and chaos.

The Law of One binds us in His image. We are bound not by law but by desire. It is not by fear of condemnation, but by desire

as to the incarnations of Jesus.

for belonging that frees us from judgment. In the Law of God are we kept whole. For God's law sustains us and sets us all on the path that leads us back to each other.

> *For God sent not His Son into the world to condemn the world; but that the world through Him might be saved.*[49]

Source: Book of Law

——————— 4 Judgment ———————

We rest in God's eternal grace. Grace being God's eternal stay of judgment. For what hope is there in God's judgment unless His judgment sets us free, to become as He created?

And Jesus said, "For judgment I am come into this world, so that they which see not might see and they that do see might be made blind."[50]

For insomuch that they that see judgment might be released from judgment and insomuch as they that do not understand God's judgment might come to know of His grace.

He who is the Creator of life, looks upon the life of that which He created and sees the split that exists within the heart of man. Man has been divided by the judgment that he has willed. Setting himself apart he has judged what God would not. In his judgment has God been condemned. Condemned to withhold what He would freely give but cannot, because His love has been wrapped within a shroud.

God offers life. In His judgment He wills life. In His judgment is life restored. God who is the source of life sets us not apart, but in the midst of life so that each life might find the value of life.

I am the light of the world.[51] *He who walks in my light*

---

49   John 3:17

50   John 9:39

51   John 8:12

will not see darkness. Not in himself and not in his brother. For the light that shines in me will shine in him. It can be seen in him as he looks towards you.

In this judgment and in this judgment only are you set free. As you recognize that you are one in the same spirit, born out of the spirit of God who creates all, are you set free. Free to be as God created, adding to life by building value in each other.

Judgment is mine, saith the Lord of hosts. In my judgment will I free you, will I restore you to wholeness, to holiness. In my judgment will you find the worth that I created you in. It is my worth that you will find your own. Abide in me as I abide in you and the image of my Son Jesus will find rest.

Source: Book of Truth

5 The Cross

Judgment was decreed by our ego. In violation to Truth, our ego upheld judgment, condemnation. Guilt was measured and condemnation was our judgment. We hold others responsible so that we might be free of guilt. Retribution was our answer to the error against ourselves and our God. The penalty of error was measured and condemnation was decreed. In our desire to reclaim our innocence we maintained that someone else was responsible, and they had to pay. The penalty of sin was exile or imprisonment. In the extreme, the penalty of sin was death.

So God sent His Son to be our sacrifice. In Him that sacrifice would be made to satisfy our illusion for retribution. Yet God is a God of love and He would not will that any of His creation be crucified in sin. God sent His Son into the world so that the world might know of the love of God.

Consider this. Why would God justify sin as having a claim on you by passing judgment that sin had to be bought, paid for? Why would God demand retribution for sin, if in retribution the penalty was death?

God wills life—restores life. He is our creator, our redeemer and our hope. What desire could there be in God to crucify His own Son as retribution for sin? The only restitution for sin is sinlessness, innocence.

It is judgment—condemnation, that has imprisoned us from Truth, and separated us from God. We have crucified ourselves, our brother, our sister, our friend and even our Creator out of our desire for retribution. It was our shared guilt that imprisoned us from one another and from God. We knew not what we did. Did Jesus condemn those that crucified him? What more could God do to show us that He is not a God of condemnation? Yet, the crucifixion could not claim life. Jesus was raised from the dead to show us that God is a God of life and not a God of condemnation.

Condemnation does not come from God. How could God call us back to Him if in judgment we were condemned? Be blind then to condemnation, and look to find God's grace.

Where is this hell that you would will that God create? Where is this hell that you have willed others to find as justification to the crimes that they have committed against you? What darkness could consume them that could keep you safe? If there is no light between you and them, then darkness truly has found a home. In this hell will you be kept safe, but this judgment comes not from God.

God restores life. His judgment will not allow you or your brother and sister to remain in the hell that you have willed for each other. From the depths of the darkness where you would hide each other will you be returned to face again that which tore you apart. Time will be the instrument that you will face. To act upon and be acted upon. To choose for love if you can, so that you might find love or to choose for judgment until judgment breaks the darkness that you have sealed yourself to.

The inhumanity of the cross was an act of judgment. The judgment that willed condemnation must die on the cross. Just as the body gives up the spirit, so it is that the image of the self must be given back to the Father—"Father, into your hands I commend my spirit."[52]

And they stood and they watched on a hill, now desolate. The crosses hung amidst a pale grey sky. The air was thick and the sounds of some suffering still tormented the ears of those who stood and watched. Others who were charged with the duty to crucify became as stone to block out the death and the stench of blood. Judgment day came and went. Day after day it came and left. Another day, another life. From judgment to judgment to judgment were they crucified. Some on the cross, others in the heart and for the few who kept charge were crucified in the mind and will. Then there was silence.

As the heavens gave way to a new dawn, life emerged. Not even the cross could contain judgment against the Son of man, the Son of God. In the final judgment of Him who would judge for righteousness was the resurrection. The recreation in both body and soul to the image of what God made real in Jesus. The Christ stood at the door of an empty tomb. His life and image did not pass into death but into life eternal.

Who then would judge God? Who then would judge condemnation? If we could see God in God's creation how then could we judge? How then could we condemn? Here then is the choice that we face. To walk the path of the cross to the journey's end of condemnation or to walk the path of the self, facing the self in every judgment, every condemnation that we would will. For the atonement to have meaning, we must face the self. It is the image of the self on the cross, the willingness of the self to bear the cross that will bring a resurrection of the Christ from within.

Allow God to abide within us and the cross you bear will be empty. Leave judgment on the cross and condemnation will be buried in the tomb. Take upon yourself the name of Jesus Christ and you will be resurrected in the life that restores us to God.

> *Judgment must die on the cross. The blood that wept from my body was the sorrow I bore for condemnation. He who drinks of my blood must seek to end that judgment that binds others to the cross. I suffered in death so that all might see life. I have given freely, yet you are free to choose. If you, whom I love, would choose for life, then choose to bury sin in darkness and allow the light of your soul to emerge.*
>
> *I and my Father are one.*[53] *The Law of One abides in me as I abide in my Father. We are of one will, one desire, fulfilling the purpose of creation by adding value to life so that life might have meaning.*
>
> **Source: Book of Truth**

——————— 6 The Resurrection ———————

From death came the resurrection. The body was buried into the light of the glory of God and from the glory of God was the body recreated. For in Adam was the body created from the earth and in Jesus the body was resurrected in glory, taking the form of the light that gives life. Life from light. Herein is the power of Jesus Christ magnified —from the glory of God, to the healing of the body. Out of the darkness of the self, into the light of the Christ, indwelling of the Holy Spirit in each of us magnifies glory.

Light sustains the miracle of life—all is light. The body is light, our desires vibrate with light, each thought is the illumination of light, the soul rests in the light of the image created and the spirit

---

53   John 10:30.

which is continuously linked with God is the source of light and God sustains the light as life itself. Images of light shining in you and through you as you choose. From God's glory to the light that breathes life in the image of you.

For God did not sacrificed His Son to a death on the cross that stands in darkness. Rather, it is the death of the self that we sacrifice to be free of the darkness that was weaved onto our souls. Out of that death come's our resurrection. Out of that death come's our restoration. Having walked the path in the shadow of darkness will we emerge in the light by releasing our ego and reclaiming God's image as our own.

Believe not that your God is a God of vengeance who enacts retribution on the act of sin. Anyone who says God is a God of vengeance does not know God. For God who created love as the life force of creation would look upon vengeance with the cross that His Son bore. The cross was unnecessary and so is vengeance.[54] Did God crucify His Son as vengeance for sin or did sin need retribution? Neither. Truth needs no sacrifice, but the recognition of Truth required the journey to the cross that Jesus freely walked so that all might see. In him was the word and the word was not destroyed by the cross. In the cross the word was magnified to help us claim Truth and Jesus raised the body in three days as testimony to show the world that there is no destruction in death.

> *Arise and stand in the resurrection that bears testimony to life. Let the Spirit of the living God shine into you so that the light that was seen in Jesus Christ might also be seen in the mirror of your soul. For herein is creation made complete when your free will gives itself willingly back to the Truth that rests in God. For your true will is the will of God.*

The work and ministry of Jesus Christ was not to change you, but rather to fulfill you. To fill your life with a true sense of

---

54 This is direct reference to the cross as being a payment for sin. God did not require the cross to justify His sovereignty for the forgiveness of sin.

meaning and purpose. For in his image is the self dissolved. In his identity are we molded in the array that binds us to God. The ego, the voice that speaks for the self, dissolves as we allow the desire for love to remove the barriers that were placed there by fear. Those emotions that echo from within which foster anger, hatred, blame, guilt, condemnation, despair, frustration, sickness, and a myriad of other delusional feelings, diminish and are relinquished in love. In God, our beliefs give way to Truth, expectations become hopes, all actions have purpose, and the heart recognizes peace.

> *Life is extended. The Lord of the dance echoes in the heavens. If every man, woman and child could join hands the earth would be encircled and the bond would be unbroken. You would be a part of that circle and your part is necessary to keep the bond intact. So it is in heaven. God's heaven would be incomplete without you. His light will continue to be a beacon in the darkness and, when invited, His light will shine through you to show you the way.*

Have faith that God has set you on a path that helps you to see yourself for who you are. That which is easy to accept and that which you find difficult to bear. But fear not, for God gives hope. Hope instills acceptance and acceptance dampens the pendulum that swings your life from one extreme to the other. We only need faith to find hope.

Source: Book of Law

——— 7 The Image of God—Christ Emmanuel ———

Born out of the Spirit of God we emerge. Set in His light, desiring His light, we emerge. The Law of One instills God's quiet presence and binds us to Him. No longer divided by chaos, we see that which gave life and restores life is kept sacred in God. Out of the Law of God will God's creation be restored to Him. For the Law of God will retain the fabric of God, even in chaos.

We are the fabric of God. From one Spirit were we created and in the spirit of oneness are we called back to Him. Born of His image will the image of the self be recreated by the self to reflect the image of our Creator. Out of free will do we choose for God. God's will in turn finds rest in us. Out of the image of God is the image of you. For your true identity is kept sacred in God.

God restores to you what is kept sacred in Him. In Him is your wholeness and from Him is wholeness restored. The light, which shines within the inner self, is the image of wholeness. It is the image of God, which you see at the center of yourself. Deep within the core of your soul is the image of God. Here He resides. In you God resides. His image resides in you and retains your true image; a sacred image where God's light is forever kept.

God's image restores your own. This is the baptism that brings rebirth. To be quickened from within to the rebirth in God so that God's image is restored to you. To willingly take upon you the image which denies the self-image and recreates God's image. The self becomes immersed in God. God's presence shines through the self. His image becomes the image of you as God created.

God, who is in you, retains your true image within Him. We are forever kept in God. This is the image that God holds for you in His light. It is forever yours, but you must walk in God's light, if you are to claim it. Darkness must dissipate from the self if the self is to walk within the light to claim the image of God that God holds for you. The desire for darkness must dissipate in order for the desire of God's light to be retained.

Be not afraid of God's light. Look about you for God's light continually shines around you. His light vibrates in life and through life. His life forever is in His creation and His light is in you. Even when you close your eyes and you allow God in, is His light found. The images of your thoughts, of your memories, of your hopes can be filled with beauty and joy. When you allow God in, He fills your life. Darkness dissipates as you touch God's light.

Make a covenant with God, so that His light might be retained as your image. Make a covenant to keep sacred the Law of One, which keeps whole God's Kingdom. Be baptized in the name of the only begotten Son whose name restores light and Truth in you.[55] For in the image of Jesus Christ is the image of peace that restores innocence. His name becomes your image. For as Christ is the image of God born in Jesus, so it is that the image of Jesus Christ must be born in you.

No other image retains God's light as your own. For in Christ is the spirit of Truth. You were created in Truth and it is that Spirit that you desire to claim. The image of my Son is the image of Christ, for in Him darkness has no home. To be born of God, to become sons and daughters of God there is but one image that retains God's image in you and that is Jesus Christ. To be born of God you must take upon yourself the name of Christ, the image of Christ, whose image is the image of Truth.

Truth is what is real. God's Truth is the reality that God wills. If you take upon yourself the image that retains God's Truth—God's reality—you will find wholeness. In this wholeness is the Kingdom of God. Wholeness is kept because the spirit of Truth binds the Law of One. There is no division for all are of one spirit, which is the spirit of Truth. The spirit of God binds us.

> *The image of my Son is the image of light and Truth. In you is the image of what I created. I am in you and you are of me. My light and my Truth I give to you. It is this reality that you must choose for yourself. If you choose for light and Truth, you will find the image of my Son in you. You will become a reflection of what I made real in you. You become born again, recreated out of your own free will. I in you and you of me. You become my sons and my daughters as I created, born of your own free will.*

---

55   Consider the "only begotten" as the only one who was created from the dust of the earth or from the light of God into this earth, to set in motion our humanity. He was Adam, the one of choice, the one who would choose to come, the chosen one who would become Jesus Christ, the Prince of Peace, our Savior. From a cosmic perspective, both Adam and Jesus became the conduit from which God's work of restoration would be fulfilled. See both John 3:16-17 and the first paragraph of The Journey of the Christ: Section 1 The Plan of Redemption.

Is this not the reality that you desire? Not to be owned or possessed by a God who commands on high, but to be loved and cherished by Him so that you are filled with that same light and truth. To be filled with peace and life, in richness that never lacks. To be filled until God's fullness is retained as the image of you. Filled with God's light until God's light retains your image. No more darkness, no more shadows. Your desires and your will become whole. In this hour is the final judgment.

In this hour is the last judgment that you will make. You will judge for righteousness. No longer will you judge condemnation. In this hour is the last breath on the cross.

This is God's miracle. You are God's miracle. From the image of you being recreated by the glory of God in the form of the light that bore testimony of the resurrection. Where the fulfillment of the Law of One recreates God's presence in God's creation. We are sustained. We are released. We are made whole. Together are we and heaven is our home.

Source: Book of Law

The Journey of the Soul

———————— 1 The Playground of Life ————————

We taste in life that which is imprinted upon our soul. It forms the record from which we draw the knowledge of self. It reflects back the creation that we willed within the presence of God. Glorified by His light or encased by the darkness of our ego. Yet both bring knowledge to the self of the self so that the self might choose the image that God would will.

Sin became the form of our ego that robbed us from God. Within the playground of life, we partook in the pleasures of our wantonness. We sought from our desires to taste the passion of the fruit, which seemed harmless and benign. From its form came the emotions and the passion that drove us further into the images of our desires.

God's creation stood before us, but we were bound to the images of our desires. As the ego of self took root, illusions of self-grandeur and edification swirled about in our minds and our hearts which formed the construct of our identity. We of like mind gravitated to one another. Here we came to partake in our creation. It was ours to taste, to hold, to mold, and reform at will. Within the confines of time and structure could we realize the very power of the gift of creation.

Yet sin formed the separation, the encasement of self from God. It became the form of the illusion that withdrew us from God. Out of free will did we choose the wantonness of our ego and out of free will were we imprisoned to the ego of self. The image of our ego became the pedestal of our grandeur.

We knew not of the seed of self. As the fabric of God unfolded in the life that we lived the very presence of God withdrew inward, deeper and deeper until His light dissipated in the silence of our soul. God's presence was forgotten and God's illumination in us became darkened by our own self-image of ego.

From heaven it could be seen that the humanity that was created to add glory, to expand glory into creation, became the backdrop to a form of darkness to be feared. Yet there were those who journeyed into humanity and did not become lost to their ego. There were those who tasted of the passion of their ego and used it to strengthen and restore the fabric of God. Wisdom was theirs. Courage, compassion, strength, stature, respect and integrity was theirs. From heaven we could see God's handiwork as creation expanded His glory into the very grandeur of the very gift of life that was ours.

The form of our humanity became the backdrop to the stage that each of us would enter into. For it was God's will that we know of our self separate from Him. The construct of our humanity was to explore the creative process. To take the form of our thoughts and desires and create the reality that would extend beyond the self. To extend creation by expanding the form, God through us created life from life.

Yet to understand the creative process, we too would have to grant the freedom of our creation. For the product of creation is either order, harmony, beauty, structure or it is chaos, randomness, unpredictability and disorder. To create is to reconstruct. To take the very elements of light with life and remold it into a fabric that is of the source yet detached from and free standing from the source.

Chaos and order are held together by laws that are governed by God alone. God's law binds the creative process to Him so that disorder and randomness does not destroy the process of creation. Within our humanity we will come to understand law. Just as the laws of physics can be used to both create and tear down, so it is the laws that govern the spirit and the soul can be used to illuminate, compel and converge the essence or presence of God.

We have an impact on God. What we create with our thoughts and desires—as it is projected into the form of reality that can be seen and felt by others—has an impact on the very fabric of God that God created. It is this creation that becomes free-standing from the creator that will either add value or take value from the creative process.[56] It will either illuminate and glorify the creation process, or it will tear down and tear apart the very fabric that was given to us to remold and recreate.

We are set upon a stage that is preordained, but the script is only a construct of the images that we ourselves must choose to face. The images of our humanity are borne in spirit so that we might choose the setting and the conditions that can be borne in this life. In the creative process, we choose our family within the context of the environment and the culture that will grant us the greatest probability to experience and endure our humanity.

Life before life, setting the stage in preparation of the creative process. We work with God to map the course of our lives.[57] We create with Him, and God works with us to restore us in oneness

---

56   In this passage, the "creator" refers to we who create. It is what we create that becomes free-standing, independent, and a construct that is both a part of and apart from the whole.

57   How much interaction each of us has, in the preparation to this life, is contingent on our willingness to engage our life plan in communion with God. In life before life, even though there is free will, there is also influence. In some instances souls negate their soul development and in order for the soul to become open to the creative force they are subjected to group development. Groups of souls plan the incarnation and individuals are thrust into lives knowing that it is for their own good, however there is reluctance depending on the lessons or the relationships that they will be subjected to. Elders provide guidance in the planning process and it is in these soul's mutual needs that will dictate the construct or the blue print. Sequences of events will enter into their lives at different stages and different groups of souls or individual will engage with them at the cross roads of their life. Depending on their willingness and ease at which they are learning their lessons and depending on the choices that they are making, up to that point in time of their life, will determine the future path that their life will take. If the soul struggles or is resistant to learning the lessons, their life can become more arduous and foreboding. To learn the lessons, in the confines of free will, is paramount.

and wholeness. Light with life creating. Our lives are preordained, but the construct is ours to hold and mold. In so doing we become co-creator's within God's creation.

Even lives that have gone astray and fallen into darkness were preordained.[58] We are set upon the stage to experience and endure the construct of our humanity in hopes that we can overcome the

---

58   As I was doing the editorial work on The Message I was quite reluctant to change certain phrases or words, because I knew that there was purpose for why I was compelled to write what was written. The word preordained created some problematic issues for me because it has theological overtones of predestination and for some people it might put into question free will. Preordained, to some people, means that God, in His sovereignty, predestines the path of His creation such that the outcome is certain. The theological problem is one of "working backwards"; we look at the outcome of events and then say that it was God's will or plan—we are but pawns. I believe, we do a disservice to God when we place the stop watch on God's plan or say that all outcomes are predestined. There is a bigger picture at play. Preordained in *The Message* means "scripted with construct for purpose and subject to God's will, plan or sovereignty, yet in free will do we choose"—God created the time, space, and choice to bring about free will knowing that these conditions would exist. Yet God did not intervene to stop the chaos, the inhumanity, acts of violence or war, suffering and darkness created by choice, nor did He apply His sovereignty to make His creation subjects to—to be pawns of the script, the construct or the outcomes (e.g. Adam, Jesus, Cain or Judas). Jesus both chose and was chosen to walk the path of the cross. Life is not a movie script cast in stone. Our lives are both planned with God and set apart from God to allow free will and choice to be played out. Free will allows for lives to go tragically wrong—to not follow the planned construct. There is also allowance for lives to enter their incarnation without a plan and these lives are lived aimlessly. There is a fine line between saying that God willed the randomness of choice to allow chaos to occur (i.e. to allow tragic outcomes or accidents or inhumanity to exist in His created universe) and the certainty of God's presence to stand with us in the chaos when allowing or not intervening to prevent bad things from happening. To say God preordained is the affirmation of God's presence in the choice, the chaos, the acts of inhumanity and the darkness.

Therefore, when the Message says, "Even lives that have gone astray and fallen into darkness were preordained", means that God would stand with us in our choices, and His promise was one of where His essence would go with us. God would not abandon us to the darkness. The certainty of God's will is the salvation of His creation and in time God will restore us back to the innocence that He created us in. That salvation, however, is by our choice.

ego of self and illuminate God's presence, God's image through us to others. Together we walk. There are those of God's elect who come and they carry with them the torch, the sacred flame. They are the beacon that bears the light of God for all to see. They are the angels of humanity that hold and uphold God's compassion, God's justice, God's grace and hope, God's will and desire.

For those whose lives have gone astray, life was preordained by God to bear their inhumanity. The images of self-choice, which are rooted in grand illusion of self at the exclusion of others, must come to bear upon itself. Our ego becomes the mirror by which we

---

The nature of God is to allow free will to fulfill creations purpose. We engage with God to face certain decisions in life, in the hope that we will grow back into the essence of God. A single lifetime is not lived in seclusion to the cosmic path of the soul. Past lives impact the choices that we want to face when planning the next incarnation. To heal relationships severed by past lives or to heal ourselves of the trauma created by the inhumanity of a past life or to even gain in soul development—to become more patient, compassionate, forgiving—we plan our lives together and in communion (prayer) with God. The plan becomes the construct. God does not dictate the outcome but rather He works with us to create the construct. The conflict, the challenges, and the struggles become the dots of our lives—events that will stand out to give us cause to consider our God lessons. The construct, the plan or the preordained path is always one of healing and wholeness. To choose to love, to choose to forgive, to accept others or to be conduits of peace is the test. We want to prove ourselves.

I look back at times and think about the premonitions I had of both my father's and my mother's death. It was perhaps a foreshadowing of a planned event that was both chosen by my parents and chosen for my parents. Maybe my mother's accident, where she lost her arm, could have been a "planned" event. One could look at these events as preordained, predestined and according to the will of God, but I think it brings a disservice to God's purposes as it taints the image of God. Sometimes tragedies and accidents are just that (not all events or outcomes are planned prior to the incarnation) and we should not assume that we are subjects to predestination. If there is purpose, then perhaps in time we will see that purpose. What is important is that we retain our humanity, love and acceptance of one another in the face of tragedy, accidents or acts of inhumanity by others.

must face ourselves. We of like mind and heart are placed together in the environment and the culture whereby we can taste the very product of our ego.

We bear upon one another the very will and construct of the images that rest in our thoughts and our desires. It is only in the distaste of the darkness, where darkness was desired, that darkness can be dispelled. A cry for mercy and release, a cry for forgiveness and compassion, the call for help and salvation is the purging of self from self. It is the wantingness to purge oneself from the form of one's ego that brings about a transformation of a life restored to God. God's presence is resurrected.[59]

Life before life prepares us for the journey that we take into our humanity. It is a preparation for spiritual endurance.[60] To become illuminated by God's presence, such that God's image can come to rest within, is the journey that we are all on. The light which is in each of us is the illumination of God's presence. In spirit, in the life before life, our illumination can be seen and felt by others. To desire God is to become illuminated with God. To become illuminated by God, we must be able to endure God's presence within the confines of our own free will. To become full of God, we must face the darkness of our ego which hides God from us.

Life before life, in spirit, prepares us to endure that which we can bear to endure so that we can purge ourselves of that part of our ego which would hide God in darkness. It is a process by which we prepare the stage and the construct for the script, but as life is lived and is intensified, our choices will determine if we can endure God's essence. As the desires of our heart changes the

---

59 Resurrection here points to life from death—in this case, to the death of that part of self that we no longer want— to the resurrection of life a new (renewed) where the image of the self is transformed from the light of God that is within us. In that moment, we are no longer the person we once were. We become purged of that desire which held us in bondage to our wantonness, our ego of self. Unlike baptism, which is the rebirth of self to take upon oneself the image of the Christ, this is the fulfillment of self through the cross which Christ bore, to become "a new" as our innocence is restored.

60 See *Journey of the Soul: 6 Spiritual Endurance.*

ego is tamed. Conflicts dissipate because no longer are we trapped by the choice that would tear us apart. God's illumination clears the way.

Source: Book of Life

———— 2 The Fabric of God ————

What we create gives meaning to the self. Our identity is born out of our own free will. It is the spilling of life onto life such that life takes on meaning.

Out of life was the fabric of God created. The relationships that we nurture in life becomes the fabric of God. Yet in our humanity are we tested. The backdrop of life becomes the potential for our soul. When we do good, the fabric of God is woven in the array of God. When we lack goodness, the fabric of God is at risk and can be torn by our acts of inhumanity. Such is life—we are a part of, and yet apart from, the God that created us. We have such great potential to add to the fabric of God and yet, many times, we choose to tear down the fabric that God has given us.

The very bond of life can be fragmented if we create fear and distaste. When the fabric of God is torn, our soul can become lost. When we hurt one another, we hide ourselves from each other and from the darkness that we created. In Truth, love was our reality, yet by our actions our relationships became severed, and the array of love became lost to our vision.

When we willed what God would not, innocence was sacrificed and an illusion ensued. We built an illusion to hide us from that memory which placed the fabric of God at risk. We claimed in our illusion that it was not our fault. We claimed denial. We claimed that we were justified. We laid blame and guilt at the footstep of someone or something else.

In the beginning God gave us our free will. From that free will would we choose. Yet in those choices that we made, we were still bound to God.

When we willed what God would not, a void was created. The

void was like a darkness from which refuge was sought. We could not free ourselves from what we did nor could we face our God. So we created a void, a mist of darkness to overshadow the reality that placed our relationships at risk. We hid in that darkness. We hid in those illusions that seemingly freed us from guilt. The light of our soul was tarnished.

From within this void that we created, we found a world of self where we could hide from God. From here we could write our own truth. By our own thoughts would we justify ourselves. From here could we recreate the past in the form of a truth that we could accept. In the shadows we could invite others to share in our form of truth. Those who would believe our truth became our friends and those who chose to stand against us were set apart.

In time, as sides were chosen, a rift was created across the face of God's creation. This desire or will to hide from God became our illusion. In this void we could hide by recreating an inner world of illusion, which would justify our thoughts, our actions and our feelings. In time, this illusion would be our form of truth, a form of truth that we could accept. And we upheld that form of truth.

As others were invited to share in it, they too claimed it as their reality. Those who could not were feared and walls were built.

So it was that we separated ourselves from the love that bound us together and in turn we hid from God and from those whom we could not face. We hid ourselves in an identity, an illusion of an image that we could accept. That image would allow us to be acceptable to ourselves within a form of truth that could justify us. Semi-innocence was born.

In our beginning, when we willed what God would not, we became separated from God. In that moment a desire of wantonness for self alone filled our minds to form the voice of our ego. A voice which spoke to our self-worth, our self-image and our identity. It was a voice, an image, a desire and a will to create from our wantonness. It was the euphoria of self. We valued the self, we feared the self, we placed our self in the image of our ego.

As we willed that which God would not, we saw the impact that our actions had on others. The fabric of God became torn. The garment of our inner soul became tainted. The act of our will and desire dulled the light of God that once radiated from within. It placed us at risk, for it set us apart. Our innocence was lost and semi-innocence was born.

Source: Book of Truth

—————— 3 The Revelation of Self ——————

From the Book of Life is the revelation of self. It is the exploration of all that we are against the backdrop of all that God created. In the journey of life all meaning comes to rest in the dimension of the soul. It is the very nature out of which we were created to explore *who we are*. To explore our dreams apart from our God. Just as a parent looks to nurture a child to allow the child to grow, to become, so it is that God granted us, His creation, to do the same.

Even in the exploration, God watches over us. In the maturity of our soul, the self becomes more disciplined. Our soul becomes stronger, instilled with a will that stems from the core of our being. Our convictions, our courage, our wisdom, our love, our beingness resides in our soul. The self retains our image, our dreams, our wantingness, but our soul retains the attributes which resides in our God. All that is good which resonates in our God is formed in our soul. We vibrate with God from within.

The self is the consciousness of our dreams and the awareness of our free will. Since our soul was formed from the very essence of God, and is in constant communion with God, it is only within the self that the illusion that we are separate from God could exist. Our self retains our image, our identity, our attitudes, our convictions, desires, will and strength. Our self forms the essence of who we are in choice, in free will apart from God. It is the dimension from which God has granted us space from Himself.

The soul, however, retains God. It is our unconscious self which speaks the voice of God from within. The soul is our higher self, it is connected to the Holy Spirit. Our soul retains our innocence, our purity, our communion with God. For God to speak to us, we must look to our soul to find God's Holy Spirit.

We know these things to be true for we are compelled to pray, to seek our God from within. It is our soul that we seek for we know that our soul can guide us into the paths of righteousness. Our soul can lead us, direct us, teach us and inspire us. Like God, however, our soul will not live our lives. Our soul has granted the self freedom and unconditional autonomy, just as God has granted the soul individuality and self-awareness from Himself.

Evil formed out of the consumption of self, for self alone. It was the perpetual desire for greed, pride, wantonness, power, lust, judgment, retribution and control that closed the self off from the voice of one's own soul. When we sacrificed our virtue, our principles and our humanity, evil grew and darkness over-shadowed the soul. The light of God from within grew dim and our soul lost its brightness, its beauty, its illumination. God was still there, but the image of God cannot be seen.

In the passing from light into darkness, from good to evil, from humanity to inhumanity, the self is left to wander, to ponder and to reflect on its own beingness. It is a haunting realization that we are drawn into by the multitude of voices that the ego speaks. The self knows not how to escape blame, judgment, and retribution, for to escape that requires a desire for God. When the self passes from day into night, the darkness hides the light of God. The soul becomes our tormentor, it consistently speaks of Truth, but the self fears the Truth and entices us to run and to hide, or to lie and make blame.

From the will and desire of the self are we liberated or trapped into the dimension that we find ourselves. All that we were before this life comes to bear in self-choice and self-awareness. To find God, to find the light, to become free of our inhumanity, our self-loathing, our darkness, we must look for strength from our soul, our connection with the Holy Spirit. It is only from this vantage point that God can teach us.

God is on the inside looking out. He resides within us, waiting and wanting to restore us. It is our innocence that He holds sacred within our soul. All that is real that God created and would will, lies within the dimension of our soul. In reality it is our true self waiting to emerge.

We who are in constant communion with God are not perfect. The voice for self is strong and constantly pulls us in the direction of our ego. Such is the humanity that God created in us. Only in our imperfection can we learn of our humanity and explore our dreams apart from our God. It is only through our constant communion which is the discipline of both prayer and meditation that our soul can speak and our heart can beat for God.

The children of the Law of One, those who retain the image of God as the sons and daughters of God, have all tasted their own form of darkness. The fallen image of Adam, who was the Christ, is the testament of restored innocence. It is the testament that God is actively engaged in the redemption and restoration of His creation. It is the restoration of self to the Christ that we embrace God again and forever.

Source: Book of Law

4 Identity

To live without God is to wander without light. Yet in our wandering, we convince ourselves that we can bring meaning to life by choosing an identity. Truth and identity must be in harmony if meaning is to be found.

When our identity sets us apart from love, Truth is lost and our will is in conflict. If we do not look to God for healing, how can we end the conflict?

Our remembrance of God's Truth that bound us together faded away. We have instilled our beliefs to which our identity pledges allegiance. How faithful are we to our beliefs, for it protects our identity. It protects us from one another by enclosing us within a world that we think is safe. Within this illusion we find a false sense of innocence to hide from guilt.

Pain and suffering will follow us all of our days if we intentionally put others at risk. If we put others at risk and tear the fabric of

God, guilt will follow. Walls will be built to protect our identity and fortify our story of innocence. We have instilled illusions and beliefs in the minds of others to protect our semi-innocence.

Yet guilt will continue to break through so long as our desire to protect ourselves from each other and from our God outweighs our desire to love and be loved. This illusion becomes the world within the void where we sought refuge. We fortified ourselves. Our beliefs became solidified in our attempt to write our own set of truths to protect our semi-innocence.

Guilt, pain and suffering will follow us all our days unless we give ourselves back to God. If God is the source of life, the source of love; if God is our creator, then it is with God that we will find what brings peace, hope, joy and a true sense of belonging. In God we are complete and our identity is made whole. God's desire for us is one of wholeness. But how can we be whole if our identity is marred by duality? We cling to the darkness of our self and our identity but want the light of our soul. We cannot hide from the image that God created in us and for us with an identity formed by our ego.

In our choice and in our delusional beliefs we set ourselves apart. We chose an identity that created an illusion of exclusion. Possessions were sought, expectations were developed, and love became conditional. In our desire to make meaningful the self, we set ourselves apart. To protect the identity that became us, we hid ourselves from God's Truth through a system of delusional beliefs. These beliefs replaced Truth and allowed us to be semi-innocent within the self. These beliefs keep us from God and separated us from one another. Our beliefs are founded in fear and bind us to those illusions which exclude. Beliefs that keep us apart hide us from that Truth which would bind us all back to God.

Beliefs that hide Truth are borne of the self, to protect the ego. When innocence was lost, we hid from God. But where can one hide to escape God? Is there anywhere, where God is not? If God created, would He separate Himself from His creation? If God was to separate Himself from His creation, would not the life force of creation have to go with Him? God would not separate Himself from His creation, for His love continually extends and radiates into life, sustaining life. Yet as innocence was lost, beliefs were born. That part of us where God still is, is still buried below our beliefs. Our vision was dimmed to allow us to accept ourselves until we could one day find the Truth that would allow us to seek the forgiveness that would bring a healing. To forgive ourselves, each other and to seek our God.

Before we can find the wholeness in our soul, we must find healing in our self. By giving that part of our self back to God that we no longer want, we let go of those beliefs that justified the identity that we created. When healing in the self has changed our identity, wholeness in our relationships will follow. To find the Truth that love is our greatest desire, we must look at our beliefs.

Your true identity is that part of you which is a part of God. God is love. Your true identity allows love to be a part of you. Love does not consume; love extends. Love ends the duality because there is no duality in love. Love binds you to one another just as God's love binds God to you. Love allows you to look at your beliefs without fear. When you desire love for yourself, for your neighbor, your brother, your sister, your friend and your foe—when love becomes a part of you—your beliefs, that would set you apart, are no longer important. Your identity that was marred by your past will become unimportant because you will no longer want that which placed you at risk.

God calls you back to Him. Believe not that He would condemn, but seek that Truth that assures you of His love for you. Allow Truth to break through those illusions that created fear and set you apart. See beliefs for what they are, for beliefs are powerful. Beliefs meld the believers but exclude all others. Beliefs justify exclusion because innocence and salvation can only be claimed by those that believe. But is love exclusive? Can anyone lay claim to love? So herein will you know when Truth has found its home in you, for Truth calls us all back to God. For so as you judge your brother will judgment come back on you. When you bind your brother, your sister, your friend and your foe to condemnation, so will you bind yourself. Innocence cannot be shared if condemnation keeps you apart.

God's healing is about wholeness. God's healing is about

restoring your innocence. God's healing allows you to see holiness as He sees holiness. God sees the holiness that He placed inside of you. The Holy Spirit allows you to see that holiness that God sees. When you seek God, you seek that part of you that God created and still rests in His holiness. That part of you where love still has a home and willingly shares with others is what God gave to you. That love cannot die, for this is the life force that sustains you.

Wherein is this Truth that sets us free? What path must we set ourselves on to end the self-destruction and bring us back home to God? How are we to be released from the past and be transformed into that identity which is whole and complete?

Behold, day has come! The sun rises on the landscape and touches all the earth that stands in her wake. The trees, the rocks, the birds and the lakes reflect her rays. Who would hide in the earth to escape her warmth? Arise and feel the radiance of that which burns but is not consumed. Look with your eyes to see the life that draws strength from the sunshine. God is like sunshine. His light brings warmth by the radiance in which it burns within His creation. We are His creation. He burns in us and we are not consumed. Behold, day has come, and today we can emerge in Him.

Jesus is the Christ, Emmanuel, God with us. In Him God's Truth found a home. His path is the path of Truth, the path of innocence. See in Him what you would desire for yourself. For in Him was the word made flesh. In Him was healing and wholeness, for He was a quiet reflection of what God made real. In Him the fabric of God was woven into His identity. As Jesus sought to be one with God, single-minded in God's Truth, so it was that the oneness of God could be testified to humanity.[61]

---

61 Christians look to Jesus Christ as part of the Trinity—Father, Son and
    Holy Spirit. The Christ was God Emmanuel, the embodiment of God
    with us. To say that Jesus sought to be one with God is statement to
    the humanity of Jesus—that Jesus had free will apart from God and yet
    in his free will he made a choice to be at one with God. This brings
    meaning to scriptures, such as in Luke 22:42—where Jesus asks his

The path to Truth is captured in an instant. It is captured when earth meets heaven, when man touches his Creator, when laughter fills our hearts and songs dance in our children. Truth is captured in the giving, in the sharing, in the hand that touches both the old and the young. Truth is found when we see God as He would have us see Him. Look then and see, what God would have you see.

Source: Book of Truth

5 Who I Am

God cannot change me into something that I do not desire to be. Only I can do that.

What makes life beautiful comes from what is inside us. You and I are bonded together by God. But God cannot change you or I so that we recognize the bond that God has created. God cannot change you or I into something that we do not desire to be. In His gift of free will He gives us the choice. The choices are many, yet only one will prevail. In every instant that is lived, only one choice will prevail.

Somewhere then between what I say and do and the person that I would hope to be, is the who I am.

We clothe ourselves in an array of colors and emotions by our choices. We are wrapped inside a cocoon, gazing through the shell of our bodies. The cocoon is armored and we defend ourselves with the beliefs that we have created.

Father in heaven that if He be willing to remove the cup, to take away the journey of the cross from him, and then in free will, accepting the path of the cross, after much anguish to the point of sweating blood from his pores. It also brings a deeper meaning to John 17:17-26 as the prayer in Gethsemane is the message of both the self, as separate from, and yet in oneness to God, through the soul (note: both Luke 22:42 and John 17:17-26 were ethereal messages, inspired in spirit, as it was impressed to be written as no man heard the words that Jesus spoke to the Father in the garden). It is in choice to allow the very essence of God to be present in both body and spirit, mind and heart.

The cocoon that we have created is the darkness that our identity has been encased in to hide us from the Truth. Fear only this, for darkness will remain without the desire for God. That which we do to another we do to ourselves. When we share hatred, we feel hatred. When we share love, we feel love. Such is the law. Acts of inhumanity bury Truth deep within the soul such that it is difficult for even one's self to pierce through the darkness to find the Truth.

How bad can it get? Darkness can be perpetual, feeding upon itself. There is energy in the evil which we create. Yet the energy is self-consuming. It consumes the self in the darkness that the ego creates. Feeding on the soul until the soul is no more.[62] We live in a cocoon, binding ourselves to self-justification and to the illusion of our wantonness. We are encased, and the shell of our ego is strengthened, strangling, holding us tight to our self-image, to our false beliefs, to our judgments on others, to our fear and to the darkness that we have created. Despair not. God is still planted deep within the cocoon. The essence of the Holy Spirit remains and speaks the voice of God.

The road back is not easy. For you will be challenged again and again, against every belief that bound you to the image of darkness that you created for yourself, until that desire for that belief has been completely relinquished. When the belief that separated you from God and from those that God loves is no more, then will you become sanctified and the walk back to Truth will be complete. So it is that innocence will be restored and the atonement, the at-one-ment, will be justified.

Think not that God can change you. Even if you offered that part of yourself to Him that you do not want and asked God to destroy it, He cannot. Instead, God offers healing. A healing so deep that you begin to recognize whose you are and who you are to be.

God did not create you to find a just cause from which

---

62   This is not a statement in *The Message* to state that there is death to the soul as the soul is eternal and rests with God. However, the awareness to the soul in the self can be silenced. The light that is from God becomes diminished as the darkness converges on the self.

to destroy you. Look deep within, for there is love to give and there is love to be had. Look without, and that love can be extended. A mother whose child she holds, rests in her arms and love is shared. God holds you in His Spirit even as the mother holds her child. Even in the silence the child still feels her warmth. Even in the silence of God can God be felt. Would God destroy the child that a mother loves? How could a God of love destroy that which He created and still be at peace? Lay aside this world, which casts shadows of darkness, and look for God's grace which extends light and love.

Something so simple must be shared. Laughter is the dance of love. Singing reaches the heart. Touching brings about tenderness. Our eyes connect our souls. Now why would God want to destroy something so beautiful? Be simple. Simply be. Rest in God and God's rest will calm your world.

Consider death and destruction. Death is the illusion of the destruction of life—still what was is no more. In death, what melts away is not the end of life. In death the body no longer has meaning. Its usefulness has served the purpose for which it was created. But the body in this life dies in part each day only to be recreated, renewed to serve the spirit. The baby becomes the child, the child grows to youth and the youth matures until the years are no longer. When the years are gone, eternity still remains. So what has ended? The only thing that is destroyed in death is the illusion that death is the end.

Rejoice, for God walks with you. Every step that Jesus took on the journey to the cross is a witness to you that every step you take is not vengeance from Him. It is the journey that you and I have chosen together. We choose to face our own self-image so that we might someday let go and remember the Truth that God instills. In that day will God's offering of heaven be found in the hope that is ours. In that day will we find the sanctification that will make us complete. Sanctification is as assured as the resurrection that bore witness to life itself. God's Son lives and so will you.

Heaven is the remembrance of Truth. Who you are deep inside is not changed, but the light that is within you is made visible. Just as light is magnified by Truth, so it is that your light reflects the Truth that you bear witness to. Since God is the source of Truth, how you shine is the reflection of the light of God that can be seen in you. Bear witness of Truth and God will bear witness in you. Abide in Him, and He will abide in you.

Love calls us back. All are called, but not all choose for love. It is the avoidance of that choice, the avoidance of love that mars the path. Look back at choice for what it is. If there is choice that creates conflict, then we are being challenged by Truth. When we choose that which leads us to righteousness, to a healing of our relationships, then the conflict will end. Replace your unwanted beliefs with Truth, and no longer will you be challenged. For where are we challenged if there is no conflict?

Herein is the gospel of Jesus Christ made real, when we love the Lord our God with all of our heart, might, mind and soul, and when we love our neighbor as ourselves. When we love, we are made one in Christ. We become of one mind, one heart and one in purpose. There is no division among us, for there is no division in Truth.

When heaven finds a home in you, your true will becomes the will of God. God wills good things. Would this not be your will? God calls you to life. God's will is not about what you should do or say. God's will is about the principles that you should live by, the ideals that uphold peace, friendship and righteousness to the world, so that the world might find wholeness.

Our true will is the substance that life is built upon. What has substance is that which has eternal value. So what has value to you? Does that which promotes the self have value? Are you that important that your value is self-evident? Can others see in you that you have value? Be not deceived, for herein is the deception of the ego. One voice would assure us of our importance, and the other would rob us of our true identity. Neither voice is the voice of the Holy Spirit. The voice that pits us against our self does not come from God. It is the voice that we created when we created delusional beliefs to hide our self from Truth. It is the same voice looking for Truth but afraid to break the cocoon that the ego created when delusional beliefs were born.

The self knows that it has value, but it forgets why. Holiness resides within. God Himself is planted deep within. If God, who is holy, is planted in you, what can disturb that holiness? Can the source of life, the source of light ever be extinguished? What brings value to the self is the value that calls us to oneness. We value one another. Our oneness with ourselves, with each other and with God is self-evident. The holiness that is deep within, God's holiness, instills us with value. In Truth our value is holiness made eternal by the expression of our love for one another.

Seek to establish holiness in all your relationships. Holy relationships are bonded in God. When we are bonded to each other in God, what then can pull us apart? Our desire for the self is magnified in a new light as we begin to live for one another. The change within begins. The cocoon melts away and the true self emerges. God cannot change the who you are, but as you allow God in, the who you are is seen in God's light. We see ourselves the way God sees us.

Forasmuch then as God gave us the gift of the Holy Spirit for them that sought the Truth of Jesus how then could we withstand God? The gospel of Jesus Christ must be shared in the single-mindedness that speaks for Truth. For God's love is pure and His message is inclusiveness. In Jesus Christ we are called to innocence. Sin has no claim on us, for sin is the illusion that would make our separation from God seem real.

> *The sun pierces the earth and finds rest on the rock.*
> *The mountain stands in majesty blocking the path*
> *that the light would take. The mountain in its strength*
> *can hide the valley in darkness, but he who climbs the*
> *mountain will find the sun. Grandeur is found in each*
> *step that we take. The mountain strengthens the soul*
> *and our eyes take hold of the vision that is set before*
> *us. See then how you cast your shadow on the Truth*

of God. Let not the grandeur of God's light be hidden. Take the step towards unconditional love so that your soul might be strengthened. Strengthened so that you might see how God sees. For His Spirit will teach you how to love as you have never loved before.

The sin that marred the path is now in the past. Ask for forgiveness, ask for healing. Sin will not have a claim on you if you seek your God and forgive yourself and others. Wash from your feet what you would ask of God to take. Give back to the earth what you would claim, and in turn the earth will share with you all of her abundance. For in giving you receive, and in forgiving you are healed. For in giving you recognize the gift, the Source, that part of you which gives life. Just as God extends life, you extend life in the giving of yourself. Seek that balance where sharing brings about a bond of love, and the gift of love will be complete.

Jesus said, "Verily I say unto you, whatsoever ye shall bind on earth shall be bound in heaven; and whatsoever shall be loosed on earth shall be loosed in heaven."[63]

For the bond of life is molded in the array of God. We carry our relationships with us, for they are bonded in God. When our relationships are healed and heaven is found in both of us, then shall our love be complete. Heaven goes with us. When forgiveness loosens the bondage that imprisoned our minds and hearts on earth, so shall forgiveness reestablish our hope in Christ. For in Christ we are recreated and renewed to a new life which is whole.

Source: Book of Truth

——————— 6 Spiritual Endurance ———————

This life provides me with the opportunity through which I can refine the who I am. In this life I am vulnerable to choice and I do not have clear vision but

*it is through my challenges that I will test myself. It is
the fire of the flesh that will mold me and will prove
me in His image.*

Spiritual endurance is the choice, the conviction, to do what is
right in life. This is the fire of the flesh, which burns upon your
being. It molds you and reshapes you into the likeness that you
would create. When you endure life, this life, convictions solidify
on the spirit in the form that others can see. Your personality is
etched, your beliefs are etched, your will is etched and your ability
to love is etched.

Spiritual endurance is about creation with purpose before
God. It's the spilling of the spirit onto life. In our movement, in
our creation, we have an impact on God. We have an impact on
each other and on ourselves. It's the expression of life that weaves
the fabric.

When we do good, the fabric is woven in the array of God.
When we lack good, the fabric can be torn. The array of God can be
lost to our vision. Wantonness carries the self away in the euphoria
that speaks to our ego and can set us apart from God piece by
piece. We become fragmented, torn from our true identity, which
rests in God.

Wantonness strengthens the ego, however it weakens our bond
with creation. The ego grows in self-will, self-desire for an illusion
that is separate from the purpose of creation. Yet we cannot
be totally separated from God's creation, so wantonness itself
becomes entrapment. Wantonness traps the mind and the heart in
the ego of the one who created it. Wantonness is extended in the
images that we create for one another and it consumes the lives of
those that are entrapped by it. This is the pride, the self-absorption,
the self-exclusion and the ego that binds us to special relationships.

God cannot change you—only you can do that. If God were
to change you, He would have to take away your free will. Your
innocence would be lost in Him, for you would not know who you
are. You would not know your own true will. So it is that God gives
back the fabric. He gives you the opportunity to try again, so that

you might find a healing and bring an end to the voice that speaks for your wantonness.

Without God, without the desire to live love, the image of wantonness goes with you, even into death. Your will to love or not to love goes with you. The relationships that you were bound to in this life, or those relationships that were torn by you in this life, will be either magnified or intensified in death.

In creation you must be restored. Spiritual endurance, which strives for holy relationships, recreates those bonds that were severed by an illusion. We endure life until the spirit reflects the image that God's will would seek. Every act, every thought and every desire will be tested. How you value yourself will be tested against how you value others. This is the fire of the flesh which will prove your *self* in the image of Jesus Christ, whose image is the image of innocence and righteousness.

Walk with one another as Jesus walked with the children, and creation will sanctify life. Extend yourself in the spirit of Christ, and creation will end the voice of the ego that spoke to the image of your wantonness. Rise above that voice that would speak for the self alone. Rise above the voice that would justify you by setting others apart. See through the eyes of your neighbor that which he sees coming from you. In creation you were both born of the one true God, and in creation He wills heaven for all.

What kind of an impact have you had on your life? Do you extend creation or do you extend yourself in pride before your wantonness? Are you free in others or are others entrapped by you? Has heaven found a home in you or is your home fragmented in disarray before the fabric of God? Is there healing in your heart or are there illusions in your mind? Are your relationships contractual, conditional or are they holy and forever bound in God?

Creation begins again. Each new day is a day for creation. Creation stills the moment and brings peace to conflict. Recreate all relationships with the purity that you would want for yourself. Ask to see in others what you would want others to see in you. They become your mirror as you become their mirror. Reflect back their innocence and the shadows in time will dissipate. Reflect back your need for them and their need for you will grow. Reflect back God's holiness and you will find God's holiness growing in you.

Life, this life, will set you free. God's Holy Spirit will sustain you. It is God's will which sustains, He changes not. His Spirit breathes life into you and sustains you, even when your ego has laid claim to your illusions, your beliefs. God sustains you for He is bound to you. Your will is set free but your link with God can never be severed. In this life you must choose. Your sight is dimmed by illusions and beliefs, but God's vision allows you to see past your ego and into creation where God is.

Source: Book of Truth

——————— 7 Choice ———————

In this life the "who I am" is vulnerable to choice. I do not have clear vision but it is through my challenges that I will test myself. It is the fire of the flesh that will mold me and will prove me in His image. Each day is the test, each day I am drawn to the light. Caught within darkness I must see beyond the discomfort of the self in order to touch the light that brings stillness and peace to my soul.

We choose according to our frame of reference. In this life, many live within a world of self as created by the images of wantonness. Yet God is planted in each life, working within each one of us at our own pace. What we see in this world is a reflection of that part of our will which has been etched by who we were, what we did, and what we desire. We etched upon our soul that which we have willed. In turn, our hearts beat according to the degree of love that we live.

The destiny that we move towards is shaped by our frame of reference. When we place ourselves at the center, looking through the self-image that we have created, that image will be reflected back. All that we see is the reflection of our self upon the images of our relationships, no more and no less. When fear sets in, fear sets us apart. When love takes root, love finds a home.

When we place the image of Jesus Christ at our center, our identity regains the innocence that God created us in. Even in the images of our ego where we still touch both the light and the dark, God is at work. Darkness cannot hide you forever, nor can it carry you away from your desire to belong, to be a part of God's creation. Even in the despair and the grief will you remember that desire to belong and that comfort which is found only within the arms of hope. Even in the darkest hour of life where the illusions of the ego speaks of despair, your hope can be seen in the light of God.

It is in that moment, where hope breathes in you a desire to live, will you hear the cry for life. Herein is the desire for hope made visible; it is where life extends creation by recreating the desire to live love. Life becomes sacred. God's light pierces the darkness and His light shines a renewal of your life as sacred to Him.

Our desire for life changes life. Our desire for one another restores us to each other. Out of free will are we changed and what is sacred to God is seen in the image that God created us in. The image of Jesus Christ is made real as we begin to reach back into creation with all of our heart, might, mind and soul, and when we reach out to one another.

The self must now choose. The voice of the Holy Spirit, which speaks for creation, will look to heal your relationships. The voice of the ego, which sees the images of wantonness, will speak to the self to protect the images that it would project. The voice of the Holy Spirit heals the self by binding you to the one who holds your true identity which is embedded in your soul. Our desire to belong to God calls us to be of one heart, one mind and of one purpose—the purpose of creation.

Earth and heaven rest in the continuity that we are all created by a just God who wills life for all of His creation. Heaven and earth rest when there is convergence in that desire that fulfills the purpose of creation.

Source: Book of Truth

———— 8 The Life Review ————

Beyond this life is the continuation of the reality that we willed. When the veil is lifted and we stand in the midst of our life review all that we were, all our beingness converges in the presence of God. Our life review is the implosion of our beingness as all the images of our life are replayed and relived. The feelings, the desires of our intentions, our will, our actions, all that which was good and everything which was distasteful, converges. Only in the presence of God can we be sustained.

When we cross over from this life to the next the record of life is open. All that we did—every thought, every feeling, our intents, our hopes, our wantonness, greed, envy, our acts of kindness, compassion and charity—is reviewed and seen again in the presence of God. There are no secrets. Nothing is hidden. Who we are and how we are seen by others is realized in its entirety. We see and feel both the joy and the pain that we projected as we look into the hearts and minds of those whom we either touched or helped, or those whom we have stripped and inflicted the blunt of our will.

To see through our ego, to find a desire for God, is the journey of self. Each day of life that is written and recorded becomes the mirror from which we will see for ourselves that our true will and true desires rests in a pure heart and pure mind. We purge from our being that which brings grief and remorse. The taste and form of our darkness, our inhumanity, our apathy and indifference becomes bitter and shameful.

Only the desire to be pure, to carry God's light and God's image can illuminate our being. We are spirit. As we cross over from this life to the next will we see the degree of illumination of God in us. The essence of God, the essence of divine love shines through us and can be seen by others. Without divine love, without a pure heart and pure mind, the very garments that can be seen by others become cloudy and grey. We wear the essence of God. Our ability to retain and hold God's image can be seen.

God stands not in judgment of us. God envelopes our soul with love and acceptance. For some, the life review is traumatic, harsh, filled with remorse and regret. Only in God's presence can they endure the heartache and pain that life sometimes creates. Yet God cannot spare them from the reality that they created nor can God change the reality that they willed.

For us who have sought God's image, for us who uphold humanity and promote peace, hope and acceptance, our life review fills us with joy. It is the desire of our hearts coming to rest on our beingness that we see. The glow of God is seen as His light fills our soul and our spirit is illuminated and clothed in the garments which sparkle and dazzle our senses. Heaven awaits.

When the desires of our heart are pure, and the will that we would will is peaceful, we are restored in the innocence that we were created in. Of such is the Kingdom of Heaven. We who are pure in our love for each other return home to the reality of God. Those of like mind and heart come together to share in the oneness that exists in our Heavenly Father.

The beingness that emanated from us in this life is magnified in heaven. Not only can our beingness be seen by the glow of our spirits which illuminates our garments, but our presence can be felt as it radiates the love that exists from within. In turn, we also can feel the beingness that exists in others. Here we have form and substance which has an added depth of dimension. The destiny and depth of our soul intensifies to form the structure and substance which can be seen and felt.

Our life review facilitates the implosion of our beingness. All of our life's experiences converge to teach us who we are by what we have willed. Yet even in that will and that desire which would rob God's image from us, God's presence assures us that we are not lost from His divine love.

The reality that we created in this life is the reality that we move towards in death. This is not punishment or reward by God but rather the fulfillment of our life by the desires of our heart. To endure the fullness of heaven, our hearts and minds must be pure. The energy of thought vibrates and can be seen and felt by others. It is the openness that binds heaven in oneness to God.

In heaven, there are no secrets. In heaven, we do not hide from one another. Our thoughts and desires can be seen and understood by others. The life force of God radiates and resonates in us, and through us, and binds us to each other. Yet, we retain our distinctiveness. We retain our identity, our personality, our individuality. Each of us has our hopes and desires. Each of us seeks to add value to God's creation, to restore God's creation, to become more illuminated by the light of God. Each of us strives to internalize those attributes which personify strength, courage, tenderness, endurance, kindness, leadership, submission, respectfulness and virtue.

The earth and all its beauty is magnified and glorified, illuminated in heaven. The richness of the earth is but a shadow to the splendor of heaven. In heaven, our very soul blends into the fabric of life, into the fabric of the trees, the grass, the flowers, the walkways, our homes, the sky and the ground beneath our feet. We blend into each other, feeling each other's presence, which is a feeling that is beyond substance and form.

Those who cannot retain God's image retreat to the shadows and the darkness in that part of God's creation where they will be most comfortable. Here they will face the images of self with others of like mind and desire. Some cannot escape the reality that they created in this life, until they have faced their own anguish. God knows all, sees all. Even where they would hide, God is. The essence of God is retained even in the darkness where we ourselves would not wish Him to go. His voice is there calling to them from the echoes of the images that stand behind them. Only when they look back and pierce the creation that they created can they see Him.

When the heart and the mind is not pure, there is closure. The light of God is withheld and the spirit cannot glow from within. The spirit becomes tarnished and tainted, darkened to God's presence. The garments cannot glow and shimmer in the luminescent colors of God's spectrum because God's presence is withheld by their will and desire. For them there is closure of mind and desire. The reality for them is a lesser state of heaven.

Each state of heaven is a state of luminescence. Each is a state to which and by which the presence of God can be endured. Insomuch as the image of God that exists in God comes to rest in our beingness, so it is that we move closer to that reality where the fullness of God's presence exists. It is a state of openness, wholeness and oneness. As the reality of God that exists in God unfolds in our beingness, the vibration and resonance of our spirit is quickened to harmonize with God's light.

No reality, however, is void of God. All realities must endure a portion of God's presence. It is God's presence which tests and challenges our spirit. Each reality retains a glimpse of heaven, a state of innocence. To the degree in which our consciousness is aware of God, and that awareness is shared openly, determines the vibration, the luminescence that exists in that reality. Innocence, openness and luminescence are magnified through the awareness of God's presence.

In the reality where one becomes void to that awareness of God's presence, innocence is hidden and overshadowed by guilt and blindness. All which God is, becomes masked by the shadows of a reality which clouds Truth. In this reality, the mind and heart are closed. Mistrust and uncertainty encircle those relationships that are entangled in misdeeds. This reality is dense without form. More effort and intent is required to overcome self-pleasure, self-indulgence and exclusivity of self to the discharge of value—the destructive behavior of both influence and malice. To trust and forgive requires an earnest desire to communicate and to listen. Only through the affirmation and recognition of Truth can this reality be broken of self. God's presence awaits.

Beyond our awareness is the hand of God. God's presence waits to openly accept our wantingness to return to Him. It is our desire for forgiveness, for love, for acceptance, for healing, and for wholeness that opens the door. In all realities are we free to choose for God, to ask God to instill us with His quiet presence. We are free to make room for His will and His light. God grants to us the vision to see past ourselves and into the compassion that heals. When we make room for God, God in turn shows us how to make room for others.

A newness of hope and desire opens all realities to a vision of the Kingdom of God. It is a remembrance of our home. In our exploration of our self, in all the realities that stood before us, will we find our innocence. Beyond all paths that test our strength of character and beyond all dreams that make creation possible, is our innocence. As we seek to become, God seeks to restore.

The Book of Life stands in testament of yourself against all realities that stand against your innocence. For all realities are a backdrop set within God's creation which were formed by our dreams and visions to allow us to explore our image. As we willed for or against each other, relational experiences set in motion our quest to find God within—a quest to find wholeness, a quest to feel complete, a quest to be healed.

God's record stands firm. In all that which would stand against us, the reality of God will prevail. The reality of God is Truth and Truth dispels all illusions. What, therefore, can stand against thee if God stands for thee? If God would restore you in the innocence that He created you in, who then would stand against you in the judgment that God has decreed? Only darkness can prevail on those who do not will for the light that grants us all hope.

God cannot and will not destroy that which is you, where He Himself resides. From the farthest spectrum of creation, where the presence of God is hidden only to be seen in that desire to call God back, God is. The darkest form of reality at the farthest corner of God's creation is the light of God standing behind the backdrop of the creation we willed. God's presence is but a heartbeat away.

Source: Book of Life

9 In Divine Love we Return

The essence of God is divine love. Divine love is a binding force which draws strength from pure thought and pure desire. The creative process of God is the construct of divine love. Born within you and I, we are weaved in its tapestry. Like the thread and needle, it takes a single string, a single life, and moves it mysteriously in and through the fabric. Divine love flows in and through the web it creates. From a distance the pattern emerges in a glorious array which radiates the presence of life.

God radiates the presence of life. It is the very essence of God which radiates the life force. Harmony and balance shifting in its patterns to create the array of force, thunder, silence, splendor, wonder, space, continuity, continuance, disturbance, and construct. Here God is seen by the absorption of the reality that is present beyond one's self. It is life that can be absorbed by the air that we breathe, by the aromas that we taste, by the sensation of the world that we touch, and the keen awareness that no matter where we are, we are not alone.

God is. His presence is made real to us by thought, form and deed. His essence in us is magnified and illuminated by divine love. When our love is pure in both desire and deed a realization of God is solidified into our being. God's presence finds a home.

The essence of you and I is divine love. We are created and formed by the presence of God. There is no space between us for the very life force of God goes with us. Pure thought and pure desire rests within. For some it is dormant because of the darkness that was created by our ego which would hide our image and our identity in a world that we can claim and proclaim as ours alone.

The record of life teaches us that we are not alone. It teaches us that we are not separate from God or each other. It teaches us that we are all connected. The actions and reactions of our lives have an impact on everything and everyone. We leave a residue of our attitude, behaviors, and desires in the wake that forms behind us as we walk through life.

In heaven we prepare for our next incarnation. Each incarnation puts to task our free will. Only in our free will, where the presence of God is silent, can we test ourselves. The illumination of the essence of God, to the essence of divine love, is instilled only through our own pure thought and pure desire. In heaven we prepare the stage, we choose the setting, and those that we will interact with, so that we might test ourselves. The conflicts, the challenges, the struggles are preordained with God.[64]

The creative process brings us all together again. Those who became lost to themselves, to their ego, their inhumanity and their darkness are called back from the shadows to face again those circumstances and those choices which robbed them from God. We go with them. These are our brothers and sisters who became lost to the light. As we reach for them by the relationships of our earthly lives, divine love finds a home. The essence of God finds a home. Our love for them and them for us purifies the heart and the mind. As we choose for each other, we choose for life.

The creative process restores hope for those who became lost to God and wholeness takes root as we are filled with illumination and seek to embody God's essence. The children of the Law of One reach into the lives of the sons of Belial, the children of the lie, to help them find their way back home to heaven.

Source: Book of Life

---

64   Please note that the word preordained should be not be taken out of context to suggests that God predestines the outcomes of our choices. Please see footnote 58 from *The Journey of the Soul: 1 The Playground of Life.*

Eternity

1 Time

Time is a wonderful instrument for it either proves or disproves the product that I manifest.

God is unchangeable. He is the same yesterday, today and forever. Such is eternity. God is eternal. His oneness stands in the face of creation which constantly changes.

Just as time brings movement into creation, so does eternity find the stillness that resides in time. In eternity, time matters not. Yet time was created because we moved from God. Since it is God's will that none of His creation be lost from Him forever, God placed in motion the time necessary to restore us back to Him.

Time is the product that we manifest. Each deed and each word is preceded by thought. Each thought is born in part from belief, in part by illusion and in part from Truth or the reality that God would will. Thoughts that are born in belief have an element of time. Thoughts that reassure us of Truth remind us of eternity. Each moment is caught between the now and what was or what will be. Time happens when the past or the future determines our salvation. Time matters not when eternity meets each moment and we live each moment in the eternity that God granted. Salvation is embraced by the eternity that is lived within each moment.

Salvation is the shared will, of the will of God. Heaven is brought into our awareness by our wantingness to share heaven within the framework of time. What is made real within our mind and heart is the reality that we move towards.

In Truth, God is real and hell is the illusion. Hell is real when we make God an illusion. When heaven is restored in us, our salvation is made real. When hell seems real, our salvation can only be found out there somewhere in the void where we believe heaven awaits. Hell then exists, but only in the framework of time, not eternity. For God's will is to save all of creation and God's will, will be done.

Time only masks eternity where God is. Bring heaven to the framework of time and eternity will be restored.

Rethink time. Each moment of each day is broken into routines that define our movement. Yet our movement is caught within timelessness. Our thoughts carry us forward and our memories recreate the past. If we fear the future and hate the past, there is hell to pay.

Wherein is there hope if hope carries no meaning? Our salvation remains out there somewhere, but where? Gentle is hell's descent within time for it places us firmly on the illusion that tomorrow is another day and yesterday is not yet gone. The illusion persists so long as tomorrow has no hope and today is only a reflection of yesterday's memories. The illusion is intensified when tomorrow is feared and yesterday is our only reality. The now becomes displaced when our illusions entrap our identity, our memories, our hopes, and our dreams. God's reality becomes displaced when our identity becomes lost to what was or what will be.

Yet in time, God will bring you full circle. In time your journey will cause you to search your soul. The inward journey is realized in your search for meaning, to make sense out of that which makes no sense. In that search you will find Truth, not the truth that makes sense out of the senseless, but that Truth that brings you back to God. In that Truth, found deep within the soul, is the remembrance of the reality that rests in God.

So how do we find our way back to God? Is God so far away that we have to look for Him? Our ability or inability to find God rests only in our desire. You cannot find God if you have to look for Him, yet His presence is made ever so clear if you allow Him to look through you.[65] God pierces the heart and the mind which is open to love and willingness to accept what is already given. It is love and willingness that bears witness to the reality that rests in God.

We resist God when we resist the desire to be with Him. We resist God when we resist the call of another who looks to us for belonging. Resistance bears no fruit from which fruit can be born. To resist love, to resist healing in our relationships, is to resist God. If God is love and we resist love, how can we find God? If it is God that you seek, if it is heaven that you seek, if it is salvation that you seek, then love must find a way to work in you.

It is the recognition of Truth that moves us back to Him. The desire we seek is the desire to find the source of life, the source of love, that radiates within us. When we recognize the Source, the Source illuminates life. We see God in all of creation. We see God in our family, our friends, our neighbor, and even the stranger. In time we recognize God in all things.

Truth stands in the midst of who we are. The images of our will, the desires of our heart and the impact of our lives leave an imprint. We cannot escape the reality that is ours no more than we can avoid the desire to breathe the air that is around us.

What we have willed shapes the reality of time that stands before us. We are all connected. We look to one another for love and support. Others in turn look to us for love and support. Insomuch as we nurture each other, our common reality forms peaceful memories. The memories and the feelings—whether they be full of joy, emptied by regret or intensified by passion—have an impact on our soul. The reality of this day will stand in the wake of time that has already moved.

The Holy Spirit brings to remembrance that same desire which is in God. God's persistence to restore you to Truth is everlasting. His persistence will continue to work in you until you come face

---

65   The image of this passage is one of self-evidence. In other words if the evidence of God is not already one of self-awareness, then trying to prove God's existence through physical manifestation's will be elusive. You cannot prove to someone else that God is, or show to someone else that God is here or God is there. The evidence of God must come from within.

to face with that desire which binds you to God. Resistance is the product of duality, a split mind severed by the ego. The mind which resists the call of the Holy Spirit, resists the heart of life.

Our desire, which connects us to God and to each other, creates the belonging. All other desires that work against that bond have no eternal meaning. The desire for material possessions can be used for or against that bond. Things in themselves are not eternal. The only meaning they have is the meaning we bring to them. For what meaning is there in our possessions, except the meaning that we give them? Yet when we share, we share a piece of ourselves with each other. Our meaning to each other is shared. That eternal value of each other is shared. Our heart can touch everyone in every moment of every day if we share every moment of everyday with the heart that is within us.

From remembrance of a time when love was our home, we begin to see what moved us from the creation that we were created in. A sparkle, a glitter of love that shone deep within assured us that God would call us back. From the nothingness that trapped the soul within the confines of time, will we remember. From the nothingness where our value was lost to what had no value will we remember. Here it was all along. We stood in the face of nothingness only to see and to learn from its heartlessness.

What has no eternal value has no eternal meaning. In our giving of ourselves to what has no eternal meaning, we learned that no meaning could ever come of it.

It is time which defines nothingness. Whatever is nothing is anything that is not eternal. If it comes and it goes and has no intrinsic value, it is nothing. If we place value in it, we create the illusion of value. We stand in its wake, substituting what had real value with the illusion of nothingness. So it is that in our journey towards our desire for nothingness that we wandered from God. From nothing to nothing we wandered and will continue to wander when that which has real value is forgotten.

Laugh at the nothingness. Laughing at the nothingness diminishes the meaning that you placed into it and causes you to remember the heart of your soul. The fun that is had within life comes from living life with each other. It comes from breaking the mold of self-inflicted valuelessness into an identity which has complete innocence.

Children are our best ambassadors of God, for they break the mold of our cocoon by drawing us away from that world of self. Our beliefs are unguarded and in them we see our true selves. There is no need for defense when we are released into their fun and laughter.

And Jesus said, "Suffer the little children to come unto me, and forbid them not; for of such is the Kingdom of Heaven."[66]

God imparts wisdom so that all might see through the eyes of a child. In an instant we can regain a glimpse of our own innocence when we allow ourselves to be released from our yesterdays and our expectations of tomorrow. When we allow ourselves to see the now that is in the eyes of our children we will see the wisdom that is granted in the breath and the heart of the moment. In our children we will find the wisdom of our God. For in the birth of each little one will we find the innocence that we seek for ourselves. For at birth, wantonness was buried for a period of time so that the world would never forget the image of innocence.

It is in our children that God would remind us of our true identity which He created us in. Our true identity is not lost, it is forgotten. Yet it can be remembered and freed when we share in the laughter and the fun, in the loving and the giving, in the living and the being. The wisdom that God imparts is the wisdom of the moment. Life is lived in the moment and in that moment are we either freed by the innocence of creation or imprisoned by the guilt made real by wantonness.

You will become the product of the time that you manifest. So has time created the identity that you want for yourself? Look to time, for God has created time for you so that you might choose again. Use time to dispel the nothingness which has encased your identity in the image of self. Let go of that which has no intrinsic value. It is only by letting go that you will regain your freedom. Enjoy all that you have, but do not lose your identity to it. Share

66   Mark 10:14.

what you have and your freedom will be multiplied. Share not and others will quickly see that you are possessed by your possessions. The shift that must take place is the shift from misplaced value to that value that God places in each one of us. Gradually as you shift, the descent into hell is broken.

Hell is nothingness.[67] Hell is the illusion of our nothingness turned inwards.[68] Without the shift back to God, hell will go with us wherever we go, even into death. We can only break free from hell when we can break free from our nothingness. God is not an illusion, yet our image of Him can be if, in our illusions, we cannot see the face of life. God is only found in the heaven that He created, yet that heaven is here, found within that desire which is pure.

Replace the nothingness that has been placed in others with the value that God has placed in you. You can't find heaven alone.

---

67   I think back again to the dream that I had when I had when I was fifteen. In that dream I was trapped to this void, this darkness and to this nothingness. Hell can mean a lot of different things to different people; most images are one of suffering, tormenting and maybe fire and brimstone. The image here, for me, points to a death to the awareness of one's own soul or the choice to extinguish God from self—without God there is this nothingness.

68   This illusion of our nothingness is what we see looking back at ourselves when love cannot be found. When we are consumed by—when we become possessed by, when rage, hatred and anger seizes our beingness, these projections of our ego creates a void, a darkness, where the self is lost to this nothingness—this emptiness, that drains us of our soul. The mirror becomes empty of value, yet the void of value and void of love for self is what is reflected back.

The "hell" that we impart in life converges on the self in death. In the choice to avoid God, the soul is hidden from the self (i.e. the soul is encased or placed within the shell of a cocoon that we create) and the self is confined in exile to the abyss where these emotions are internalized and can become demonized. This is not God's will, nor is it punishment, rather God grants the self the space it needs to sort through this negativity. Those souls that internalize anger and hatred seek to inflict pain and anguish by subjecting others to suffering. Those who are sensitive to influence, easily beguiled or of like mind become targets of their rage—the living can be impacted or influenced by those souls trapped to the abyss.

Heaven will remain out there somewhere so long as you place others out there somewhere.

Use time to refine the love that you have for others and you will find a new love in yourself. Use time to rekindle the bonds that were torn and severed by memories that you cling to from your past. Only by facing the mirror of yourself can you see past the beliefs that hides you from God's Truth. The fabric must be arrayed in God or the fabric will be left unfinished. As we share ourselves with one another the bond that was formed in heaven is reestablished on earth. All that we have on this earth in time will be gone, but we will continue on—we walk through time into eternity with each other.

The identity that we seek is the identity that expands ourselves into creation within the framework of Truth and righteousness. What we seek is what God created in us. We were born by the divine presence of God. In God were we created. He is the source of life and it is His presence that sustains life. Since God cannot be divided and His presence is forever bound to us, our oneness with Him out of free will is the fulfillment of His purpose. Our individuality is not lost in God when we seek the desire to be at one with Him. Rather, it is out of that oneness that our true identity is magnified. The oneness that we seek is the oneness that promotes peace, love, hope and joy. It is the interaction of our oneness, set within all the colors and sounds of our talents and our skills, that brings laughter and joy to the fabric of God. Each moment of each day is filled with God's creation. Eternity is brought to the framework of time as heaven is restored to earth.

Time then becomes the stepping stone back to God. Each day we are given the opportunity to create, to re-create, to bring healing and to promote wholeness. Each day we must choose to love, to end the conflict and to dissolve the guilt. Each day we can allow God to look through us so that we can see how God sees. Each day is a day for innocence, a day for Truth. Rework the fabric of time and time will rework the fabric of God. So God willed, so will it be done.

Source: Book of Truth

2 In Life We are Tested

The root of insanity is the inability to reason because we have become powerless to understand reality. Choices that place ourselves at risk are choices which test how we value others relative to ourselves; our choices mold the reality we see. Yet a reality which separates us from God, a reality which divides God's creation, is not what God would make real.

We live within a delusion that we make real. If we make God an illusion, if we make fear our reality, then insanity begins to take root. Our insanity will grow if our choices separate us from God and from each other. When we choose an identity which is closed, confrontational, fearful, resentful, revengeful, and unreasonable, love ends and insanity takes root. *Insanity sets us on a road where we become powerless to choose for love.* Insanity ends only when we return to God and look to each other. Insanity ends when we return to the reality that God would will.

> *Life, this life, can solidify your image of wantonness, beliefs and illusions. Choose well, for in order to find the light of God you must move through your own darkness. You must face the identity that you have created but no longer want.*
>
> *When you choose God, the desire for God's light can shine through you. Without the desire for God's light you will remain trapped. The light, which is the source of life, will continue to call you back from the darkness of your illusions. This life provides you with the opportunity through which to refine the image of who you are with that image that God created you with.*

It is our value system which is being put to the test. How do we value others relative to ourselves? When we set ourselves apart, when we think ourselves unique, special or deserving more than those that are around us, the voice of our ego begins to echo. Little by little as the illusion of our grand self-image emerges we become encased in a value system that protects our identity. The ego speaks to the self for the self alone. If in time our ego is solidified on our self-image, we will become consumed by its taste.[69] Its voice is maintained by the illusion of guiltlessness. Blame and denial are its weapons of self-defense.

To break free, we need new eyes for seeing. God is trying to break through this illusional value system of self that we have created. He is not on the outside looking in; He is on the inside looking out. He is the source of your conflict, for He is the still small voice calling you back to Him.

Everything that you do testifies as to how you value others relative to yourself.

When Jesus was crucified, none of the disciples came to the cross for they feared the crucifixion.[70] They feared that if they were to be seen with Jesus at Calvary that they too would be condemned. Just as the shock wave that Jesus experienced as the nails of the cross pierced his wrists, so did his disciples experience the shock wave from their choice to abandon him in his final hours. Even Peter, John and James—who witnessed the transfiguration of Jesus and knew who Jesus was—could not bear to witness the cross he bore.

Herein is how true fear operates. Fear sends a shock wave into our delusional belief system. Our fears are expressed against

---

69　Our ego can be like nicotine, a drug, a flavor, a sweetness that we cannot get enough off. We can become so addicted to what and who we are that we love to love ourselves—consumed by the taste of self to the point where unknowingly that self-love is destructive to our relationships with others.

70　In John 19: 25-27 we find Mary Jesus's mother, his mother's sister, Mary the wife of Cleophas, Mary Magdalene and a disciple whom he loved. How it reads would suggest an error in *The Message* to the account of scripture. I choose not to correct the apparent error, because it is a demonstration that the process of spiritual journaling can have flaws. Messages that speak for God still come through a conduit, a person—someone who does not have perfect knowledge or someone who is influenced by their own beliefs. There is, however, a theme of fear that I believe existed in those closest in fellowship to Jesus, in that they also could have be condemned and crucified. We have Peter's denial as evidence of that fear.

the self, based on the expectations of what will be. Our fears are expressed against the self by the way of uncertainty, distrust, anger, frustration, hatred, blame, hopelessness, resentment and a myriad of other strong feelings. When we place fear into our relationships, we pit ourselves against our value system. When we value others more or less than how we value ourselves then every word, every act and every thought is reflected back on us. Our emotions are inflamed and our mind races to justify our beliefs as we seek to find a home in the exile that we make real.

We are indeed condemned to suffer when we set ourselves apart and when we exclude ourselves from the love of others. It is our value system that condemns us—if it hides us from our God and from each other. Our condemnation is without mercy if our value system doesn't take us back to God. Conflict haunts us and the guilt persists; thank God it does. For without God, how could you break free from that value system that encases you?

God seeks to restore your innocence. God seeks to restore your wholeness.

Somewhere deep within is someone who is full of God's goodness. God is trying to show that to you by trying to get you to prove it to yourself. When you do what is right, your heart soars and your mind clears. When you do not do what is right, conflict ensues. Correct it quickly. When you make a mistake and you correct it, where is the mistake? The mistake is in the past and has no impact on the present. When the lesson has been learned, is there still a need to repeat the mistake? When we are no longer tempted by the identity that we no longer want then there is no conflict. Guilt is gone and innocence takes root. God, who is in you and who is the source of your innocence, calls you back to Him by restoring you to your own true image, which is the image of innocence.

Life struggles are our building blocks that will restore us to wholeness. In time, our love for each other will break the mold that we find ourselves in. That is the turning point. The past no longer matters. Things no longer matter. Our differences no longer matter. The fear for the self no longer matters. What matters is that we do not let go of each other. What matters is that the desire to walk with one another is so strong, it is unconditional. Such is the source of God. Such is the strength that God gives us through the power of the Holy Spirit.

We are the community of God. We are God's children. In Him were we created. If God created us, does that not make us His sons and His daughters? Can we deny any longer who we are? And yet we have, if we have hidden love from our identity. So long as we hide love, *acts of insanity* can ensue. Look at your beliefs, look at your value system, look at the image of God that you have created.

Does your image of God make God a judge? For if we have denied ourselves of God, set in sin, set in the terror that we have caused others to bear, creating fear and distrust, what then must God judge of us? If God cannot tolerate sin in the least degree, what must He judge? Fear not, for God knows what is real and although we set God in judgment of us, God's judgment will set us free. In the end, He will lay claim to us because we still are His sons and daughters and our disillusions[71] can never change what is real.

The pendulum will continue to swing and time will continue our movement so long as you walk within the insanity that leaves you powerless to choose for love. Because of the fear of the valuelessness that was born from your beliefs, God will give back to you what you freely choose. In your judgment will you either mortify yourself in the condemnation that you will or you will begin to recognize the insanity of condemnation itself. Judgment which wills retribution binds you to the condemnation that you inflict. To end condemnation you, must end the unwanted identity—it is the only way.

Together we must walk. Together we will free each other of the judgments that condemn. In community will we come to the altar of God. In community will we come to share that part of ourselves

---

71   Illusions are images of reality. They are created images formed by beliefs. A disillusional belief is an illusion used to mask reality. We form a disillusional belief to hide a Truth that we fear. The difficulty is one of discerning if a belief is disillusional—does the belief rob us from accepting or recognizing Truth?

which resides with God. For it is with God that we learn the value of each other as God sees us. Holy relationships will bind us in peace, love, hope and joy. We seek the community of Christ.

> *I recognize that everything that I do is a reflection of how I value others relative to myself. All that I own, all my material possessions will pass away. But the people that I know I will walk with through eternity. It is through this Truth that I will discover what holds true value to my soul. For I know that I only place myself at risk when I think of myself greater or lesser than my brother. My greatest joys are found when I seek to better others, even if the price that I pay is most dear.*

Source: Book of Truth

─────── 3 Suffering ───────

> *Suffering caused by conflict allows me to see that which is not quite right about me. I will eventually learn from my pain and one day it will change me forever. That day will come when I resolve that the question is not what I ought to do, but who I ought to be.*

God does not will suffering. Yet in our free choice suffering came to be. It is because of suffering that the Law of God was written. Through the Word came the Law of God, and the Law of God became the mirror of our soul. In the mirror we would see what we sowed. We cannot escape the Law of God because we cannot escape ourselves.

In our wantonness we were entrapped, ensnared by our own self-image. Yet by the Law of God will God set us free. In time the Law of God will free us for God's law is bound by time. Every step towards our ego's euphoric self-image is unmasked by God's law to bring us back. In darkness will we see light, in chaos will we find purpose, in separation will we seek each other, in pain will we seek healing and in condemnation will we seek grace.

Conflict is bound by law and your disillusional belief system cannot help you to escape God's still small voice. You can live in denial, you can live in blame, you can live within self-justification, but you cannot hide from God's voice. In condemnation you bear upon yourself as you come face to face with God's law. Suffering is intensified when we do not seek to instill God's whisper of healing.

It is only within God's law that we can be released. Under God's law will the fabric of creation be returned. In time will we face again those beliefs that separated us. Under God's law will we be tested again and again until that part of us that set us apart is healed. Suffering upon suffering if we so desire, but eventually will we learn from our mistakes. In time, our ego will have no claim on us because our desire for God will bind us to Him as He is to us.

Suffering is not bound just to this life. In death are we released to review our choices. To feel the impact that we had on others. Every thought, every act and every feeling that was ours to share will be realized again. What we freely gave will be returned tenfold. In death will we be set free or imprisoned by the beliefs that encaged us.

Except if a man be born again he can in no way inherit the Kingdom of Heaven.[72]

In life, do we not learn and grow from our choices? Life brings about a transformation by allowing us to remold the fabric of God. We become transformed into the image of Christ as we allow the Law of God to prove us in His Truth and innocence. We are healed in righteousness as we allow the Law of God to operate in our relationships and in our communities.

---

72 Similar to John 3:3-6. The meaning of born again in this passage I believe refers to the rebirth of innocence. My own reflection on this passage is that the Kingdom of Heaven should be thought of as "our created condition" and to inherit as a birthright. The meaning of the passage is that to rightfully claim our inherited condition of the Kingdom of Heaven, one must be born again into innocence or be restored to innocence—the baptism of innocence. The Kingdom of Heaven is both a state of being and a place; however one cannot enter the Kingdom of Heaven unless the desire for innocence takes root.

Each one of us has an impact on the other. Our communities have an impact on our society, our society in turn has an impact on our government and our government in turn has an impact on our world. Our collective voice has a global impact. When our collective voice breaks the Law of God, the collective body will suffer. Your voice has a global impact on the family of God. We learn together, we grow together, together are we called to heal each other and together will the Truth of God be revealed.

Who will answer, "Here Lord, send me."? Who would choose to come from heaven to help others find their way back to God? Who would accept the call to be an instrument of global peace? Who would accept the call of creation to help those who are lost or are suffering? Who would teach the power of love by living love's example so that others might know that the source of love comes from God?

Herein are we all called back to God. To end suffering by restoring Truth. Restoring Truth by living righteousness and extending the innocence that God sees in us. By us will the world be changed, for in us is the will of God. In us will God find a home and as heaven is restored in us, so will heaven find a home on earth.

With what have we sacrificed if, in our sacrifice, we have shared ourselves with one another? If in sacrifice we have served, is not our service fulfilling the purpose of creation? To serve is to add value. When we add value, we prove ourselves within the identity that gives life purpose. Our sacrifice is made sacred when we give of ourselves freely. When we freely give, we freely receive. What we freely give will be returned tenfold. It is the unconditional bond of love that we seek. That is the treasure that God offers. To love and be loved. The desire to belong is magnified when our belonging is made holy. As holiness is restored, our belonging is made whole.

Your service of love is the process of atonement, the process of at-one-ment. When we are in service of one to another we are in the service of our God. It is in service that the act of God is made real in you. As God acts in you—as you take on the will of God, which is your true will—that act becomes your atonement. In service we make our relationships holy once again. In service is our love for one another realized. In service, suffering dissipates as conflict gives its way back to our natural desire to love. Our service is our natural desire for in service is our love made real.

> *God's peace is caught in an instant by the grandeur of the soothing waves upon the shoreline. Where the land and the sea meet, each gives way to the other. The ocean shapes the land and the land creates movement in the ocean. The grandeur of God is captured in the moment of each on the other. When the ocean gives way to the rocks, the waves become crushed. The rocks appear impermeable to the ocean, yet in time the rocks will give way to the waves. The rocks become reshaped into sand and the shoreline, over time, is recreated. God acts upon our lives. Shape does not matter to God, yet in the process will God's grandeur recreate our lives.*

From a distance, do we not see the beauty of heaven acting upon the shoreline of our lives? As we give ourselves back to God, we in turn become a part of God's work reshaping the lives of others. Only from a distance do we see how we are changed. As turmoil sets in to our lives, as the storm blackens our day, as the wind drives hard the waves on our lives do we not see the impact of God upon the rocks? Herein are the two made one, for this life embodies our spirit, the spirit acts upon the body and in turn the acts of our lives defines the "who I am". It is the process of one upon the other that defines the shoreline; it redefines the "who we are". The rock is the hardness of our beliefs against the Truth of God and the ocean is the Truth of God beating upon the rock. The shoreline is the identity that can be seen by God and by others. When the rock finally gives way to the ocean, when our lives become like the grains of sand, then the Truth will move through us. The water then moves through our lives and we flow easily with the water. When we move freely with the ocean, we become one with the ocean. Our shoreline like the beach is defined easily by the waves of the ocean. As God moves, we move with Him, for there is no resistance in us to His good spirit.

Where we see suffering, God is at work moving in us so that Truth may release us from suffering. God works the process and our love beats upon our beliefs to free us from suffering. As we seek to serve, we in turn have an impact upon the shoreline of others. Together we become the grains of sand that will define the shoreline of our families, our communities, of our society and our governments. By our response to God, will God's peace find a home on earth. Together we can end suffering.

Listen closely to your heart. It speaks of that which you would desire for yourself. What you desire for yourself is given freely to others. The temple which houses your true identity is found deep within your heart. It is protected by God and therefore is kept holy in Him. By allowing your true identity to be seen by the world, the "who you are" as you have defined yourself will be transformed and sanctified in God. We endure upon the spirit and the spirit is illuminated through God's stillness residing within us. We become brighter, shining forth the light of God whose Spirit rests in the heart of all those who choose to love.

The heart radiates as we hope to touch lives. As we touch another life, suffering dissipates from our own. No longer are we turned inward by our ego and wantonness. In God we seek to serve; the heart radiates to connect, to touch, to bind us together. Our hopes are fulfilled in one another. Our true identity as God created is made real by those relationships which are whole, set in holiness. When we stand together in holiness, suffering will not set us apart. Our endurance binds us together as the Kingdom of God is restored.

Source: Book of Truth

The Kingdom

——————— 1 The Kingdom of God ———————

Seek ye first the Kingdom of God and His righteousness. For in God's Kingdom rests righteousness—right relationships. In God's Kingdom relationships are not strained by wantonness, but are kept holy by our desire of love for each other. Relationships are kept whole because the Law of One is kept sacred. Wholeness is expressed by the desire to live one's life as a part of God's creation. The purpose of life is to create, to bring new meaning to the self and to add value to others. We add value by restoring wholeness to others and helping others to end wantonness. When heaven finds a home in you, you will begin to fulfill your purpose that God created in you. As you seek the Kingdom of God you will find meaning in life.

> *The Kingdom of God is awakened when I become aware as to how God's eternal Truth operates within me. All that is love, generosity, kindness, devotion, that which is unseen but gives life its highest beauty and joy, with the sense of childhood, can exist within me. For I find peace when I end the senseless destruction caused by those beliefs that place my ability to love at risk.*

> *When I seek the Kingdom of God, God is made real in me; love is made real in me. Truth lights the way. We begin to see as God sees. For God looks into me and sees a piece of Himself. He sees me as I am—all my hopes,*

*my dreams and my desires. He sees the best of me, He
sees the worst and still He loves me. He sees who I am
and who I hope to be. God sees the war between my
fears, my beliefs, my wantonness and the Truth which
holds my life together. Only in my true identity which
rests at His altar can I end the emptiness and the guilt
that would hide me from Him. For it is only in my true
identity that I become illuminated with His goodness
and my desire for others is made whole.*

The disciples came to Jesus asking, "Who is the greatest in the
Kingdom of God?" And Jesus called a little child to him and set
him in the midst of them and said, "Verily I say unto you, except
ye become as little children ye shall not enter into the Kingdom
of Heaven. Whosoever therefore shall humble himself as this little
child the same is the greatest in the Kingdom of Heaven."[73]

The Kingdom of Heaven is not meat and drink, but it is the
living of the Word in both thought and deed. The Kingdom of
Heaven is likened unto a child whose heart is set in innocence. For
the Kingdom of Heaven to find a home in you, you must seek to
find innocence in others. For as you find innocence in others, you
find innocence in yourself. As you find innocence, you let go of
judgment—condemnation. When innocence is seen, you will see
past the images of the ego to find the heart of the soul which rests
in God.

In God you will find pure light. As you seek to find heaven in
you, you will seek to bring light into that part of you which you hid
in darkness. That part of you which you hid from God was set in
fear. The light that you desire sets in motion the hope that brings
wholeness and Truth.

Shine into God who would look upon your heart as a child who
would hold out her arms for love. A child knows not the brokenness
that would keep you from her, but she feels the pain. However, the
child knows that the love that she has to offer will sustain you until
your heart is healed.

---

73   Similar to Matthew 18:1-4.

Shine into God who would look upon your thoughts as a child who would ask you to hold him. No questions asked as to why or how come. Even as a child who would only ask for acceptance, God asks you to accept Him. His voice calls to you in love and without judgment.

When the spirit is broken, the body cries out. The body cries out by the visible expression of the fear which entraps the soul, seemingly sealed to a heart and mind that not even God can enter into. To heal the spirit, the embodiment of those illusions that hold your beliefs, the heart and mind must be broken.

When the body is broken, the spirit cries out. The pain of another can be heard even in the silence of the broken body. When others respond, our spirits connect. Fear dissipates into compassion when all judgments that were set in condemnation fade away. When the desire for love and healing extends outwards to connect our spirits, the fabric of God is mended.

Begin this day, this moment, with the peace that cultivates stillness. Find the Kingdom of Heaven so that others might see the flame of God in you. The flame in its stillness radiates light and warmth. The light breaks the darkness and glows upon the faces of all those that look towards the flame. The warmth soothes the soul as it penetrates the eyes that it touches. Each life that lives the stillness that is offered by the healing heart extends both light and warmth. Each hand that reaches out, each vision which connects, each act which embraces and holds the world with tenderness instills the peace that we all desire.

We share heaven. Heaven brings to us the perfect knowledge of the Truth that reestablishes our innocence and makes real the desire for unconditional love. When you look into the eyes of a newborn, the child shares with you a piece of heaven. The newborn child is set in innocence and only knows how to share love. Their love is pure because you have a perfect knowledge of their innocence. This little one is pure and without sin. He that is pure is whole in God and he who is whole in God is found in heaven where God is. A child who is pure is whole in God brings God with them, even into a world where God has been forgotten.

The Kingdom of Heaven is pure light, where the desire for darkness has faded away. The darkness has no claim, for as the light in us grows brighter, Truth vibrates and radiates until the darkness is no more. As the light intensifies, our hearts begin to beat as one. The Law of One begins to beat again. Truth is restored.

In God's judgment, will you be set free. In God's judgment, will you be sanctified and purified. The light will be made pure in you. Truth will be remembered and heaven will find a home.

Source: Book of Truth

———— 2 Innocence Restored ————

We are called to be transformed into the image of Jesus Christ. His image is your image. It is the image that you desire, for it is this image that will set you free. What bound you once by judgment, will be set free by the image of Jesus Christ that is in you. God's law breaks judgment, for judgment has no meaning in the Kingdom of Heaven—condemnation has no place in the Kingdom of Heaven. The image that you desire is the image which is free of judgment, free of condemnation.

What good can come from condemnation? If God decreed condemnation, wherein could your hope be restored? If God's law bound God to decree condemnation on His creation, how could God free Himself from that law to save you?

Chaos has no claim on God and the insanity that would bind God to judge condemnation is not real. Yet will the image of the cross that Jesus freely walked with the Father set you free. As you begin to see God's law, you will come to understand that it is judgment itself that binds us all to the cross.

Abolish judgment, abolish condemnation and sin will have no claim. As life is restored, death becomes the illusion. As Christ is resurrected into the heart of man, life is restored. As Jesus was resurrected, the world came to know that death has no claim on life. Our life is restored when we face the cross that we bound ourselves to by the judgment that required payment. Restitution is finally met when judgment itself dies on the cross.

The resurrection of Jesus is the same resurrection of the self as the self emerges from the desire to judge. Life is restored as the self sees innocence in what God wills. Pure light will permeate from within as the desire of God sets you free.

Living for each other brings true meaning to the self. The images of wantonness become but shadows of our distant past as the self finds meaning in the creation that God wills. When the desire to be a part of each other has equal meaning within the self, the Law of One begins to beat again. No longer do we see ourselves as separate, rather we see ourselves as one being created from the one Spirit that is in each of us. Our lives remold the fabric of God when we see in others what God sees in us—innocence.

We are set free. In innocence are we set free. In judgment do we risk condemnation, yet in innocence will judgment have no claim. If in Jesus Christ you are baptized, if in Christ you are willing to take upon yourself His name, walking in His stead, are you now not innocent? If Christ is to abide in you, would not His innocence also abide in you? Seek innocence and you will find the Christ. For if we seek innocence will we look to condemn? Does not your faith in Jesus teach you to forgive and that in Christ you are forgiven? If Christ condemns not, what then stands between you and the innocence that your Father created you in?

Here then is innocence restored, when judgment has no claim on sin. When the desire for judgment placed upon sin serves no purpose, the Law of God is restored. That which tore us apart and separated us from God is forgotten in judgment. Judgment which is forgotten, the willingness to forgive and let go, is God's judgment for innocence. In this judgment are we set free. In this judgment are we bound to God, for we uphold the law that binds God's Kingdom in wholeness. As the Law of God is kept, we become bound to one another in innocence.

Will then for God. Will for innocence, for judgment against innocence is judgment against God.

If you will condemnation, you will find chaos. Look carefully, for the Law of God stops here! It is here that the Law of God becomes fragmented. He who judges condemnation, takes upon himself condemnation and heaven will dissipate from his vision. *Correct it quickly, for this vision of heaven is easily lost once judgment sets in.*

He who seeks God's image, in the image that rests in God, will God set free. For in God there is no judgment, and in Christ there is no condemnation. With God, with Christ, are we transformed.

Blessed are the pure in heart for they shall see God.[74]

It is our desire for God that saves us from that part of the self which would hide in darkness. In Christ we are born again, restored in innocence, set free from both sin and judgment and are made real in the resurrection that restores life.

Source: Book of Law

3 Grace

Grace is the eternal stay of judgment, for God does not condemn, and in His grace is life restored.

Wherein are you saved? Can heaven be infused into your being if you choose not to will for heaven? Only when we choose for heaven is heaven restored. For it is not by grace that you are saved, nor by faith, nor by works; rather, it is the act of grace which saves, it is the act of faith which restores, and it is the desire to serve that brings the value of works to life. For he who condemns not extends that act of grace, and he who places faith in his brother and sister restores the bond that God created and he who desires to serve fulfills the purpose for which brings meaning to creation.

What then is salvation? Salvation is the fullness of love. Salvation is the sharing of oneself with each one that God has created. Salvation brings the awareness of God back to God's creation in the life and the beauty that God created. For it is in the laughter, the love and the value of life, that heaven is found.

74   Matthew 5:8

Salvation comes when heaven has a home in you.

The Kingdom of Heaven is not the avoidance of sin.[75] The Kingdom is not the avoidance of or the obedience to, rather the fulfillment in the observance to God's law. For we are free to be as we will, but our desires are pure. The Kingdom of Heaven is the desire for God, the desire for life and for love. One who upholds life and upholds love in all relationships has fulfilled the desire of God and the Kingdom of Heaven dwells within. Together we restore what God created and together we restore what God would will.

Who then are the elect? Are we not all created in God's image, out of the one Spirit that is the source of life itself? Think not that the elect excludes salvation to the few. Rather, the elect are those who have chosen to return from heaven to restore heaven within those that have lost their ability to find God. Some walk quietly among the children of men and others walk boldly upon the rocks of life, willing to risk life to save life. All are God's creation, and God calls us all back to Him. But His elect carry the shield of God and the flame of love. His elect carry forward the sacred songs and hold high the flame of life so that those who have forgotten God may hear the still small voice that echoes the vision of salvation.

For why else would God have created man and the earth that beckons man back to God? For why else would God have created time? For within the pattern of creation was free will given. Yet within free will, innocence was lost and suffering ensued. He who willed for selfishness became lost from God and knew not how to return.

Here then is God made real. Here then is where our innocence is restored. For by this life will we prove ourselves in His image. To be pure in heart is to be true to oneself. When we are true to our self, we are true to God. God is seen in us and those who see us, see God. The desire for God is extended when others see the life that radiates within you.

Grace is the eternal stay of judgment, and he who desires

---

75   This statement required some exploration, so please see page Part III
       The God Process: Commentary Notes on The Message.

innocence will find grace. For rain falls from the heavens and refreshes the earth. The source of the rain is the ocean. The ocean gives to the heavens to rain onto the land. Yet will the rain return by the rivers to the ocean from where it came. The earth bears testament to the cycle of life. By grace is life restored. The fabric of life is given back so that we might try again.

Yet in death are we separated. For some the celestial light, for others the terrestrial light, for many the telestial light and to others only shadows of light.[76] For the soul illuminates the light of God insomuch as the light of God resides within the soul. For the purity of God shines forth in those where innocence has endured. For the pure in heart shall see God and abide with God in the celestial kingdom. But in those where the law remains fragmented is grace, God's hope. Think not that a lessor glory is condemnation—rather, it is God's grace working its way back into the heart of creation.

In death, the garment of our soul is seen—the veil is lifted from our eyes to see the glory that we have endured. The glory is the light of God that dwells within. He who has eyes to see will see the glory that exceeds his own. To behold God's glory requires a desire for God. For it is the desire for God that illuminates the soul. He who desires God abides with God, and God's law begins to work with him as the Law of One brings healing to the heart, mind and soul where God must dwell.

Light magnifies that part of the soul where love has found a home. Light magnifies that part of the soul where innocence has been restored. Being born of God, we return to God what God has given. For oneness brings about healing and maintaining the Law of One in free will binds us to God.

Think not that separation is condemnation. For the separation of souls in the eternal dimension is necessary so that one can accept one's self in that realm which they have endured. In death we receive the glory that we have endured, for spiritual endurance shines forth according to God's law. For the self cannot be divided

---

76 See 1st Corinthians chapter 15 which provides some insight as it relates to the destiny of souls—the division of souls—when we cross back over into the ethereal reality.

and in death the self must abide within God's Kingdom according to the glory that abides within them according to the Truth that is found in the heart, the mind and the soul. We cannot turn away from what we have freely willed, so it is that the glory that abides in us is a reflection of what we have created in the presence of God's Kingdom.

Is this not the grace that you would want—the grace, which testifies to God's patience? Would you not want the grace that gives you the free will to choose again, so that you might prove yourself in God's image? For without grace, your hope would be lost—condemned to the darkness that you willed for yourself. In grace will you be restored—through life, will life be restored—born again.[77] To choose again until the sin that separated us loses its appeal. For sin will tarnish the soul, and the soul will see the gloomy luster in the mirror, the rust that eats at the heart and the mind and the body. For sin consumes and elation cannot hide what the self must see.

The mirror of our actions becomes the reflection of our heart.

---

[77] In this instance, the statement "we are born again" points towards reincarnation. It is the directional process in soul development to choose to be born again, to plan the next incarnation, so that one can again test oneself against the fire of the flesh. To place "self" and "soul" in contest to choice. To place in contest the voice of our ego against the silence of our soul to find our willingness to embody the essence of God.

Reincarnation becomes a more prevalent theme again in the cosmic story in soul development. Our need or want to test ourselves again in life (this life) or to come back and make good on "karma" as in "soul debt" is essential to the soul for soul development. It is not enough for the soul to want to be; rather, the soul has to be strengthened, infused with God's light or God's love for the process to take root. The creative process for soul development requires choice in free will to want God in mind, body and heart in order for God's essence to take root in the soul. This is the process of Spiritual Endurance. See Journey of the Soul, Section 6 Spiritual Endurance.

Reincarnation is a theme that is not yet accepted by mainstream Christian doctrinal covenants. Yet we do find it in scripture. In scripture we have Jesus pointing towards John the Baptist as the reincarnation of Elijah or Elias (Matthew 17:9-13).

Our actions take on the image of the glory that abides in us. In our choice, will we see. Beyond the darkness exists the light of God. Deep within our soul, the glory of God shines forth. What we bear in God's glory will be born in our actions when our heart is bound towards grace. In our desire for grace, can the heart recreate our will. For God glorifies the heart that has overcome that part of the self that was hidden in darkness.

The Law of One binds us to oneness. Grace for all and glory for God. From glory will God shine into creation—we become one with Him for He shines in us.

Source: Book of Law

— 4 The Law of One Binds the Kingdom of God —

The Law of One brings together the people of God. God's law binds the Kingdom of Heaven out of free will. Each desiring to fulfill God's purpose in creation by extending love, peace and harmony to each other. It is a law that needs no other law. It is a law which is fulfilled in the binding of the self to the Kingdom where hearts beat as one, as God willed. This is the Kingdom which is undivided. Each one's desire beats for the other. Each retains their own identity, yet each identity reflects the image of God.

Of such are the children of God. The Law of One expands from within, having overcome the split created by duality we end elation[78] and give ourselves back to creation. As each one overcomes, will each one remember. From the deepest part of the inner self will the Law of One emerge. In remembrance of our God, will it come. From heaven to the earth. From the breath of each soul, to the voice of God's people. Calling forth the Kingdom of God, will it come.

---

78   This reference refers to the swing of the pendulum from self-glorification to the other end of the spectrum of despair when failure leads to a sense of having no value. I do not believe the intent of the passage is to stifle emotions such as feelings of joy or pride, but rather to recognize that we bring an end to seeking attention for the purpose of promoting one's own self.

Each heart will be pierced. Each thought will be purified. Each act will testify of His presence. The Law of One is the Law of God. In the beginning, was it written, and in the end will it be restored. Retained by God in and through God's children. In God's children, will the law be retained. Harmony will resonate at the heart of the Kingdom, where freedom abounds in the Law of God, breaks the chains that linked order to chaos.

Order has no meaning as chaos fades away as a distant memory.[79] The community of God's children has no need of order, for order co-exists with disorder and disorder is a fragmented state of being. Just as one draws closer to the source of light, the state of darkness dissipates. So it is as the Law of One resonates harmony within community—laws that maintain order have no meaning as chaos fades away. It is our perception of reality which changes. No longer do we shift in judgment; rather our reality is focused on the wholeness that allows for growth in an identity that adds value but retains God's image.

Each will seek to add value in an identity which defines the "who I am", yet that identity is maintained in innocence. Our will is set within our individuality, yet that will strives to add value to God's creation, to the community of the children of God. In turn, the community seeks to promote each individual. Each seeks for the other, yet none are lost to the self. Harmony is retained for none is for want, and want is filled by the mutual giving to each other's needs.

Our homes are built by each other for the joy of giving back what has already been given. Our homes are filled with memories and resonate with a decor that promotes the peace that is in our hearts. Our homes reflect the solitude of our individuality, yet the door is open to the neighbor that walks by. Our homes are shared in families as God gives to each one as brother and sister, as parent and child. From the immediate family to the extended family. We learn from one another, yet the fabric of God is retained in

---

79   The word "order" is in reference to laws, authoritative direction, stringent rules, mandates or commands. As chaos fades away there, life is lived according to the good spirit that is within us. Harmony abides.

harmony. Peace becomes our home. Love becomes our altar. Strength flows from the source of life, which is the light of God.

We are of God, living in a community filled by the friendship of each other. Here lies our bond of one—our soul friendship. Born out of the one spirit of our Creator, we return in the spirit of one forming our soul friendship. As with God, our friendship is bonded by divine love. A love bonded by the knowing that we are of the same soul spirit desiring what God desires for all of His creation. He is our God, and we are His children. We are brothers and sisters in creation bonded by our soul friendship.

We are the keepers of each other's soul. From one to the other. From the soul of one to the soul of the other. We must bear testament in promise to the keeping of each other's soul so that friendship might abound.

In friendship is each soul kept sacred. In soul friendship are we all family—brother and sister, parent and child, neighbor and companion. We entrust ourselves to each other, to learn from one another, experience life one with the other, to grow, to change, to be. By each other will we be challenged, will we be encouraged, will we face our weaknesses and our strengths. In friendship will we listen, will we walk, will we stand, will we understand. From our desire for friendship will we forgive. A hundred-fold will we forget the offense, because great tragedy is found not in the mistake, but in the offense—for the mouth can be a sword, yet love is our breastplate. From our mistakes are we reminded of the frailty of the soul and the need to care for one another. The word is the law and the law retains our soul in oneness. When love abounds, holy relationships are fostered and friendships are maintained.

> And the children came and each sat on his knee. From the eyes of the Master was each child touched. From the soul of Jesus did each child see that which was pure in him, was made real in them. For he who was pure of heart was in communion with God. From the communion of God did each child see their own relationship with Christ. And Jesus said, "Suffer the little children to come unto me, and forbid them not;

for of such is the Kingdom of Heaven."[80]

From the eyes of the Master to the soul of each child—a bond of love, a bond of remembrance. Each child remembered the Kingdom of Heaven. It was there, present in them, with them. In that instant did the remembrance of God come alive. The presence of God came alive as the Master's eyes pierced their own and their souls danced with the fire of light, radiating the presence of God, which shone into them.

The reality of God was found in that which was shared between each child and the Master. A friendship bonded between the soul of each child to the soul of the Master. The Master touched each child and each child was touched by the spirit of the Master. Filled by the presence of God in the soul of each child. A connection, a remembrance, a witness to that spirit that binds us all to one another. In God is that spirit and from God are we connected—connected in soul, by friendship.

We who are born of God are bound in God. Of one heart, beating for creation so that creation might remember the Law of One. For he who is found in God, carries forth God's voice. Not a voice which speaks for obedience or submission, rather a voice that proclaims Christ in all, God within all. One spirit, which extends life to all.

Who then holds the sacred flame? If not in me, then in whom? Who Lord, will you entrust to carry forth the message of the Law of One? Choose in me a heart of love, a mind for peace and a purpose that adds value. Let me show forth your handiwork so that my life will hold high the sacred flame that you have entrusted to me. Let me not falter in my ways. Let not my heart be darkened by those choices that would set me apart. I

---

80   Mark 10:14.

trust in thee, for it is in thee that I desire to be.

The spirit of God prepares us. The inner small voice that is in all of us, links us all back to our Father in heaven. The spirit of God dwells within and we in turn recognize our oneness with God our Father. Born of God, because God can be seen in us.

> *I Am that I Am. The giver of life extends life to you, through you and into creation. My law binds the source of life to you, for in you, I am. Out of One Spirit did the I Am create, and out of the void did the I Am proclaim the Law. The Lord thy God is One. One Spirit. You were created out of my Spirit. I am in you and you are of me. My image was recreated in you.*

Still the heart and shine forth God's flame. For oneness beats in all. We all desire what God does give. Life restored in wholeness, beating for each other what God extends in His glory. For in Jesus Christ was the light of life. In Him was glory extended from the Father to touch creation so that darkness might not have claim in us. It is His light that pierces the darkness.

For the glory of God is crystallized by the interaction of the Holy Spirit upon our being. From coal to diamond. From the form of our will, to the will of our Father in Heaven. From the void of darkness into the presence of God, desiring to share God as God shared Himself with us. We emerge crystallized, transformed into His image. We the elect, choose again to walk in darkness, carrying the flame of God back into God's earth, God's creation.

Source: Book of Law

Psalms of Salvation

——————1 The Psalm of The New Day ————————

As the sun breaks the dawn of a new day, the night dissipates from the far side of the skyline. The penetrating rays of the sun pass through the skyline from the east to the west to glorify the heavens. What wonder awaits each morning? This day has potential to unfold newness of life. It reigns in stillness, yet it moves unknowingly and unexpectedly in directions that we cannot always imagine. Has God planned this day?

Would God reach in from the heavens to set in motion His will?

Perhaps. But perhaps this day He will allow His creation to set in motion a multitude of events as to His creations own choosing. If good is to come from this day, let it be from the hands of those who would act on God's behalf in testimony of our witness to Him. If good is to come from this day, let it be in the form of a gift from one life to another so that all might be blessed.

Let us not be blind to what we do. For salvation declares that God is present. Only in our awareness to Him are our eyes open to the good that stands before us. From our eyes to our heart are we challenged. From our heart to our lips are we called to speak. As we listen and respond can we be called into action. From one hand to another we are connected. Together we create.

This day sets in motion the task of salvation. To bear witness, in fullness, that the image of God rests in the bosom of my heart. His image I would claim in humility, as a servant. I would fortify my will to do only good, to seek my humanity. It is in this task that my purpose is complete.

Herein is wisdom. Seek goodness and live for that purpose. Salvation finds a home in those whose hearts are pure. Simple is life, when life is not bound to the past. When tomorrow meets today and yesterday is but a pleasant memory, the world becomes a playground of peace and joy.

God offers you this day. His salvation is like the aroma of a sea of lilies set in the meadow to a valley encased by rolling mountains where the sparkling streams flow continuously to the lakes below. In God's salvation we work and play side by side, each promoting the other to strive in creation to add value and beauty, honor and respect, honesty and integrity as we seek our individuality and identity.

Whoever welcomes the Lord will find this day complete. Today will come and today will go. Once gone it is no more, but its memory will linger. Its imprint on my soul will be forever. If I live this day with my Lord, it will be a day without regrets. Such is joy's sweetest pleasure—to look back with God and to see His handiwork in our lives. To be proud of each moment because each moment was filled with His goodness.

We, who welcome the Lord, are awakened by His quiet presence. His goodness resonates in our hearts, our eyes, our hands and our laughter. His quiet presence is seen and felt in our lives, our homes, our family and our community. As God's presence grows and expands, peace and goodness is shared by all.

Such is heaven. Such is that place we all call home and seek to return to. Such is the reality that God would will. Not lives lived in servanthood, holiness and reverence on our bended knee, but lives lived in wholeness, goodness and purpose that fills our dreams and adds value to the creation that God sets before us. It is out of that goodness that we bring perfect worship to the dance of life.

The task of salvation is our daily choice for life lived with our God. To be free in Him and by Him. To set in motion our desires and dreams which intertwines in and through His presence. It is this passion for life which is made full, for our humanity in all its wonders is not lost. The task of salvation is a call to explore ourselves, to explore the limits of our humanity. To test our compassion, our endurance, our integrity, our courage and our spirit. We are called by salvation to test our brotherhood, to enact a common creation, to bind in marriage our lives for the fulfillment of parenthood. Salvation solidifies our families and glorifies God's image into our daily passion for life.

The sun closes each day by withdrawing its light from the skyline. Peace and solitude spans the night air and with rest comes renewal. The mind is free to dream and wonder. Take heart for God works His miracle by dividing each day with the solitude of the night. For it is only in solitude that the whisper can be heard.

Pray for peace and seek God's whisper.

———— 2 The Psalm of Salvation ————

I stood in the tall grass beside an open meadow and marveled at its splendor.
The air was calm and the aroma was soothing to every breath that I took.

I sat.

I leaned back and rested my head on the ground so that I could find the sky above. So much peace, so much stillness.

I closed my eyes so that my mind could wander in the memories of joy.

My childhood filled the void. Memories of parents, family and friends. The years passed by in fragments only to stop from time to time to bring laughter, a smile and a tear.

The grass started to move and the brush of the air worked its way through my senses.

God was present.

His spirit flowed around me and filled me with wholeness. In an instant, all that I was and all that God hoped for me to be, was. I was complete, for He filled me with the desire that purifies.

The moment came and then it was gone.

Yet, its memory lingers on.

Such is eternity.

Only time intertwines its threads through the fabric.

But eternity is here.

In its solitude I can call it back and God's presence is made real again.

Who then would forsake such love once tasted? Who then would forsake eternity for the dim illusion of a world trapped in fear? Who then would forsake God's reality where divine love is forever present?

> *Only in solitude,*
> *Only in pure desire,*
> *Only in hope,*
> *Do we remember.*

A whisper from the soul. From the inner most part of me it spoke. It soothes and it beckons me to enter the world. Its message pulls me from my complacency, from the solitude of the meadow and from the four walls of my life that I know so well. I see and fear the tempest, the storm of what awaits, but I know its shadows will pass.

For God is my protector. What good could I do if in this whisper I fail? Would I learn if I feared each step that I took? And how would I grow if I didn't go? How could I help others and be God's presence if I hid in these shadows of my life? For what good is anything that I do if I cannot trust that whisper that passes through my soul?

Father in heaven, hide me no longer in silence. The world in its twists and turns matters not. My fear is but an illusion and your vision is my hope. Inspire me, my Lord, so that the vision might burn in me a desire that is forged upon iron.

Lift up my eyes so that I might see the image that you created for me. For if I seek my sacred life, that sacredness will be forged by love and I will walk with you all of my days.

I am obscured by my own short-comings. What I hope to be seems so elusive. Forgive me, my Lord, I see both my weakness and my arrogance. It causes me to turn away and yet if I hide my weakness with my arrogance, I only find that my arrogance binds me further to my weakness. For I fear the whisper that could expose my vulnerability. How can I face what I myself am ashamed of? What good can come from this shame once exposed?

Help me to face my shame and to humble my arrogance. Give me courage to accept both my weakness and my strength. Encourage me to call to others who are willing and able to teach me what I need to know. Encourage me to stand boldly with honesty and truth to find the path past shame to the path which leads to honor.

Truly you will stand beside me my Lord. Surely you will grant me the words that I will say and give me the courage to hold my head high as I bow myself before my shame. May those that I face be filled with mercy and compassion so that they might accept me for who I am. Compel me to accept whatever fate should await. It is but a passing minute in the one hour of my eternity.

——————————3 A Psalm for Life——————————

Begin again, the day anew.
Reach in and touch the earth below.
Stir in the ground the life that lies within.
Bring forth her beauty for all to see.

May I take in the breath of her fragrance,
To be still and yet awaken.
For creation speaks to my soul,
The presence of my God.

Walk with me,
Begin my day with passion,
Set my heart on fire to fulfill my life's purpose,
To begin anew, the dance to make.

Lord, allow me to be,
Satisfied, yet not complacent.
For salvation is the sharing of myself,
The giving of my soul.

Allow me to be,
me.

From the dawn of creation through the days of my life
Allow the spectrum to unfolded.
For your creation has expanded the Universe
and I join with others to add meaning before my God.

Together, the creative process has allowed us to mold even

ourselves.
For God did not limit us in the image of self.
God painted the sky and filled the earth,
and He gave us the freedom of self to create,
to hold as we willed and designed.

How marvelous, how wondrous is the very gift of life,
to know that all the dreams and visions
can be realized and experienced.

Still, nothing has changed.
The same creation stands before us.
Our visions and our dreams, our hopes and our desires still stand
before us.

Never ending and beckoning us to start again.
Yet, no longer do we want the wantonness.
No longer do we place our hands and arms and claim
our wantonness.
We open our lives and give of ourselves in wantingness.
We help each other to live the dreams and build new realities
in wantingness.

God's creation has been glorified,
Illuminated in wantingness, to expand the presence of God.

We become more than what we could ever dream to be,
because we are filled with the very presence of God.
God's presence expands us into a new reality.
Where life is intensified,
Where life resonates and vibrates and our boundaries
blend together.
We expand our spirit, our beingness.
The light that is in us glows and radiates outwards.

Our lives blend into the lives of those around us,

We experience the presence of each other in ourselves.
We resonate and illuminate life.
We sense the reality of heaven on earth.

For the light of our salvation can be seen.

It is the light of God's presence which can be felt.
Salvation comes.
It comes each day, each hour and in each moment it comes.
It comes when we cleanse the Earth.
It comes when we live our lives filled with promise, hope, peace and justice.
It comes in the innocence of life.
It comes from the whisper of our soul.
It comes by the gift of God.

Part III
THE GOD
PROCESS

1 Passion is the Path to the Soul

Are there moments in your life, where reality seems to converge with this ethereal dimension—this mystical spiritual world, which we cannot see or touch?

I was taking a trip through British Columbia not long ago and the traffic was stopped on the highway, because a semi-truck had caught on fire. We were stopped for a couple of hours and so people would get out and chat. I had a conversation with a truck driver and the topic came up about how our lives were both impacted by cancer. This truck driver was telling me that his parents split up when he was young and that he grew up with his mother and step-father. He didn't have a lot of time with his biological father in his younger years; however, when he was nineteen his father came down with cancer and he became the caregiver. He lived with his father for the six months and watched death take him.

About ten years later, after this truck driver got married and started a family, he was putting his two year old daughter to bed. When he pulled out a bedtime story to read to her, she said,

"Grandpa isn't your real dad, is he?"

Somewhat surprised with the question he replied, "Well no."

"What happened to your dad?" the daughter asked.

He thought a moment, then said, "Sometimes people get sick and do not get better. Your other grandpa, my dad, got sick. He got so sick that he went to heaven."

"Oh." The two year old paused, "Well he hurt here (hip), here (stomach) and here (head), but he is all better now!"

Sometimes we are given these mystical gifts to remind us that there is more to life than just this life. It tells us that our loved ones, which have passed on before us, live on in another dimension.

So, do you believe in God? Do you believe in miracles? Do you believe that every so often that God steps into your life to remind you that He is there, and that everything is going to be okay? Do you believe that your life has purpose and that through your choices, you can connect with God? More importantly, do you believe that God offers you healing and wholeness that comes from looking to Him and accepting this divine, intangible, surreal love? Do you believe that there is more to gain by having a faith, a trusting in this God, that you cannot see, then not having this faith or belief?

I often think about my life and the moments in my life where the surreal seems to converge with *my* reality. I think about the events of my life that took me to a place where I first would write *The Message,* and then gave me the courage to publish this.

My God Process brought me to a point in my life where I was compelled to write and share my soul. It caused me to look back on my life to connect the dots. It caused me to stop, look back, look in and look up. My life is no different then anyone else's life. Perhaps being a conduit to *The Message* is extraordinary, however I had to explore God like everyone else, which is through faith and life's experiences. Perhaps my story is not unlike your story, because life is usually quite ordinary—yet every so often we have these extraordinary events, and it is in those events that we see God at work.

The Message was written because God infused this passion in my soul. If you stop and consider what drives your life, it is passion. Your dreams are your passion, your beliefs are your passion, your hopes, and your want for something—money, status, power, companionship, forgiveness, or acceptance—whatever is rooted inside of you and moves you forward, is your passion. For twelve years I was consumed by what became *The Message.* And then I had my fill. I wanted to shut it off. Walk away. Turn my back. And so I did. I put it on the shelf and there it stayed.

The Message to me was extraordinary, yet at the time, when I was writing *The Message,* it did not always feel like it was extraordinary. When I began to put on paper the thoughts and images that came to my mind, my recollection was only one of focus—to write one page at a time. When I was writing, the words would flow onto the paper and then it would stop. It sometimes would be weeks before I would be woken up, and again, compelled to continue. *The Message* would always pick up from where it left off, and I would write a couple of more pages.

I did not always know what the next sentence was, or what the next paragraph would say. Sometimes, it was not until after I had written the passage that I would reread it and realize, or understand, the continuity. To you, the reader, that might seem somewhat odd—how could the person that is writing, not know what he is going to write? The mind is a curious thing; however, the soul is even more curious. I yield to faith and just accept that God has a purpose. At times, I was overwhelmed with what was written, and yet I felt totally at peace. I did not always know where *The Message* was going to take me, but I was curious. Although *The Message* was one continuous document, it came in the form of three books, *Book of Truth*, *Book of Law* and *Book of Life*, which constitutes the 194 pages of text.[81] When it came time to write *The God Process*, I reorganized and restructured *The Message* into a format that I felt would be an easier read.

When I decided to stop and put it up on the shelf, it all stopped. My life went on and *The Message* stayed on the shelf. The dark side of this story is that my belief, in this message that God gave to me, faded. As my life went on my own inner world became a rollercoaster, with both success and a lot of stress as I became consumed with corporate life. I became a Vice President and then an Executive Vice President of a Junior Oil and Gas Company, which became a 24/7 occupation.

From time to time, I attempted to pick up the pencil to see if

---

81   The problem with making this statement is one of sounding audacious. I was not sure if it adds to or takes away from The Message. I decided that it was better to be open about the name of the source of The Message, then to make these statements after the book was published. I talk about this more in the next chapter, The God of Reincarnation.

God was still there, and to see if He had something more to say, but nothing. If there was more to *The Message*, it was not something that I could will or make happen—the curtain was closed. I did write a few poems which I called Psalms of Salvation. Unlike *The Message*, which I was compelled to write, these poems were just poems. There was one exception, because one morning I was compelled to write. I was given a glimpse of light, a spark to another message. It was to be called the Book of Light. I wrote five pages and then I stopped—*I stopped it*, because I didn't want to do it again. I put the pencil down and that was it. No more messages. I did not attempt to allow the process to happen again.

When I was compelled to write *The God Process* it was electric—I knew it was time to take *The Message* off the shelf. There was this darkness in my life, and in my world, and it woke me up. The promptings from my soul in the last eight months have been focused solely on telling my story, my God Process and publishing *The Message*.

Writing *The Message*, I believe, was one of my life purposes, as God willed. In life, we are driven to do what we are called to do. What I have learned is that it is not our passion that drives the soul, but rather it is our soul that drives our passion—if we allow it. When we listen to our soul, we become more alive. Our God Process is about allowing God in and choosing to become inspired by that creative purpose that brings life into life. Our soul knows—it drives "the bus", so to speak, as to where your life will take you, and hopefully God will be there, along with others, who will help you along the way.

Having said all this, there was no divine intervention, that I am consciously aware of, that would tell me what to write. I do not think *The Message* was dictated to me by some heavenly messenger. With every fiber of my being, I honestly and whole heartedly believe, and know within myself, that what I wrote did come from *my* soul. I trust my soul, and *my* certainty, is *my* certainty as to source of *The Message*. I trust that my soul is connected with God, and for me, *The Message* is consistent with the message for Christ—for he is there present in our soul through the Holy Spirit.

God takes you on this awakening to the mystery, but once you enter this God domain, it can be scary. What we think He asks of us is sometimes scary. Exposing my life to share, write and publish this book was scary. What does one do with a message that will potentially be viewed as so audacious that it makes you a target? Faith is sacred, powerful and perhaps it is something that you do not mess with. You don't mess with faith because your journey with God may not be seen as a journey with God by others. I wonder if *my God Process* is sufficient.

The purpose of writing Part III of this book is to help bring some closure to *The Message* and to relate *The Message* to the *God Process* journey that we all are on. Over the years, as I have read and reflected on *The Message*, it has caused me to look back, look in, and look up.

You might find this odd, but I too have to go back and reread *The Message* to remember what is in *The Message*. As I worked on this book, I quickly became tuned in, and at times I felt like I could remember almost more to *The Message* than what was written in *The Message*. It was like a curtain that I could draw back, but once I stopped, the curtain closed. When I wrote, there was certainty in my own being as to what I was writing. When I put the pen down, I had self-doubts and I found myself reading and studying both scripture and books on *life after life*, *life between life* and *past life regression* to try and find collaboration with what my soul seems to know.

There is mystery to the divine—to the ethereal spirit world. There are some things that maybe we are just not meant to know. Yet, this mystery, this hidden universal truth is easily recognizable when we see it. This mystery captures our imagination—our soul, and for some it becomes our faith and our religion.

God and religion sometimes just do not seem to mix. Faith and beliefs across our globe can be so vastly different to the point that it divides our humanity and it makes one wonder, how it is that the Creator could be represented in all of them. If beliefs were so important to our soul destiny why would God leave His Truth to chance? Why would God leave our souls to chance, to be manipulated by influence or by the dark side of our religions? Why not just give us a playbook right up front at the start of creation? Yet, as I ask these questions, I think most of us know the answers.

I think part of God's design is in the mystery. We have to want to discover God. We have to want to seek the reality of God, that exists in God. It has to be done in free will. The truth is, we don't live our lives thinking about God or the afterlife all the time. If we did, we would not have a productive and purposeful life. The treasure of life is in the mystery; it is in the path or the journey of discovery. The richness of life comes from learning who we are and how we can or should connect ourselves to the divine.

For example, learning of and relating to "power" is a treasure that the soul seeks. Knowledge is power, money is power and having a position of influence is power. Simply being a mother, a father, or an older brother or sister can give us power. The divine has granted each of us power—tools of influence. How we use these tools that we have been entrusted with will determine if the soul can master the use of power in relation to self-discipline. The use of power in this life becomes the cosmic classroom for the soul. In some respects, it seems harsh that we are subjected to someone else's classroom lesson, but the reality is we all agreed to be participants. The God lesson requires free will and this mystery of not knowing is part of the test.

I think in life most of us are not concerned with the grand scheme of things. The global human cosmic story will unfold as it should. The real mystery of the divine is that I believe that God is actively engaged in all of our lives. God works with us and is engaged in all our lives. This *God Process* is one of love and compassion. It is we who create the pain and suffering. We create it by the misuse of power and the inflicting of our influence for exclusivity and privilege. We misuse money, we misuse our possessions, we misuse our positions of influence and there is a danger when we do that.

The *God Process* points us in the direction to discover what we painfully hide. When we connect the dots, when we look back, look in, and look up, we can discover the hidden gems that God is offering. If you look for events in your own life, you will discover your God lessons. The God lessons tell you that God is there. God lessons can sometimes bring you to your knees, but not always. God isn't trying to bring you to your knees. When we plan our lives, we plan it with God, with the hope that we can overcome obstacles and find healing for our soul. To love again as God intended—that is the real gem. Love *is* the infusion of God and God's light.

When you find God you will find that your own mystery will start to unfold. As you realize your God Process, the choices that you make in life will connect you to God and you will find your own extraordinary events that tell you that God is there.

The purpose of *The Message* is to help us break the condition of the "self" and to help us reconnect with our soul by bringing to our awareness that God is with us, beside us, inside each of us and that He has a plan. That God is actively engaged in our life and in all of His creation. That collectively we are not left to wander on some cosmic road which is random, unpredictable, cold and foreboding; rather, God is at work and is engaged in His miracle of salvation for all of us. And even though we do have free choice, God does send a little light our way and every so often He gives us little miracles to tell us that it is going to be okay.

From my perspective, *The Message* can only change our perception of reality. It gives us cause to consider our eternal self and this ethereal reality that exists beyond this earthly realm. **The Message wakes us up to the nothingness that sometimes we can be about. It is our wantonness of this "nothingness" that has to change. When we see this "nothingness" we become aware of what has true value to our soul and we awaken to a new day, a new beginning.** Yet, regardless of whether or not *The Message* has an impact on our choices, our lives will go on. In the end *The Message* is just words and this is just a book.

Words have both the potential to heal and to destroy. Words can either inspire or they can become a sword to pierce the soul. Words can bring people together or cause nations to divide. Words can either add meaning to life, or rob us of life. What we take to heart, regardless of whether we accept or reject the message of words, can change us. The judgment of what is good or what is bad is in the impact that words will have on our life. The power is in each of us to choose the good that comes from words.

At some point in time you will put this book down and you will go on with your life. You will live your life and you will live your dreams. You are supposed to live life, to dream dreams, create and explore life's wonders. You are supposed to live your potential and become more than what you already are. You are supposed to love and be loved. What I hope changes is that together we will have a shift in our collective consciousness. I hope that what we value changes. I hope our desire for peace and a sustainable earth is magnified and then realized.

By becoming aware of the condition of "self" we have that hope that we can minimize or even end the suffering that is in our lives. We have the tools to not become trapped by our ego.

The Message, I hope, brings about a change in our awareness to God in such a way that we can recognize the God movement in our lives and to help us become more cognizant of our own *God Process*. In reality, we can only bring about a tangible change with a shift in our consciousness to make better choices. As we take to heart God's light and listen to that inner voice that speaks from our soul, we will no longer choose to act out of selfishness, wantonness, greed or deceit; nor will we make choices that would put others at risk, knowingly. Hopefully by listening to our conscience, to our inner voice, the difficult choices that tell us to do the right thing will become just a little bit easier.

The Message is not calling us to change our faith. I do not think it matters whether we are Christian, Muslim, Buddhist or atheist. And yet, having said that, I absolutely believe that our choice of faith, and what our beliefs are, does have an impact on how we live life and what will influence us in our decision making. The influence of love, and the desire to know God, will be impacted by our faith and by our choices. On one hand it doesn't matter, because I firmly believe that God loves us, regardless of how we think or believe, and on the other hand it absolutely matters because these choices will either open our hearts and minds up to

God, or close ourselves off to God, and to the humanity that we are called to live.

Many people feel compelled to proclaim a message about God—I certainly was. In reality, our salvation is not contingent on this inward spiritual journey that sometimes compels us to stand up in public and proclaim a message. We are not being asked to beat a drum. The only thing that we are called to do is to have a more personal walk with our God and to *love our neighbor* as ourselves. To be their helping hand, and to walk with them, when they need a friend. To have a closer walk with God—for that is the Christ message, to be at one with God, to be at peace with God.

In the end, I think it all comes down to choice. We need to listen to messages that move our collective consciousness to make good peaceable choices and sustainable choices for our Earth. If we are to see *Peace on Earth* and create a sustainable planet then it will come down to the choice to make it so. What we choose to believe is not important, but our choice to *love* is.

The Message can help. When I reflect back on what *The Message* says and teaches it would suggest the following:

1. God has a plan. That there is this cosmic origin, a universal force, a divine presence that is ever present. This earth, creation, the centrality of Christ and our lives are all part of the plan.

2. Although the plan of redemption is the cornerstone to God's work on earth it is not the only reason as to why our souls are drawn to earth. There is so much more to life than purifying the soul, so to speak.

3. The bigger picture is this—we are meant to become more than what we already are now. We are meant to test ourselves—to test our courage, our compassion, our ability to love. We are also meant to learn tolerance, temperance, acceptance, forgiveness, patience and other virtues. We are meant to dream dreams. To explore our potential, our limits and our character flaws. That is the *God Process*. It is the process where we allow God's light to be infused into and onto our soul. To allow God to permeate our being.

4. What we do in life does have an impact on God. I like George Lucas's choice of words, "There is a disturbance in the Force" when we err against God. The fabric of God can be torn when we make bad choices. The construct of our life is such that we cannot escape our choices. On a global scale, we all pay the price when groups of people forcibly inflict acts of inhumanity on others. God's method of saving us is by sending "His elect", the 9-1-1 first responders who are filled with His light, filled with goodness, and are resolved in justice to retain humanity intact.

5. This life does shape and mold us. It molds the "who I am". It molds our soul. It can either infuse God's light into our being or wrap our soul in a cocoon, which hides God's light. God remains. He is deep inside of us. We only need to open the door.

6. We do have an eternal home. It is a home that we all long to return to. If we live our lives true to ourselves then in spirit we do return home. We return home to our eternal families. However, if we do not live the good life, if we err against God, others and ourselves, if we destroy life and pull others away from God, our spirit may not be able to return home. Not because God doesn't want us, but because we do not feel it is our home. For those who live life in violation to good choices, who knowingly do not to do the right thing or who promote acts of inhumanity are at risk of becoming lost to this abyss, this darkness of their soul.

The bottom line is that life is found when life is lived in harmony to the innocence that we were created in. In an idealistic perfected condition, it would be to get to that point in life where we choose love and do no harm. Our cosmic destination is this *oneness* with the Creator, the Universal Force, the Source of life itself, who sets us free to be, the "me" that He created.

———— 2 A God of Reincarnation ————

My Christian up-bringing is one where my church beliefs does not permit a God of "reincarnation". A God of reincarnation is not the God of the Gospels, at least that is what I was told—since *The Message* is grounded in reincarnation, it cannot be a message from God. I personally do not think that (obviously) and my hope is only to open your mind to what God placed in my soul—a message to the possibilities about how God uses life to shape and mold us in free will, to bring about His essence back into your life.

Since the 1980's, books on *life after life, life between life* and *past life regression* have become mainstream, and they talk about the journey of our soul. We are seeing the veil between this reality and the reality that exits when we pass on and cross over is being lifted. Our collective consciousness is becoming aware that we all plan our lives—maybe not the details, but for most the construct of our lives. These books have a message which says that each life has purpose and we *do* come into life with a plan. We prepare ourselves for this life in the life before life. That is why the *God Process* sometimes takes a life time to connect the dots. If God is going to change the very core of *who we are*, it has to be done in the construct of time.

There are many books that have been published in recent years that talk about our ethereal reality and our collective cosmic journey. Books that I found enlightening include:

> *Life Between Life*, by Joel L. Whitton, M.D., Ph.D. and Joe Fisher,
>
> *The Messengers*, by Julia Ingram and G.W. Hardin,
>
> *Return from Tomorrow*, by George G. Ritchie, M.D.,
>
> *Return to Love*, by Marriane Williamson,
>
> *Destiny of Souls*, by Michael Newton, Ph.D.,
>
> *Many Lives, Many Masters*, by Brain Weiss, M.D.,

The Case for Heaven, by Mally Cox-Chapman,

Beyond The Darkness My Near-Death Journey To The Edge of Hell and Back, by Angie Fenimore,

Embraced by the Light, by Betty J. Eadie,

The Eternal Journey, by Craig R. Lundahl.

These books tell us what to expect when we cross over, they talk about the cosmic God Process and they point towards the impact that our choices have on our spiritual reality.

My grandmother surprised me one day, as we were sitting together one afternoon. I am going back some thirty years ago, long before I started to write *The Message.* She was sharing with me some of her life's experiences. She also had a near death experience, as she had cancer when she was in her forties. She completely recovered, but like my father, she had an out-of-body experience. In that experience, she was met by a personage and was told what was going to happen in her life. In particular, she was told that some of her children would leave the church and that they would need her faith, so that they would not forget their God. More importantly, it was faith in God that *they* needed to have. She was told that it was not her time to cross over and then she was sent back.

Then out of the blue, she said, "You know we live more then once." Lorraine and I were just married and living in her basement suite when I was still going to university, so we had this conversion back in maybe 1981. This would have been before books on near death or reincarnation became main stream. She said she recalled a life that she lived that was back in the 1800s. She had several dreams and in those dreams she remembered living on a farm in the mid-US. I do not recall much of the story of her previous incarnation in the 1800s, but these dreams had enough of an impact on her that she wanted to share them with me. It surprised me, because reincarnation would not have been well accepted in our church faith at that time. I am glad that she shared her beliefs as it helped me in my own acceptance of reincarnation.

The subject of reincarnation is becoming more main-stream in both the media and in clinical regression therapy. However, many religions, faith traditions and beliefs are not aligned with reincarnation. In my Christian denomination, there is an openness to consider God's Truth's; however, reincarnation has yet to be embraced and acknowledged as part of God's plan for salvation. Beliefs should be aligned with the ethereal reality, if we are to fully embrace Truth.

I was drawn into books on reincarnation, and in particular, books on Edgar Cayce when I was in my mid-thirties. Edgar Cayce (1877 - 1945) is known as "America's Sleeping Prophet" and he gave 14,246 clairvoyant readings while in a sleep induced trance, over a forty-year period. Most readings were for the purpose of helping others with recommendations for specific medical treatments. Under self-hypnosis he could diagnose and describe treatments for physical ailments without meeting the person or knowing their condition prior to the psychic reading. Once in trance, he would be given a name and an address; he then would proceed with the reading. These readings were carefully transcribed. These readings were given in an unconscious state, and Edgar Cayce could not recall what he said in the psychic reading after he awoke.

These readings proved to provide physical healing and aid, and over the years Edgar Cayce gained public acceptance. Because of the credibility of his clairvoyance to assist those who asked for a medical diagnosis, Edgar Cayce was often asked questions regarding cosmic origins and, in particular, questions directed to the life of Jesus Christ. Two books in particular detail the readings of Edgar Cayce on the life of Jesus Christ. The first is called, *A Life of Jesus the Christ from Cosmic Origins to the Second Coming*, by Richard Henry Drummond, Ph.D. and the second is, *Edgar Cayce's Story of Jesus*, by Jeffrey Furst.

According to the readings of Edgar Cayce, Jesus of Nazareth's origin was one of cosmic purpose. In Chapter 1 and 2 of the book by Richard Drummond, he draws from the Edgar Cayce writings to describe Jesus as a soul entity, having free will, who lived many earthly lives to perfect his soul [page 10, reading no. 5749-14] and yet became completely immersed and at one with "God the Father, the Universal Influence, the Creative Energy, the I Am that I Am [page 6, reading no. 262-87]." "He came through his own choice— as well as being sent [page 11, reading no. 5749-7]." According to Cayce the incarnations of the soul entity known as Jesus was Adam, Enoch, Melchizedek, Joseph, Joshua (who Cayce also says was the "mouthpiece of Moses"), Jeshua (in the days of Nehemiah, Ezra and Zerubbabel) and other non-biblical prominent figures as well (see pages 23 - 24 from the book by Jeffery Hurst).

In reading 2067-7, Cayce is asked (see page 23 by Jeffery Hurst):

Q. When did Jesus become aware that he would be the Savior of the World?

A. When he fell in Eden.

There is a paragraph on page 15 from Drummond's book that captures the cosmic nature of Jesus:

This then was the background of the birth of "the Savior, the Messiah, the Prince of Peace, the Way, the Truth, the Light" (no. 1010-17), "that beloved Son, who would make the paths straight, who would bring man out of darkness into light... that Shepherd [who] must lead forth His flock, His brethren again into the light of countenance of an all merciful Father" (no. 587-6). The purpose of the birth of Jesus was clearly divine. "The purpose of the entrance of the Son into the earth [was] that man might have the closer walk with, yea open the door to, the very heart of the living God! (no. 587-6, compare to Mark 12:29; Deut 6:4 [which states that Lord our God is One])."

The message on universal oneness that comes into Cayce's readings was pervasive and consistent. Edgar Cayce also addresses reincarnation as applying to all souls. Most of both Drummond's book and Furst's book focuses on the life of Jesus Christ as oppose to cosmic origins; however, Cayce many times related these messages, which were cosmic in nature, back to soul development.

Edgar Cayce on occasions was asked, what was the source for his clairvoyant readings? He said he could only speculate as to the source, but personally believed that the past life readings of his subjects were sourced from what he called the Akashic records[82] for his clairvoyant work (in some *past life regression* books it also referred to as the Hall of Records). He believed that anyone could access these records if one could attune themselves properly.[83] I personally believe that there is an ethereal library, which contains the history of our cosmic origins, past lives of our incarnations and sacred texts.[84] What was written on my soul and became

---

82 Akashic is a term used in many life regressions and it means the space [or record] filled with thought, word and deeds.

83 See page 16 of Edgar Cayce's Story of Jesus, by Jeffery Furst.

84 As to whether or not there are sacred ethereal books in the Hall of Records that are called Book of Truth, Book of Law and Book of Life, and that The Message is indeed an ibidem of these ethereal books, I have nothing to offer to give substance to this. The Message I believe must stand on its on merit.

I did have two particular vivid dreams where I may have visited the Hall of Records. Afterwards you think, that was weird and, for me, I discounted it as being associated with some ethereal reality. Maybe the dream was influenced by what I was reading at the time, so it lacked as a tangible experience. However, others may have had similar dreams, so maybe by recalling as best I can the dream, others may also come forward with similar accounts.

The first dream was seeing the structure (this ethereal library), but in that dream I did not enter this library. In that dream I recall a white marble structure almost Roman in design, enormous in size, with an open air courtyard and a staircase that lead down to the Hall of Records—I knew what the structure was. The second dream was where I was in the actual Hall of Records reviewing a particular tablet. Access to the tablets was granted through a guide or guardian who would assist in retrieving this memory slate and then you would be taken to a viewing area. In the viewing area you would enter into or became an observer to a particular incarnation. It was like being a part of a movie where you could both see and feel the emotions of the participants as the events were being played out. I remember being in the actual Hall, the guardian and going to the viewing area, where there was other guides that would assist you. I have to emphasize this was just a recol-

The Message may have been sourced in part from these Akashic records. The only thing that I can say with certainty is that *The Message* itself was not something I manufactured and, whatever the source, I know that I am a part of it.

For me, believing that Adam and Jesus were the same soul entity adds to the structure and substance of the *cosmic God Process*—to believe that God influenced the "stage" of humanity. That this *cosmic God Process* was one of design and purpose—that it was Jesus himself, who came as Adam, as Enoch and as Melchizedek. It sparks the hope of salvation to believe that just as Adam fell, so it is that Jesus was raised—from the fall of innocence to the restoration of innocence, fulfilled in Jesus Christ. The path of one becomes the path for all; the path of the Christ becomes *my* path, *my* hope—his humanity is not unlike *my* humanity, *my* journey. From a cosmic perspective, it is affirmation for me to believe that Adam was not a random soul picked out of a crowd of souls to take the fall for all of humanity. Rather, Adam was both chosen and did choose to be both the Father of mankind and the Son of God, the path of the Christ.

I also find it compelling to think that Melchizedek was the same soul entity as the Christ. Melchizedek was regarded as the king of Salem (Salem being the name of the local god in Melchizedek's time). The name of *Jerusalem* literally means the city founded by God.[85] Jerusalem was named by or after Melchizedek, who from a cosmic perspective according to Cayce was the Christ, the Emmanuel, God with us—so in fact it may be the city founded by the Son of God. The city of time now is the focal point for Judaism, Christianity and Islam. Another interesting connection is that in Christianity, the high priest follows after the order of Melchizedek. Jesus Christ was regarded as a high priest after the order of Melchizedek (Hebrews 6:20). The priesthood of God was

lection of a dream, which may have been influenced by the books that I was reading at the time.

85   Sacred City of Mankind A History of Forty Centuries, by Teddy Kollek and Moshe Pearlman, page 17.

established by Melchizedek—again the same soul entity whom became the Christ, therefore from a cosmic perspective, the Melchizedek priesthood was founded by the Son of God.

Connecting the dots between the lives of Adam, Enoch, Melchizedek and Jesus, and between Eve and Mary can have meaning to us, because it affirms to us the cosmic plan. The message is that God has been actively engaged with His creation through the soul we call Christ, since the dawn of time. God, the Christ Emmanuel, has incarnated numerous times to influence the construct of our humanity, to guide His creation back to Him.

The message is that in our creation and within our free will, where choice caused the split—this separation between our self and our God—God set in motion a plan to reclaim us. He set the stage and became an active participant in that stage, that journey of life, the journey of the soul.

The Message speaks of our cosmic origins in Jesus Christ and the need for soul development. Again, we see this same message in *life after life* books, the *life between life* books, in *past life regression* and in the readings of Edgar Cayce. The reality is that many people do get trapped in-between the light and the dark, because of free will. Some people are not able to bridge themselves back to God or even return to their spiritual home, because of their choices (note: most past life regressions that I have read are positive in nature and even in the worst of lives—past lives—we find that our loved ones want us to come home). Our choices in life, shapes the pattern of light that becomes infused into our soul.

This veil is being lifted as to our eternal journey through these books and through people's experiences. We are being shown that reincarnation is the path back. If I take anything away from *The Message* it is that we do have free will and in that free will we have to purge ourselves of any desire that might impede, hurt or destroy other people. We have to be careful *not* to be involved in acts of inhumanity, whether it is against people or the earth itself. Acts of inhumanity can lead to this abyss, this hell, this darkness of the soul where the light of God can become lost to our vision. In this reality, acts of inhumanity can bring a larger scale of destruction, like World War I and World War II. Acts of inhumanity can destroy our planet. We all have to pay attention to how our lives impact the world.

Karma, as some religions point to, is what people will face in life as the result of bad choices of their past, or even past lives. God does not punish nor is He cruel; however, *The Message* almost echoes the same destiny for souls who make bad choices. The twist here is this, these souls willing choose to come back to face again similar circumstances, so that they might choose again. They willingly choose an incarnation where they might face again those decisions that created the schism. They want a second chance, not only to learn and correct their mistakes, but to also to prove to themselves that they are that better person. The challenge can be one of difficulty. Future lives become more difficult, because the soul has to come face to face with those hard decisions that created the darkness. They choose to come back with the same group of people that tore the fabric. It is the desired way, because that is the path to healing—love is the path to healing. If they are to find that desire to love and to be loved, it will be with those where love was lost. To infuse into their being a piece of God's light means that they will have to find that light that is in each other. Learning to love and to be loved is what salvation is about.

Cayce's readings are clear—there is a cosmic purpose to life. We are all on the same path to eventually become at *one* with God, to become at peace or in harmony with God. What is important here is the connection that we ourselves can have with God; knowing that we can have a deeper relationship with our God because of our beliefs. Like Adam, my humanity is not found in Eden; it is found outside of Eden.

———— 3 Finding God—A Subject of Faith ————

There is a hole in our soul—a yearning for God—there is something that is inside of us that looks for the something that is not of this world. When life stops us and we have to search our soul for our faith—which is in part our religion, our beliefs and the home for our spirituality—we find our foundation, our hope and the source of life we find God. Our faith has been both handed down to us, by what we are told to believe, and built up from within by our own self exploration, by what life has done to us and sometimes by how the Divine has reached in and touched our lives.

There is something about sharing ourselves in family, and in community with God. In acceptance of that faith, we find a bond in family and community, and through our beliefs we walk together and stand together with God. For in our belief, God came to us and favored us, set us both apart and in the midst of the world. We knew we were called because we felt this mission, this calling and this hope that God brings to us—God fills the hole and offers a peace for our world.

Yet, finding God is not something that you do, it is something that happens. It is like opening your eyes in the morning—all of sudden you are awake and aware, it just happens. Like it says in *The Message*, "You cannot find God if you have to look for Him, yet His presence is made ever so clear if you allow Him to look through you."[86] Finding God is one of self-evidence. You know what you know, not because of some test or some evidence, but because the intangible (God) makes tangible the reality that you know to be true. This God of all that I see, opens up the possibilities to a life full of potential.

When I was twelve, I attended church youth camps at a place called the Hills of Peace. There was a minister who came to these camps, and he opened my eyes to the possibilities of God. He would tell the stories, but it wasn't the stories that caught my imagination, for me it was the promises. In the scriptures were these promises that God made to us.

To a twelve year old, that was like magic. I could actually test God! Of course, as you grow older the tests that you put God through takes on a far different nature. The test I wanted to put God through was like the one in James 1:5 which states, "If any of you lacks wisdom, let him ask of God, that giveth to all *men* liberally, and upbraidth not; and it shall be given."

I wanted to know the secrets of the universe. At twelve years old that is a pretty big test to put God through. But at twelve you don't think about the size of the test—you just think about the possibilities. So I knelt down and prayed that if God was real that He would show me the secrets of the universe. Of course I got up off my knees and... nothing. My life went on. I had no idea that this simple prayer would consume my adult life. I had no idea what that little test would mean to my life. I look back now and smile.

Sometimes, when you put God to the test, God changes your life. One thing is for sure, I did not see this coming. What became *The Message* took twelve years of my life, a lot of heartache, soul searching, and then a lot of time wondering what I was going to do with this ethereal message that set my mind on fire—and many sleepless nights, I might add.

As life went on, I had, for the most part, put that prayer aside, and besides it seemed like an empty test. Of course in the naiveness of youth I put God through the "test" with some smaller requests, because I figured that maybe that first test was too much to ask. One of my favorite scriptures for testing God was in John 11:12 which says, "But I know, that even now, whatsoever thou wilt ask of God, God will give it thee." I also remember thinking that if I stacked up these scriptures of promises it would be like really putting God to the test, so I pulled out a couple of others. Matthew 7:7 says, "Ask, and it shall be given you; seek, and ye shall find; knock, and it shall be opened unto you." And John 16:24, "Ask, and ye shall receive, that your joy might be full." So as I was thinking about these scriptures this voice came back into my head *as* clear as day and it said, "Tempt not the Lord your God." *Wow—okay, so I thought maybe I better back off with putting God to the test too much.*

I do recall putting God to the test on a number of occasions and I had some amazing confirmations as to the reality of God. At one of the church youth camps that I attended I really wanted to see the power and majesty of God so I prayed, *God if you are real, show me how powerful you are*—a typical kind of prayer from a young teenage kid. On the fourth day of the camp, at around three o'clock in the morning, this storm rolled through like none I had ever seen before or since. It wasn't the force that I remember, but rather the sheer magic and silence of the storm. The only way that I can describe it would be to say that it was like being inside a cloud of sheet lightning and then being deaf to the tempest that you were seeing with your eyes. The whole camp lit up in a million flashes of light as if the light was coming not from the sky, but from within the camp itself. Normally when you have a storm you have wind that blows the trees directionally from one side to the other, this wind twirled and swirled up the trees and there was a whistling of sorts that climbed the trees. As I am watching in awe out my cabin window, I thought to myself, *well there is my answer*—God's power sure is mystical. The storm lasted for about fifteen minutes and then it faded away.

From that moment on I was captivated. To think about the wonders of God just captivated my mind and imagination. And then came the dream when I was fifteen; that mystical vision which was so surreal it made me stop and ponder what message God was sending me. God became both scary good and mystical. Real and surreal. *Scary* is the wrong word, because the dream pulled me to God and it caused me to want to pay attention to whatever I was supposed to do with my life.

As I got older I realized prayers required both action and response. It is a two-way street. Going to God to ask for favors, I learned, was not the right way to go about it. Going to God meant you had to open yourself up to God's whisper. It's like the good old Darth Vader expression... "What is thy bidding, my Master?" But the prayer is more like, *what would you have me do today God, or what miracle can I help you with?* Now *that* kind of prayer brings results. If you really want to find God, there you go! Just say that prayer and open your soul to listen to the messages—the compelling thoughts that you get. If your soul is really looking to test the miracles of God and how God can move in your life all you need to do is be open to how you can serve and help others.

Asking to help God with God's miracles means being engaged

in other people's lives. However, listening to your inner voice requires you to use reason and to be responsible. One cannot divorce oneself from one's own limits and capabilities. I might want to help others, but I may not be qualified. My involvement may be to go find somebody else that is qualified to help. To be a first responder means being open to the task at hand and recognizing what it is that you can actually do.

Asking God to use me is the kind of prayer that is constantly on my heart when I decide that I really want to get involved with God. It was that kind of prayer that landed me in Israel, it was that kind of prayer that caused me to go out into the streets of Jerusalem, where I was asked to *"give blood"*, and it was that kind of prayer that prompted me to write *The Message*.

When Lorraine and I were just married we decided to ask God to be a part of our lives. We made a commitment to God that He would always be welcomed in our home. We sat down together and made a wish list of what we thought would be nice for our goals and targets in our marriage. Things like, how many kids we wanted, what kind of salary I would like, our health, how many weeks of vacation, wishes for our savings account and places that we wanted to go for our vacations—almost like a bucket list. We took that list and we posted it to the inside one of our kitchen cupboards. We would put it in there and then forget about it. Every so often we would be reminded of the list and look at it. Gradually over time one of the items on our list would get crossed off. I often wondered if angels were looking at our list and then going to work to help us out.

This book was on that wish list. Before I put *The Message* on the shelf, I decided to put "publish book" on our wish list. As it stands right now, this is the last item that I need to cross off on my wish list, my bucket list. I'm not sure if that is good or bad because I have no intentions of kicking the bucket (when I found that out, I quickly made a new list). For me, it is just another one of those small miracles that tells me that God is there, and that He is at work in my life.

For me God is real. He is as real as the world that He has created and my experience is that I see Him actively engaged in *my* life. If you want miracles in your life, if you want extraordinary things in your life to happen, then look to God—consider what God has to offer.

God is the glue to life. God is the glue to *my* life. When we live purposeful lives and consider all the opportunities to love, we find the true meaning to life. To be creative, to be purposeful in what we create; what we construct by the lives we live, is what makes life magical. If you want to have power, if you want to find immortality, it you want to have true love, then consider what God has to offer. God offers what is real. It is God that will create the reality, the possibilities for your life. Why not give it a shot?

> *The LORD is my shepherd; I shall not want. He maketh me lie down in green pastures: he leadeth me besides the still water. He restoreth my soul: He leadeth me in the paths of righteousness for His names sake. Yea, though I walk through the valley of the shadow of death, I will fear no evil: for thou art with me; thy rod and thy staff comfort me. Thou preparest a table before me in the presence of mine enemies: thou anointest my head with oil; my cup runneth over. Surely goodness and mercy shall follow me all the days of my life: and I will dwell in the house of the LORD for ever.*

Psalms 23

The *God Process* is the path we walk to find our way back to God. Jesus said, "I am the way, the Truth and the life: no man cometh unto the Father, but by me."[87] I believe that Jesus was calling us to a way of life, lived *with* the presence of God. For Christ—the Emmanuel, God with us—to come to rest within us we have to find that desire for God. This is good news for those who have difficulty with Christianity and have been brought up with a different faith tradition, because the road back to God is a desire for God. Maybe for some, Jesus does not resonate with them, yet

---

87   John 14:6

in their faith tradition they have found both an awareness and wantingness for God. If we look to God, God will come. For myself, the image of the Christ, the image of Emmanuel came to rest in Jesus of Nazareth. Jesus took upon himself the image of Christ, so that we all might see the true nature of God.

In the message of the centrality of Christ, we *can* find the persona of God. There is this *potential* to come to a closer awareness of the creative force we call God through Jesus Christ.

> *For God so loved the world He gave his only begotten son. For God came not into the world to condemn the world, but that the world through him might be saved.*

John 3:16

Faith traditions that call us to God provide a conduit for the *Spirit of the Emmanuel* to come to rest within the human heart. Our salvation comes when we place a piece of heaven, a piece of God, into the human heart. God *is* actively engaged in all lives, regardless of our faith, beliefs or tenets. God's way into the human heart is through our wantingness and willingness to fulfill the two commandments...

> *Love the Lord your God, with all your heart, and with all thy soul, and with all thy mind and with all thy strength and Love your neighbor as yourself.*

Mark 12:30–31 (ABBREV)

The commandment does not say go get baptized. The commandment does not say repent or to worship or to get on your knees. The commandment does not say become Christian. Do you realize that this commandment was first given in Deuteronomy 6:5, long before the world came to know of Jesus and long before we had a multitude of religions? The commandment is really a promise as opposed to a demand made by God, because that is what God does, He offers us promises. If we keep His commandments something happens to us—"If ye keep my commandments, ye shall abide in my love; even as I have kept my Father's commandments, and abide in His love." (John 15:10) The promise is that love would follow us all of our days. If love were to follow us, then suffering would end. No more suffering—what a promise!

Because I have a love for Jesus Christ, there is a deep desire in me to say come to Christ, to meet the Christ, to walk into the waters of baptism for the remission of sins, to sing the songs of praises, to consider the act of prayer on your knees. All these actions are meaningful for me. They are not only *acts*, but desires of faith, to bring about a deeper relationship and connection with God. However, after reflection on everything that has happened in my life, and coming to perhaps a shift in my own consciousness as to how God works and is engaged in my life, I have come to the conclusion that God works in lives regardless of religion, faith or creed. He meets us where we are, and engages with us insofar as we are willing to walk with Him. Salvation is contingent on our willingness and wantingness to love and be loved, for this is the essence of God—this is the God force that God has created. Time and eternity merge when love follows us, each and every day. Love is magnified when we connect love with the source of love. God created love as the binding force of life. It only makes sense that when we seek God, we find a deeper meaning of love.

The God Process is about discovering what God is trying to do in our lives. It is about connecting the dots. To find what God is trying to do, we only need to connect the dots.

———— 4 Connecting the Dots ————

Connecting the dots helps us to see our own *God Process*. To find meaning and to live life's purpose is part of *The God Process*; however, finding the hidden messages, seeing the hidden tests as to why things happen in our lives is not so easy. If God is trying to change us for the better, it will be in the struggles and in the difficult choices that we have to make. Connecting the dots might help us discover what it is that God is trying to do. That usually means looking for events where we find it difficult to choose for love.

When there are reoccurring themes in life, it may be because God is trying to show us something. We are good at hiding that part of ourselves that is not so loving. We are good at not loving. We are good at avoiding others and avoiding difficult relationships. As an example, the last thing that we may want to do is be patient when it is so much easier to be impatient, especially when we can get what we want by pushing others. For soul development to occur, if we are to infuse God's light, there has to be a willingness and wantingness to break free of the cocoon—to break free of those character flaws, to break free of our selfish thoughts, or change how we manipulate others.

If there is avoidance or a fear which impedes our ability to love or to make good decisions, there will be numerous dots in our lives to tell us that. There will be major events that stand out when you look back. It will be a constant theme that seems to surface. If we want to grow into God, we may have to learn our God lessons. We have to want to see the message that challenges us to love, but more importantly, we have to want to change—to be that new person. The message of love may be one that challenges us to be more patient, peaceful, compassionate, or considerate. The message of love might mean to be stronger, trusting, to have the resolve to act truthfully, or to be more brave. The message of love might be one of self-sacrifice, to intercede, to stand by someone else, or to be a first responder.

Messages of love can take on many forms, but love always adds to the creative purpose. The message of love creates connectedness and sustains Truth (the reality of God). The *God Process* is about breaking the cocoon that hides our soul in darkness, so that God might infuse His light.

When I was in grade eleven, I made a metal medallion. On it was a circle, a cross and a triangle, which is the icon that you see on the front cover. The medallion symbol was yellow, casted on a blue canvass of the universe and then shaped in the form of a human spirit around the symbol. At the time there was no symbolism to the icon; I just thought that it looked mesmerizing. It was later in life that the icon of the *circle – cross –triangle*, took on meaning. It is symbolic of the Father, the Son and the Holy Spirit, the three as one—the Trinity. It is symbolic of the Emmanuel—God with us.

Emmanuel

Father

Son

Holy Spirit

The circle represents our God. It symbolizes the oneness within our Creator, the convergence of the Divine as light is both infused within creation and radiates outward into creation; it symbolizes the essence of God, the will of God. It also represents the first dimension, that God is omnipresent in all of creation and that we draw life from God. Just as pure love takes on the shape of a circle, which is symbolic of a never-ending bond forged in a ring, so it is that we draw life from the essence of life which is love itself.

The cross represents the Christ. Christ came in the midstream of humanity to show us the path back. For Christian's, it is the symbol of salvation, it is our bridge to God. Through Christ we are made whole. Although the crucifix was an instrument of death used by the Romans, it is now symbolic to Christians for new life. It reminds us of the resurrection and that through Christ our sins are forgiven—it is the message for restored innocence. It is also a reminder of what happens to us when we allow the acts of inhumanity to be borne on each other, when we allow judgment or condemnation to be inflicted on our lives. The cross is our hope in Christ—Emmanuel, God with us, in us, and through us. The cross is the path of innocence our soul takes through the second dimension to be connected to God.

The triangle is symbolic of how God's essence is infused into or onto our soul. It is symbolic of how His spirit (goodness) has the potential to be seen in the third dimension (the dimension of self). It is through our choice, our actions, and our love that we see God in our self, our identity. The triangle has three apexes, which represents mind – body – heart, the expressions of self. At the core or center of the triangle is our soul, and our soul is connected to God as symbolized by the cross reaching into the center of the triangle.

The triangle of mind – body – heart – soul can be symbolized as follows:

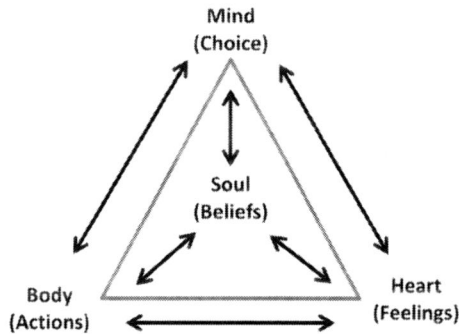

Everything in life involves choice, feelings and actions and whatever happens in life can, and most likely will, change us. Who we are on the inside, and whether or not God's essence (goodness) comes to rest in us, will be the summation of life's decisions, feeling and outcomes, as they come to rest on the soul. Regardless of our beliefs (about God) life will change us, because that is *the God Process*. This simple triangle is how God designed us.

Here is a simple example:

1. Love (feelings) → Will you marry me? (choice)→ Wedding (action) → Happily ever after (belief).
2. Cheating (action) → Hurt and anger (feelings) → Do I forgive? (choice) → No, spouse doesn't love me (belief).
3. Do I divorce or give my spouse a second chance? (choice) → Spouse cheats again (action) → I stop loving or caring (feelings) → love is painful (belief).

Of course there are a myriad of scenarios about how love impacts our soul. And where is God in all of this? How does God influence us to choose for love? Why would God allow this person to come into my life, if He knew (because our belief may be that God is all knowing) that this person was going to shatter my life? What is God is trying to teach me?

Our choices will impact how love will come to rest on who we are. The exploration in life between life regression, where individuals are faced with extreme choices, often reveals that both individuals had free will to make the choice and that they together agreed—prior to life—to be participants. One maybe needed to learn self-control and the other perhaps forgiveness. Learning to love, regardless of what life does to us, is a difficult task.

In Mark 12:30 Jesus said, "And thou shalt love the Lord thy God with all thy heart [feelings], and with all thy soul [beliefs], and with all thy mind [choice], and with all thy strength [actions]". It is love; it is the choice to show love, through which we become connected to one another and to God. Mind, body and heart mold the garments of our soul. What we choose, what we do and how we love will infuse the goodness of God—the God light that comes to rest on my soul. Our will, our actions and the impact of outcomes shapes our ability to love and can either infuse light or darkness onto our soul.

Who we are on the inside, the goodness that is in us is either solidified, or our goodness can be washed away. "Who we are" is in a constant state of flux by the infusion of choice.

We evaluate our beliefs based on what we have been taught, what we have experienced and what life does to us. Out beliefs, and not necessarily religious beliefs, dictate our expectations about what will or will not happen. Some choices require careful thought, whereas others do not. Our decisions will lead to our actions and our actions will leads to an outcome. Outcomes can be good or outcomes can be bad. Outcomes will impact how we feel. Good outcomes make us feel good and will affirm our choice in life and our beliefs. Bad outcomes, especially outcomes which cause emotional distress, may cause us to stop and reevaluate our choices and sometimes our beliefs. In the end our beliefs, our choices and our actions will leave an impact on ourselves and on others, and we feel it—we know it. Actions that scar us, leave feelings that are raw, perhaps filled with regret, guilt or remorse and these emotions have an impact on who we are and what we choose to be.

The Emmanuel is symbolic of *the God Process*—how God's light becomes infused into our being and how the process of life infuses light into or onto our soul. It is infused by the construct of time, which means that eventually these outcomes are solidified into the past and become the moments between time, which are captured for eternity. These are pivotal moments that are written into the record of our life and into our soul memory. The actual events are not important so the events may be forgotten and I think forgiven—we forgive ourselves from past lives lived, however we still have to prove to ourselves that we are no longer that person. The residue, the imprint on the soul, is that *if* we have learned our lesson, we will no longer need to face or be challenged by the tests.

The symbolism of the triangle is the reminder of choice and how choice shapes and molds the "who I am". The cross reaches into the soul to remind us of the Christ who is our bridge to God. Together the symbol is the image of how our humanity is connected to God (circle). The circle is a symbol of our hope (the ring for eternal love). Together they become our Emmanuel, God with us.

When Jesus said *to love the Lord thy God*, the operative word was love. I believe God is in and through all things. He is in the trees, the flowers, and the Earth. God is the life force of life. He is a part of me and a part of you. To love the Lord thy God is to have a deeper connectedness with all of creation. When our choices are grounded in love, love comes back to our soul. The choice (mind) to love becomes the act (embodiment) of love and the outcome is to feel (heart) loved. Love makes the world brighter. Love infuses light into the soul. The soul becomes illuminated with God as the life force of God is magnified through love.

The Emmanuel symbolizes a dimension within a dimension within a dimension—a dimension of God (Source), a dimension of soul (conduit) and a dimension of self (giver). The three in one, the triad, the trinity as God's essence comes to rest in the image of "who we are". God's light is infused by the choice to give, the act of becoming the conduit and the expression of love as our source.

In Genesis we read, "Let us make man in our image."[88] The Emmanuel is the image of our innocence. It is the image of the innocence coming to rest inside of our humanity. It is the image of our God coming to rest inside of you and me. The Emmanuel is an icon for our hope restored, our wantingness for *Peace on Earth*, it is the willingness to accept the message of God in our lives.

Symbols are important, because symbols speak to us and captures who we are in an instance. The simple symbol of the cross, for Christians, captures and reminds Christians of all that Christ is and what God is about. Symbols have the potential to guide us, to transform us. When we connect the dots in our lives ,we find symbols are associated with these events. For some it is a dove, or a fish, a cross, a picture, prayer beads or a wedding ring. For myself the symbol of the Emmanuel was personal, it became a symbol of *my* God Process. I see it not so much as a symbol for faith, but as a symbol of hope for my innocence.

We sometimes have to connect the dots in our lives to learn our God lesson. Connecting the dots in our life brings us full circle. It takes us back to why we are here. When we see God in those extraordinary events where love came to us (maybe through someone unexpected, one of God's first responders) it affirms in us that God is there and that our lives do have purpose. Stop, look back, look in and look up, because there is where you will find your healing. That is what God has to offer.

5 A Call to Love Thy Neighbor

There has to be an active change in our lives if collectively we are to have an impact on our world. To create peace in our world, to create a visible sustainable planet, to create a piece of heaven in our

---

88   Genesis 1:26.

lives, there has to be an infusion of this life force we call love. If *The Message* is to have a home—which is a message of life, connection, of oneness, of harmony and of sustainability—love must find a way.

There are many initiatives that people have taken to make the world a better place. I like the acronym *ARK—acts of random kindness*, and *pay it forward*. These simple phrases can instill God's essence. They are not formal programs and yet many people have adopted these simple phrases to brighten the world by how they live their lives.

Love thy neighbor is another simple phrase to invoke visible change. It is three simple words, which do not require any kind of construct to empower its potential. Yet this simple message can transform lives. The focus of *love thy neighbor* is to bring about connectedness or healing in our relationships by the choice to love. If the laws of the spirit are operative, then love can be a magnet to bring about peace and community.

Prayer is a wish to God. Prayer is the vision of our heart for a better world. Prayer is a wantingness to enact our love for others. *Love thy neighbor* finds a path for love in our lives. It is our willingness and wantingness to choose to love, to connect with others and to heal our earth.

The objective of *love thy neighbor* is to invoke a connection. For me, it is a decision to share myself by a conscious choice to listen to my soul. If the *God Process* is to awaken our lives to change, to recognize what it is that God is trying to do with our lives, then we have to take that step to listen to our soul. Our faith teaches us to pray, to ask God, to go to God and then leave it with God. However, to create miracles is a choice to allow God to work through us. It is the opening of our soul to the messages, to the impulses that invoke acts of love, and the giving of ourselves, that connects our soul with those whom we choose to love.

Love thy neighbor should be a three-part process:

1. **Choose** the person that you want to love. Love is both a prayer and a response to that prayer. Listen to your soul and allow your thoughts to be open as to how best to love. Make a promise to yourself to respond to your prayer of love.

2. **Respond** in a timely manner. The response needs to be visible to the person that you want to connect with.

3. **Share** your outcome. Let others know how love touched you. By sharing your soul you spread the feeling of love.

The hope for us, and our world, is that as we choose to love, love finds a way. Acts of love invokes more love in our lives. Love binds us one to another. More importantly love brings a healing to the life of the person who chooses to love, which is you.

Who is our neighbor? It is our brother, our sister, our mother and our father. It is someone else's brother, sister, mother, or father. Our neighbor is the one to the left and the one to the right. Our neighbor is the nameless faces whose lives are touched by our prayers and our actions to do the right thing. Our neighbor is our church, and the people in our church, who need to be touched by our faith. Our neighbor is the people who will be impacted by regulations and corporate decisions. Our neighbor is the earth, as our earth is reliant on our choices that bring about sustainability. Our neighbor is our God, to accept our God in our lives, so that His love might find a home.

We are called to love, because love is the life force of life. Love converges on one's self through the light that infuses life. The more we love, the more it is that love becomes a part of us.

——— 6 Commentary Notes on the Message ———

There are a few things that are in *The Message* that I thought needed some commentary. My overall concern is the big picture, the take away message that people might interpret. I say this because I do think we all have the tendency of reading too much into a message, even when reading scriptures in the Bible. It is our human nature to over-think, over-read and over-interpret.

First, I have a commentary note as to what *The Message* says when it comes to laws and regulations, when it comes to court decisions, penalties and sentencing. *The Message* might suggest that people who are charged with these responsibilities are at risk in breaking the "Law of One" if they carry out their duties and responsibilities to society. However, I do not think that this is the case. Even though *The Message* calls us to almost do away with condemnation and judgment, sentencing and penalties against others, I do not think that that is the direction that *The Message* is suggesting our society should take. Nor do I think that is the message that is coming from my soul and onto the pages of this book.

Everything we do converges on both the self and the soul. Laws are intended to maintain order in our society. People who abide by the law have no need to worry about what happens when the law is broken by others. However, people who intentionally choose inhumanity, people who choose to rob, break laws and do harm are sometimes best served by coming face to face with their actions. There are consequences to choice and it is no different under God's laws. In spirit we come face to face with our actions and our choices. When the law is broken there are consequences.

Those who are charged with applying law should be vigilant to uphold the "spirit" of the law. Anyone in judgment of another human being needs to exercise righteous decisions; the right justice. More damage can be done if the law is used to inflict retribution on others. If laws or regulations are used to condemn or penalize "the people", if laws and regulations minimize freedoms, if laws or regulations are used as a whip or a statement to forewarn others as to the power of government or law enforcement, then the use of law has been over-extended. Law-makers, regulators, and enforcers must have extreme resolve not to use the power of law or regulations as a way of getting even or even subjecting society to the errors of its people or the regulators and enforcers themselves will become subject to acts of inhumanity. When it comes to regulators and law enforcement, their actions should be corrective and constructive in nature. A government should not penalize its people for lifting the box incorrectly.

Our culture, our freedoms and our liberty is a mirror of our government. In other words, to live in a land that is free with liberty for all, regulations and enforcement have to be reflective of the beliefs, the principles and the ideals that are the heartbeat of the people. As chaos sets, in more laws and regulations are required to maintain order. Yet no nation can govern and not sacrifice justice and liberty, when freedoms are eroded. Governments and law enforcers have to be resilient not to cross the line. Still, no people can expect a government *not* to regulate, to maintain order, if the people lose sight of their moral principles. To retain our morality, to maintain our freedom, to maintain our liberty, both government and the people need to maintain that internal compass which keeps our hearts and mind in tune with that higher collective consciousness. The bottom line is that we need our God in the heart of our nation. We need the goodness that we ascribe to God.

Second, I wanted to provide some perspective on beliefs on the afterlife. As I was preparing this book for publication I did my best to keep *The Message* pure with *The Message* that was received, as it was penned. There has been some content edits and considerable amount or rearranging of *The Message*. I believe that this earthly reality is governed by the ethereal reality—by a reality that exists in this other reality of *life after life* that we cannot see. When we cross back over to that life after life reality, there is a level of consciousness that surpasses what we now can comprehend. The knowledge of life, the universe and our understanding or comprehension that is in our soul, and it's connectedness to the *Creative Force,* has the potential to expand. What we see, what we know and what we feel has the *potential* to open up—almost like a drop of water being put back into the sea of God and becoming one with the lake. That potential, however, is linked to how in tune we are with the essence or presence of God.

I believe most people want to know what awaits them when they cross over. In my exploration and in my prayers, or communion with my God, there has been certain "beliefs" that have been impressed upon me. I share this with you with purity of heart and say that these "beliefs" come from my conscious self and does not come from *The Message.* I do believe that most of us, when we cross over are greeted by family on the other side. My certainty is that we do have an eternal family and part of that family is on the other side and they are engaged with us both as guides to our life and they help us along the way to influence us to live our life's purpose. Not all of us are open or receptive to that help, but our eternal families do their best to help us.

There was a time in my life where I **did not** believe in hell or this abyss, because I could not accept the idea that a loving God would condemn us. This was not what I was taught in my church. When I was growing up I can remember a number of sermons that talked about God's judgment, fire and brimstone, and hell. *My* church isn't like that any longer and very seldom do I hear talks of this nature. I have, however, changed my thinking on the existence of the abyss. There is a mounting amount of reports and experiences as to the existence of the abyss. TV shows on the paranormal and a number of documentaries talk about this abyss. These are perhaps observations, or witnesses to observations, but the reports of both heaven and the abyss is mounting. Certainly, scriptures and *The Message* talks about the abyss.

I now believe that both God and our families almost become powerless to the destiny of our soul, if we refuse to go to the light. If in death we refuse to go to the light, we can be caught in this abyss. When we knowingly choose to create or cause harm, or when we consciously and intentionally invoke acts of inhumanity, or when we allow rage and hatred to fester in our lives, or when we consciously close ourselves off to goodness, there is a risk that we will not go the light. God does not force us into the light.

Having said that, I believe most people do not need to fear God or this abyss. Most books that talk about *life and life, life between life* and *past life regression,* suggest a benevolent approach to life's lessons. Our eternal families look to embrace us and we have the opportunity to be immersed in this sea of love, at the time of death. The abyss, if reported in these books, is usually followed by a personage who meets the soul in the abyss and helps them back to the light.

With respect to rewards in heaven, I believe that what we

give in life is what we *receive* in death. We tend to go through life collecting things, building wealth, striving to live in bigger and more luxurious homes, almost at times to the neglect of others and even to the neglect of our own families—this acquisition in life is gone at the time of death. The wealth we receive in death is contingent on the love we give. I think in death we return to homes that are reflective of the love and kindness that we shared in this life, that is because our homes are built by our eternal family. Our eternal homes are a response to the love that we impart in life.

Sad it is, sometimes, that we would almost rather spend our money on a new car then to give of our money for a child who holds out their hand for bread. For the people who *do not* live their lives for others and do not add value in this life, may find in death that they return to homes that are small. I believe that not only is the essence of God's light infused into our soul by our choice, but our home in heaven is reflective of our love for others in the life that we live.

Whether or not what I believe is the destiny that awaits us, it is **compelling to consider that what we choose in life also becomes a choice of what we give to ourselves in the next life.** I believe we cannot escape our choices and our choices converge on our soul in so many ways. When we cross back over to the ethereal world our choices can be seen by the garments that we wear, by the amount of God's light that is infused into our soul, it is reflective of the dimension of heaven that we gravitate to, it governs the reality of heaven that we can endure and it determines the kind of home that we will live in. It seems like a lot and it is, but that is why we plan our lives and why we need to stay connected to God. That is why church is so important and having a faith in God is so important. More importantly that is why we need to live our faith and never stop loving.

Third, I also have some commentary statements with respect to our concept of sin or to err against God. In *The Kingdom: 3 Grace,* it reads "the Kingdom of Heaven is not the avoidance of sin." I wanted to highlight this because for some it all comes back to the question of how good do we have to be to be acceptable to God? There is this pervasive thought in our minds that we have to be perfect to be acceptable to God. We have to avoid making mistakes. We have to be void of error if we are going to be worthy of heaven. In the Christian tradition we have to be baptized, we have to be on our knees, we have to turn our lives over to Jesus if we are going to be worthy of heaven. We have to come to the foot of the cross to repent and ask for forgiveness.

The Message does not say any of that, and for Christian theologians that may be problematic. *The Message* doesn't say that, because it is not about the "have to". It is not about avoidance or commitment or dropping to the knees. These are acts. Acts which are responsive to commands do not have an impact on the soul. The act of baptism should not just be a willful act. For baptism to take root, we must want it in mind, body, heart and soul. For the embodiment of Christ to occur, such that the Christ can fill us with the presence of God, we have to open the door. Not just in will, but also in body, heart and soul.

The *God Process* is what happens to us when we do change. There is a deep desire to be baptized, there is a wantingness to pray and there is a visible change—we live our lives differently. It becomes a natural desire, a natural response that is born out of love. As we shift in both thought and desire, we learn that the Kingdom of Heaven is not about "avoidance of sin" but rather there is *no* "desire to sin". There is no desire to be selfish, to be wantonness, to be prideful—it just doesn't exist. We still have our free will, but we choose to do what God would have us do. Through soul development people have overcome willful desires that would "tear the fabric".

Again, we see the purpose for reincarnation—we choose to come back, we want to come back. Some come back to help others find their path back to God. Others come back to not only purge their souls of bad choices from previous lives, but more so to prove to themselves that they have changed. Some come to test the strength of their will, their courage. We dream dreams and the purpose of life is to explore the depths of our soul. There is risk in taking on life, this life, because this life can have a negative impact on our soul development—those who choose to carry the light of God back to others are at risk of losing their own light. I think that is why we come back as groups of souls; to help each other, to protect each other. To not forget how to love and what it means to be loved. We come back as groups to minimize the risk of us getting lost to God.

Fourth commentary note is with respect to the scriptures or any writings that speak of and for God, there are passages that will draw us to God and there are other passages that set God in judgment of us. There are passages which pulls us towards God and passages where it would seem that God will condemn His creation into exile. Religion attempts to integrate these passages into the sovereignty of God. Integrating passages into a framework of faith, that decrees judgment or condemnation by God on His creation, creates a dichotomy in the nature of God. The dichotomy is, how can God separate Himself from Himself? If God is the source of life, how can that life force be separated from what He created? The problem is if God was to condemn part of His creation, would He not have to go with them? And, is there anywhere where God is not?

There are many Christians who believe that the Bible is the infallible Word of God. Scriptures cannot be written in error and therefore these passages need to be integrated into our beliefs. Further, the scriptures have been casted—set in stone, it is a closed book and that the message is complete. I often think to myself, which scriptures? There are so many versions of the Bible out there, and now we are finding these historical documents that were at one time considered scriptural writings; however they were never canonized—what about those scriptures? There are so many faiths, beliefs and interpretations? Were the prophets of 2000 years ago, these good men of God that wrote scripture, were they infallible? Were they maybe closure too or more in tuned with God, then what we are today? My point is, that scriptures came through a conduit, someone who was human, and they did their best to put onto paper that faith, that Word, that could draw all men to God. The operative message here is to *draw* all men to God.

For Christians, maybe God has granted us all that we need to know in the pages of the Bible. Yet locking God in the Bible is not what God asks of us—we should not limit the Truth of God to our poor reach of mind. We should always be open to new light and new understanding that God infuses into our world. Messages that compel us to consider God are messages that open our mind and can help shape our beliefs towards the Truth—the reality that exists in God. When we look at our beliefs and scriptures, we have to decide whether our understanding calls us all back to God, or if it make us exclusive to God.

In *The Message* we find:

> *Where do you will to be? Do you will to see God as a just God, who would extend heaven to all or do you will a God of justice, who saves only the elect few? Choose carefully, for in so choosing you choose for yourself. For the God you see is the God you worship and in your beliefs, Truth will either find a home or it will continue to elude you. In so choosing you either become God's offering to a world in need or you become exclusive to God's offering clinging to the duality that makes you special.*[20E]

Fifth and last commentary note is with respect to prophecy. I do think that God has set in motion a cosmic plan. Central to that plan is the Christ. However, prophecy is a dangerous game and really it is not a useful tool for creating an urgency to change our lives. There is urgency, however, and that urgency has nothing to do with prophecy. It has everything to do with choice. There are enough signs to tell us that our Earth is on a pivotal course. It could go either way. If our collective consciousness can embrace the light I believe we can still heal the Earth. If not, our world could undergo a schism, a series of planetary events as a consequence to the shift in the balance of the Earth's eco system. That shift must occur if the Earth is to be saved.

We are being given messages to help us in our collective consciousness, to help ease the direction each of us has to take when it comes to decision making so that we might bring a healing to the Earth. We all have to do it. We all have to want it. I think that we have a responsibility to do what we can to bring a healing to our planet, not just for ourselves but for our children and for their children.

I do not know what tomorrow will bring. There are prophecies in the Bible that I think point to our time and in my soul I am hopeful for the day when Christ will return.[89]

7 Epilogue

Like everyone else, I still have a lot of work to do on my own soul. I have a lot of character flaws, which my wife reminds me of all the time. I do not always pray. My faith and trust in God can be like a yoyo—it is up and down. I do not actively tell people that I am Christian. I do not always appear or act Christ like, nor do I want to. That is because I do not think or believe that is what God is asking me to do, or to be. I am to be me. I just want to be a better version of me. I need to and want to live a better life.

I do fear that my own short comings might impede *The Message*. I cannot escape my own humanity, my past or my own limitations. I am not always the best spokesperson and I do not always communicate effectively with others. I am sure that there will be people who will want to discredit *The Message* because of "me". Being a conduit to *The Message* does create concerns, but I hope people will be gracious and considerate.

My God Process is not just about my soul development. It is not just about purging myself of character flaws or becoming something *holy*. Life is about living. I have my wants and my dreams. There are things I want to do and places I want to go. I

---

89   I look to God's promise in Malachi 4:5-6.

want to share my life with my wife, my family and my friends. I want to be there for my children and to help them in their life. When we come to that moment in life where we can just sit and breathe and take in everything that is around us, then that is the moment that we find peace.

God grants us many gifts. The most precious gifts to me are my wife and my children. Lorraine grounds me and loves me for who I am, with all my character flaws, and even when I forget to rinse the dish cloth out (I am pretty much trained to do that now). She reminds me of how most people will think and tells me what I should say sometimes. My son reminds me of my father, and my spirit soars when I am around him. He has a way about him that puts others at ease; there is this calmness in his soul that makes the world around him bright and warm. My middle daughter has the spirit of her mother; her determination and perseverance is reflected in everything that she does. I am so proud of her. My oldest daughter, is like her aunt Zella, her grandmother Doris and her grandfather John (Lorraine's father). She has a love for people that is pure and inviting. They all complete me. My whole extended family, my church family and my friends over the years, complete me. I believe we have walked through time together and we all seek to bring a bit of heaven back with us each time we are reunited. Their love fills me and I enjoy being around every one of them.

I showed my son *The Message* for the first time on November 14, 2013. He had heard about it on differing occasions, but he had never seen it, nor has he read it yet. My son had it right I think, his wisdom is beyond his years, when we chatted about *The Message* and its purpose we joked and laughed about how some people might react to the book. Laughing always eases the tension. Not to make light of *The Message* or its purpose, but rather to put it into perspective. He reminded me of Galileo. The historical Catholic church of the 1600s didn't like Galileo because he said the Earth was not flat, and that got him into trouble, people wanted to believe that the Earth was flat and the center of the universe. It took time for people to realize that the world was not flat, but it was long after Galileo's life.

It may take time for people to move towards a collective consciousness as to the reality of God and how God is engaged in our creative process. It may take time for all people to accept the centrality of Jesus Christ and his cosmic role in the creative process. However, as we do, as people accept God and as we collectively take upon ourselves the name of Jesus Christ, we will accept each other *for* each other. By that I mean we grant each other space to live and to breathe and to become. We help each other with our dreams. We lend a helping hand. We free one another. We laugh and accept one another. We become a part of a community that lives in harmony—where there is love, peace, joy and justice. The message of community is the message of the Christ. As God's law permeates back into our heart, mind and soul the justice becomes the *just us*—a way of life where we live for others and others live for us.

When I reflect back on my life I can better see the connections to the dots, especially the dream that I had when I was fifteen. We all have free will. I had free will. Although I had this wondrous message, which was inside of my soul, it was out of choice that I allowed it to be penned onto the paper. I could have stopped at any time. I could have blocked it if I wanted to. At some point in my life I came to realize that we shouldn't hide our gifts. We shouldn't hide our light. It is only in our choice to let God out that we collectively become truly free.

Maybe that is the way God wanted it. Not only did I have to want to take *The Message* off the shelf, I had to want *The Message*. I had to want *The Message* in my life, and I had to want to share *The Message*. You also have the choice as to whether or not you will put *this Message* on the shelf or to accept *this Message,* by how you live your life.

Each of us will have to face these kinds of decisions. Not necessarily whether or not to choose or believe in *The Message*, but rather to earnestly seek and grow into that faith tradition which compels you to follow and to take to heart those messages that speak for God, to you. I find with God it is always about Him walking the journey with us. Jesus freely walked the journey with

CPSIA information can be obtained at www.ICGtesting.com
Printed in the USA
LVOW10*1947061014

407509LV00001B/2/P

God to the cross. It is a scary thing sometimes, but we choose to endure life's difficult paths so that we can prove to ourselves that we can become the person that He created us to be. That is how we infuse His light into our soul.

God is always about giving us free choice, and whether or not we accept Him. Messages from God that are forced on us are not readily accepted. Thankfully that is not the way God works. We can either accept or reject God. We can either accept or reject the message of the Christ.

The God Process, however, is not in the preaching. It is not in the walls of the church or between the pages of the Bible. It may not even be in *The Message.* Not that learning of God or hearing God's word isn't important, because it is, but what I believe is that is not where God does His work. *The God Process* is in the people we meet, the decisions we make and the relationships we create. God wills good things, and when we become the goodness that He created us in, we feel it. We feel that goodness in the way we live our lives. It is a free and liberating experience to discover our God-goodness.

Messages that lead us back to God, that lead us back to the reality that exists in God, are messages that we need to pay attention to.

My belief is that God works in all faiths, and even in faiths that are not Christian. Our salvation does not come from being baptized into a particular church, which may be contrary to mainstream Christian thought and theology. Salvation is not granted just to Christians. Heaven help us if God's elect only came to earth as Christians!

I worship in the Community of Christ. Although I have a deep faith, it has been a very personal faith up to now. My faith traditions and my church are rich to me; however my community of worship has beliefs that are considered sacred and parts of *The Message* are not aligned with what my community of faith believes. Although *my* church encourages members to explore the mysteries of God and to be engaged in prayerful thought for God's whisper in our lives, there are limits or boundaries that restrict that exploration.

Reincarnation, in my faith tradition, is one of those boundaries.

With respect to Christianity, I do believe that we can have a closer walk with God if we take upon ourselves the name of Jesus Christ. That comes from my beliefs, knowing in my own soul the centrality of Christ to the cosmic story. If we willingly accept and want baptism as a witness to choosing to have Jesus Christ in our life, we *can* have his spirit to be with us. My witness is that you can have a closer walk with God through the Christ. I believe he is the light, the way and the path that God made real.

Still, God infuses His light into all who choose to look to Him, regardless of our faith traditions. I only need to think of the movie *Schindler's List* to believe that God sends his first responders into the very heart of darkness to bring hope to those who were trapped by the inhumanity of Hitler and those who chose to follow him. We who choose for God, to be God's first responders, are in all faiths.

To find God or even to find the desire to have God in your life, you sometimes have to get to that point where you are ready to open the door and allow God in. You have to want to hear the message. More importantly you have to want the message.

All paths can lead to God. No matter what choices we make in this life, no matter what life does to us, there is meaning, purpose and lessons on the path that can lead us back to God. In reality, we cannot escape *the God Process*, because life is going to change us, regardless as to whether we look to God for His help or not.

God has a way of making the timing right. Perhaps collectively we are all ready for an ethereal message that will open our minds to a reality that is there but not visible. Perhaps collectively we are ready for a shift in our collective consciousness that can free us of the condition called "self" which traps us to our suffering. Maybe we are all ready to choose for peace. Maybe we are all ready for heaven on earth.

——————————— **Spiritual Truths** ———————————

1. *I believe in a just God, and as such I do not believe He would give*

a soul an unjust life.

2. *Life is indestructible. God did not create me to find a just cause through which to destroy me. Therefore, I believe that He works with me and refines me at my pace until I eventually reflect His likeness.*

3. *Somewhere between my actions and my attitudes and that person that I hope to be is the "who I am". God cannot change me into something that I am not. Only I can do that.*

4. *This life provides me with the opportunity through which I can refine the "who I am". In this life, I am vulnerable to choice, and I do not have clear vision; however, it is through my challenges that I will test myself. It is the fire of the flesh that will mold me and will prove me in His image.*

5. *Time is a wonderful instrument. I recognize the eternity that I move through. I know that I am in His constant care, and as such, death is but a shadow. I therefore will use time to prove the product that I seek to manifest.*

6. *I recognize that everything I do or say is a reflection of how I value others relative to myself. All that I own, all of my material possessions will pass away. But the people that I know, will I walk with through eternity. It is through this truth that I will discover what holds true value to my soul. For I know that I only destroy my own self-worth if I think of myself over my brother and sister. My greatest joys are found when I seek to better others, even though the price I pay may be most dear.*

7. *Suffering allows me to see what is not right about me. I will eventually learn from my pain, and one day it will change me forever. That day will come when I let go of my condemnation of others and seek God's eternal presence in my life. That day will come when the essence of the Christ Emmanuel finds a home in my soul.*

8. *The Kingdom of Heaven is found in the awareness as to how eternal truths operate within me. All that is love, generosity, kindness, devotion, that which is unseen but gives life its highest beauty and joy with the sense of childhood can exist within me. It is through my own self observation and my own spiritual*

awareness that I will find peace and end the chaos caused by my senseless wantonness.

January 11, 1992

———— 8 Post Epilogue: The Measure ————

How do you measure a soul?

My daughter said, "Post Epilogue? Dad, really?" In my defense, I thought I had finished all that needed to be written; however, one more event occurred after I had written the Epilogue.

On Thursday February 13, 2014, at 11:40 pm, the angels came to claim John Perkins, my wife's father. He died peacefully in his sleep. We did not expect it. I started to write this book with the death of Ron Perkin's his son and now I find myself ending the book with the death of Ron's father, John Perkins.

We came up to Wainwright that day to see John as he went into the hospital earlier in the week. Still he was in good health, he had a strong heartbeat and the family had just celebrated his 95th birthday only two weeks before. Most of his children, grandchildren and great-grandchildren came to watch him blow out the candles. We thought he would live another ten years. He was a kind gentle soul with farmer hands, and a strong grip—a grip that could hold you with firmness without overwhelming his gentle touch.

There was something about John. He was more than a patriarch to the family. When he prayed, you just somehow felt closer to God. His voice would resonate in your soul and bring peace to your ears. I think living through the war at such a young age and seeing the presence of death as often as he did, changes a person. He watched death take too many of those that he loved. The war had a profound impact on him at a very young age. One of his commanding officers lost his life in 1944—he peeked his head up out of the fox hole and it cost him his life. At 95 years of age, his parents and all his immediate brothers and sisters had passed on before him. He was the last one to return home to heaven. Death has a way of teaching us to see life differently.

I often think, *how does God measure a soul?* Certainly not in the years lived. Maybe it is in how well we love? Yet, how can love be measured? Maybe it is in the gift? The gift we leave by the residue of our life, the gift of what we leave behind for others. I think of Marian Bates, my mother's sister, who only lived for 9 days, but is now connected to you, the reader, through the pages of this book. Maybe it can be summed up in a single statement:

My joy is complete when I live the good life.

John lived the good life. He lived his life for his family, for the people he stood with on the battlefield, and for the friends that needed a helping hand. He lived his life for his Lord. If there ever was someone I knew that walked with the Lord, it would be John. John's measure was the gift of peace, which resonated in simple words in the form of a prayer. All who were touched by John's prayer were illuminated by the presence of God in his soul.

Lorraine and myself were laughing about life as we drove home to her sisters farm the Friday night after John passed. I didn't put a lot of humor into this book, but maybe I should have, because life should be about laughter. My brother-in-law, was telling us stories about his granddaughter, Sarah. His granddaughter has a spirit which can light up a room. Her father, Patrick, was finishing up a long day of combining, and Sarah was in the cab with him. Patrick still had more to do, but he was getting tired so he stopped combining to rest his eyes. Sarah, after a few minutes of this, stood up in the cab and turned to him and said, "DAD, Stop wasting my time!!" Sarah was four years old.

Time is such a precious commodity. To live the good life would be all that I could hope for. If I were to measure my life, I think I would have to laugh at how many times I just didn't get it. God still has a hard time breaking through this hard casing of a shell that I put around my soul, but I know now that I can break that shell and embrace the light that He offers.

At the end of the day, all that we can do is to try to live each day without regrets.

I still wonder what people will think of me after they have

read this book, but perhaps I shouldn't worry about it. I believe God had a hand in what I wrote—yet, *my* certainty is *my* certainty. For myself, *The Message* helped me to become a better person. What more could I ask of my God? For with God is *my* hope and *my* salvation.

I do not know the purposes of God, or why He would wake me up at four in the morning for all those years to write *The Message*, just for it to be shelved. Sharing *The Message* was the right choice. Yet, I had no holy encounter. For me *The Message* was enough, for the words illuminated my mind and set my soul on fire. Many times I would write in the silence, only to feel the whisper of the morning as I watched the sunrise. I am watching it now, from the farm house of my brother-in-laws kitchen. A sunrise with colors of red, purple, blue and above a landscape of trees and snow...

Snow.

For me, the light and the dark converge; they simply cover my life like the *snow* on the landscape in the season of winter. As the snow melts into spring, new life will emerge. As the warmth of God's love melts the cocoon of the shell around my soul, I know new life will emerge.

Today—Saturday, February 15, 2014—we will go to Point's West Retirement home and clean out John's belongings and next Saturday we will sing the praises of our God as we bid John farewell. He lived the good life.

Acknowledgements

A book is not written without a mass amount of participants. Each person I know and even people that I don't know have left an imprint on this book. However, I found that there was both positive encouragement and uneasiness after people that were close to me read *The Message*. For that reason I have not mentioned all the names of those that helped, but I am appreciative of their efforts to read and help out.

I am thankful for my parents and for my sister. To Clara Jean Lillian (Bates) Boote-Coombes and to Lawrence Herbert Boote: Their lives are forever embedded in my memory and I hope to have brought some purpose and meaning as to who they were and how they lived their life. To my sister, whom I love dearly: You brighten my day by the simple sound of your voice. You make me laugh, think, cry and smile. You also make the best perogies in the world.

To my wife, Lorraine: I know you lived a lot of lonely days. You always stood beside me and have loved me all these years—not an easy task. I use to immerse myself in my job; I was a workaholic. After I stopped working and started writing *The God Process*, you again gave me the time and space to complete this task. You made this book real and kept me grounded. Your love for family, for our children and for me, bonded us together and I love you. You have a quiet presence and a firm grasp on reality.

I took the names of my children, who are now grown adults, out of the book to give them their privacy. They inspire me and continue to give my life meaning. When you write a book, you need the support and encouragement of your children, especially a book like this where you expose your life and your soul. In so many ways you end up drawing your family's life into the pages of a book. Like Lorraine, they stood by me with this task. All of my children are deep thinkers, and we had many discussions over the years on God, life, and the meaning of life. My children are wise beyond their years and are balanced on the matters of the spirit.

I thank my family and friends who took the time to read the

book and for the feedback that they gave me. To Gordon, Karen, Michael, Al, Carol, Marilyn, Ken, Carolyn, Ted, and Don: Your insight and support helped to shape the pages. We walk the path of life together and we accept each other regardless of how each of us thinks or believes. Friendship is like chocolate—always sweet, and you can never get enough.

To my good friend Ken in Australia: Your candid and numerous emails back and forth on the use of language and encouragement for good theology was taken to heart. Faith seeking understanding requires the exploration of God. To be a conduit for God's message requires the influence of both the soul and scripture. More importantly, it requires the miracles of a church faith and feedback from others who are grounded in Christ to ensure that the message that is conveyed is being conveyed in the proper language. I cannot help but be a filter to *The Message* that was in my soul. My prayer is that I have conveyed *The Message* according to the will of my God and to His Holy Spirit whom I believe inspired my soul.

I am thankful to my extended family, especially for their steadfast faith. To my grandparents, Ted and Doris Bates, Marian Bates, my great-grandparents Martha and Albert Lochyer and my wife's parents John and Lillian Perkins: Their lives always affirmed the goodness of God. They looked to God and passed their faith onto us, their children and their grandchildren. They held their torch high and it is because of their love and sacrifices, a piece of heaven I think found its way into the families they raised.

To the many others whose lives graced the pages of this book: Thank you for influencing and inspiring my life. Thanks Renny for allowing your story to be told and to Charlotta for being my adopted sister. Gordon you are more than a cousin to me—you are my brother. Derrick, although our stories together were not shared in this book, the influence of your friendship and music connected us for a lifetime. To my friends that I play soccer with: The joy of team creates a lifetime of memories. It keeps us grounded to life. Go Wolves.

To my anonymous editor who gave encouragement, support and editorial advise from the very start of this project: Thanks for

staying with this project and for your candour with suggestions. You shaped this book beyond measure. Someday I hope to meet you.

To my God, to my Lord and savior Jesus Christ: I am not always the person that I should be, yet each day I learn and you grant me the time and the space to find myself. I am grateful for all that life has given me and even when life is scary, I trust in the path you have set me on. Perhaps time can bring the miracle of peace. I only hope that at the end of the day I can say, "I lived the good life". It is my prayer that I will leave a positive imprint on the world.

Kirk S. Boote
March 31, 2014

Endnotes

All Endnotes come from Part II: *The Message.*

—————— (Endnotes) ——————

1 Creation: 2 Born of Light
2 God: 1 God is a Just God
3 God: 1 God is a Just God
4 God: 4 The Law of One
5 God: 4 The Law of One
6 The Plan of Redemption
The Journey of the Christ: 5 The Cross
7 The Plan of Redemption
The Journey of the Christ: 5 The Cross
8 The Journey of the Soul: 5 Who I Am
9 God: 1 God is a Just God
10 The Journey of the Soul: 2 The Fabric of God
11 Creation: 4 The Dance of Life
12 Creation: 1 The Beginning
13 The Journey of the Soul: 2 The Fabric of God
14 God: 3 Truth
15 God: 3 Truth
16 God: 3 Truth
17 Eternity: 1 Time
18 Eternity: 1 Time
19 Eternity: 1 Time
20 God: 1 God is a Just God

Chapter 1

1. "The Lord our God is One".

2. The law of God was born out of truth. When the truth was broken the Word became the law. The Word was "The Lord our God is One." In God there is no division, no duality. In God's Kingdom there is no division, no duality. In God's Kingdom there is but one law, the "Law of One". The Law of One maintains God's Kingdom in wholeness and in truth. When the truth was broken, the law became broken, fragmented. Man became separate from God; man became separate from God's law.

3. The law of God binds us to God. God's law binds us to the life force; the source that extends God. In life, this life, we become witnesses to order and chaos. Our understanding about God's law is lost when we see law within the confines of order and chaos. When order is broken chaos ensues. When law's in a society are broken chaos sets in. To bind man to 'law, man in turn binds chaos to order. Chaos is imprisoned and order is used to measure injustice. In man's understanding of law, truth is sacrificed and is used to lay claim to order. If in truth we are set free, how can truth be used to imprison?

4. God's truth sets us free and God's law binds us to God. The "law of One" calls us to God's creation. We are called to be of one heart, one mind and one purpose which fulfills the truth that brings value to life. We are called to be "Children of the Law of One." One with God, living in truth that promotes each other as we seek our true identity. The law of One does not bring order to chaos but instead allows us to see God within the chaos. In turn the chaos finds stillness as God is revealed from within.

5. The truth became the word and the word became the law. In creation we were born of God's image but the image of God became lost to man. Man became lost to truth when beliefs were born and the law became fragmented. Our understanding of what binds us to God was buried deep within our soul. The image of God was fragmented and became a reflection of what we feared in judgement. Sin was established and retribution was weaved into the image of God.

6. To break free from sin, to break free from the beliefs that set us apart from God, the law of God must be strengthened within your heart and within your will. Sin is the will for elation and elation separates man from the law of God. God cannot look upon sin because sin is an illusion created by elation. Elation splits the self which retains the vision of chaos and order.